The
Diary
of
# Anaïs Nin

# Works by Anaïs Nin

PUBLISHED BY THE SWALLOW PRESS

*D. H. Lawrence: An Unprofessional Study*
*House of Incest* (a prose poem)
*Winter of Artifice*
*Under a Glass Bell* (stories)
*Winter of Artifice* (revised)
*Ladders to Fire*
*Children of the Albatross*
*Under a Glass Bell & Winter of Artifice*
*The Four-Chambered Heart*
*A Spy in the House of Love*
*Solar Barque*
*Seduction of the Minotaur*
*Collages*

PUBLISHED BY HARCOURT BRACE JOVANOVICH

*The Diary of Anaïs Nin, 1931–1934*
*The Diary of Anaïs Nin, 1934–1939*
*The Diary of Anaïs Nin, 1939–1944*
*The Diary of Anaïs Nin, 1944–1947*

PUBLISHED BY THE MACMILLAN COMPANY

*The Novel of the Future*

# The
# Diary
## of
# Anaïs Nin

1944–1947

Edited and with a Preface by Gunther Stuhlmann

A Harvest Book

Harcourt Brace Jovanovich, Inc.
New York

ISBN 0-15-626028-X

Library of Congress
Catalog Card Number: 66–12917

Printed in the United States of America

E  F  G  H  I  J

# Preface

The publication, during the past five years, of three volumes drawn from the monumental *Diary* of Anaïs Nin, which she has kept now for half a century, has brought to the author a cornucopia of critical acclaim. It has established Miss Nin's life work, in the words of one critic, as "one of the most remarkable diaries in the history of letters."

This intensely personal document also seems to have assumed a special individual significance for many contemporary readers, which goes beyond the genuine literary, historical, and biographical value of the *Diary*. Transcending the borders of age and background, its spectrum of recorded experience, thought, and emotion seems to invite direct identification, a sense of recognition, a sharing of concerns. In the numerous personal letters addressed to Miss Nin one note is struck again and again: "Yes, this is exactly the way I have felt, myself; these are the very things I am struggling with now." Many readers, especially among the young, have responded to the *Diary* with an intensity, an open directness, reminiscent of the voluble emotions released by Miss Nin almost four decades ago in the "Hotel Chaotica" in New York. Indeed, this very personal response to the *Diary* seems to bear out Miss Nin's assumption—quoted in the preface to Volume II—that "the personal life deeply lived always expands into truths beyond itself."

The specifics, the special circumstances of Miss Nin's own exploration of the "inner spaces" of the self, lucidly presented, sharply observed, open themselves to sharing: her uncertain childhood as a European "exile" in New York; the long struggle to free herself from the domineering shadow of her father; the lifelong effort to create for herself and her friends a nourishing, "livable" environment in a troubled, hostile, or indifferent world; her attempts to gain a totality of experience, a "personal relation to all things and people"; and her constant striving to capture an intuitive rather than ideological "feminine consciousness" in both her life and her art. The personal, the singular, expands under the prism of the *Diary* to become, in Miss Nin's words, "universal, mythical, symbolic." ("The hero of this book," she notes in these pages, "is the malady which makes our lives a drama of compulsion instead of freedom.")

The preceding three volumes, extracted from the broad flow of the original *Diary* manuscripts, are essentially self-contained units. Each forms, as it were, a complete "chapter" in the "book" of Anaïs Nin's life. Each volume marks a stage in Miss Nin's development. Each moves from a particular starting point toward change, greater awareness, new beginnings. At the core of each volume is exploration, unfolding, growth.

Volume I opened in Louveciennes, near Paris, when, in 1931, Miss Nin first appeared in print with a deeply felt appreciation of D. H. Lawrence, who had been quietly buried in Vence only a year earlier. This publication—through a chain of circumstances pinpointed only by hindsight—led to her contact with the unknown expatriate Henry Miller, to the "mad" Antonin Artaud, to psychoanalysts Dr. René Allendy and Dr. Otto Rank, to her own discovery of the turmoils and possibilities of psychoanalysis. Volume II (1934–1939) saw Miss Nin in New York, caught between the demands of analysis and her need to write, opting for the latter, returning to her "romantic life" in France only to be forced, by the outbreak of World War II, to leave again, to part from a pattern of life she knew she "would never see again." Volume III (1939–1944) mirrored her second "exile" in New York—paralleling, emotionally, much of her childhood experience (which gave the initial impetus to the *Diary* itself) as a reluctant refugee in Manhattan—and her efforts to establish herself as a "foreign" writer on these shores.

The present volume continues the chronology. It links up with her first "breakthrough" here as a writer, early in 1944, following the publication of a handset edition of her stories, *Under a Glass*

*Bell,* and a review by Edmund Wilson in the *New Yorker*. It is based on the original manuscript volumes sixty-eight to seventy-four. Miss Nin and the editor have followed the same principles of selection established in the previous volumes. The bracketed dates have been supplied by the editor. The omission of some characters was again necessary, and a few names have been changed and are indicated as pseudonyms in the index.

The basic themes of the *Diary*—self, femininity, neurosis, freedom, relationships, the confluence of art and life—also provide the essential strands in the tapestry of this volume. Again, there is often a "prophetic" quality to Miss Nin's endeavors and responses. Her antennae detect and register, as the radar of true artists has done through the centuries, much that was only dimly perceived at the time. Much of what she felt and sensed about vital aspects of life in America during the 1940s foreshadowed, in its implications, many of the strong concerns voiced only recently on a larger scale by the revolutionary young, by the advocates of a "new consciousness."

In this country, among the people who fielded the giant armada that defeated Hitler's Germany, that atom-blasted Japan into surrender, she perceived, amidst all the power and technology, a curious emptiness. "The drama of our present life," she writes, is that there is "nothing big enough, deep enough, strong enough." America's most active contribution to the formation of character, she notes, is the development of an impermeable shell behind which to hide. "A tough hide. Grow it early."

Most of the men she meets are "plain, one-dimensional." She deplores their single-mindedness, their lack of color. They are "prosaic down-to-earth, always talking of politics, never for one moment in the world of music and pleasure, never free of the weight of the daily problems, never joyous, never elated, made of either concrete and steel or like workhorses, indifferent to their bodies, obsessed with power."

She misses meaningful personal relationships. "Every friend I reach out here to seems incapable of big friendship." The depersonalization of relationships alarms her. "My friendships, instead of being concentrated on a very few, as in Paris, have become fragmented into many. I find only partial relationships."

"I am aware," she writes, "that what I love and seek is illusive, tricky. . . . What ought to be and not what is interests me. . . . In between, an all-consuming loneliness."

Miss Nin's continuing refuge still is the world of the young, the undiscovered, the potential realizers of "what ought to be." "When I am with mature people," she confesses, "I feel their rigidities, their tight crystallizations." She is tossed back, emotionally, into the strictured atmosphere of the Spanish father. "With the young," on the contrary, "one lives in the future. I prefer that." Perhaps by identifying with the young ("I feel as they do, I think and act as they do"), by being "open," and not yet "finite," she herself can escape finality, she can stay fluid, mercurial.

She has retreated from the "children" she used to mother in the past—Henry Miller, Gonzalo—perhaps because with aging they themselves have lost some of their fluidity, have become set, finite, predictable.

By repudiating what appeared to her stifling maturity, by escaping from the finalities of the "real world" into the free-form realm of the artist, into the self-centered emporium of the child-adult ("Both live in a world of their own making"), Miss Nin could stave off the "outside world" for a while. But caught in a culture which saw the artist either as a swaggering, hard-drinking he-man or draped in effeminate exclusiveness, even the sensitive young extracted a price ("I disguised the woman in myself to be allowed to re-enter the world of the poet, the dreamer, the child") she could not continue to pay. "I create a myth and a legend, a lie, a fairy tale, a magical world, and one that collapses every day and makes me feel like going the way of Virginia Woolf."

For the artist, who is not merely a technician or a propagandist, the American climate does not seem very propitious ("Much writing in America has confused banality with simplicity, and the cliché with universal sincerity"), the emphasis on competition, on "bigger and better," exaggerated.

"My greatest problem here," Miss Nin writes, "in a polemic-loving America, is my dislike of polemics, of belligerence, of battle. Even intellectually, I do not like wrestling matches. I do not like talk marathons, I do not like arguments, or struggles to convert others. I seek harmony. If it is not there, I move away."

At a time when there is much talk about reordering of priorities, Miss Nin's question, asked a quarter of a century ago, seems especially pertinent: "Why does everyone here believe that by all of us thinking of nothing else but the mechanics of living, of history, we will solve all problems?" And she adds: "I don't think the American obsession with politics and economics has improved anything."

The reordering of priorities, as Miss Nin has so often remarked, must begin in "inner space," before America, before anyone, can ever be re-formed. Her own struggle, in this volume, is far from won. ("I have tried not to be neurotic, not romantic, not destructive, but I may be all of these in disguises." And: "While neurosis rules, all life becomes a symbolic play. This is the story I am trying to tell. . . . The story of complete freedom does not appear yet in this volume.") But again she draws from her own experience of our growing encapsulation, our lack of contact "now that we have reached a hastier and more superficial rhythm, now that we believe we are in touch with a greater amount of people, more people, more countries. This is the illusion which might cheat us of being in touch deeply with the one breathing next to us. The dangerous time when mechanical voices, radios, telephones, take the place of human intimacies, and the concept of being in touch with millions brings a greater and greater poverty in intimacy and human vision."

With instant replay and total electronic communications on hand, these lines from Miss Nin's *Diary*, written so long ago by today's standards, have perhaps never been more "up-to-date," more pertinent.

New York
April, 1971

GUNTHER STUHLMANN

The
Diary
of
# Anaïs Nin

The first edition of *Under a Glass Bell* sold out in three weeks and I have to make plans for a reprinting.

As Gonzalo wanted the press to seem more businesslike, more impersonal, less like a private press run by writers, we had to find an appropriate place. *The Villager* had just moved out of 17 East Thirteenth Street. It was a small, two-story house. The ground level with a cement floor was suitable for the printing press. A narrow, curved iron staircase led to the second floor, which would be perfect for the engraving press. The house rented for sixty-five dollars a month, almost twice as much as the old studio on Macdougal Street. But Gonzalo hoped it would bring him more work.

The small house was painted green. There was a large front window, big enough for displays, and it could be fixed to exhibit our beautiful books.

Next door was a coffee shop for workmen. Across the way, Schrafft's (if prospective customers wished to take us to lunch).

The press is now named "Gemor Press," after Gonzalo's initials. William Hayter arrived with a printing job. Gonzalo's friends dropped in with work.

Gonzalo is active, joyous, transformed. It is his press. His pleasure gave me pleasure. He began to get up early. He kept his appointments. I could take time off to write. But for the moment, we both have to work on a second printing of *Under a Glass Bell*. The first edition of three hundred copies was sold quickly. A publisher who met me at a party said: "How did you get so well known with three hundred copies of a book?"

Installing the press was a tremendous labor. Work with electricians, window cleaners, movers; packing and unpacking; transferring trays of type into type cases, counting paper, beginning to work on engravings. The second edition will have only nine engravings instead of seventeen. It will be linotyped instead of hand-set, and will cost three dollars instead of five. We unpacked twelve boxes of paper, books, plates, tools, etc. We bought waste-baskets, scrapbooks, bulbs, blotters, files. We pasted samples of Gonzalo's work into a scrapbook, to show his ability as a designer of books.

It was all done in a week.

Gonzalo has assumed leadership. He is proud of his place, his machine, his independence. I am very tired, but content. I am proud of my human creation.

Took one thousand prints out from between blotters. Cut paper. Exhaustion. Contentment.

Intense labor.

Deep down I feel an understanding of those who revolt against the slavery of work, but I have also seen those who rebelled against the system harm themselves beyond repair.

I watch Gonzalo taking pride in his work. The guilt which often accompanies those who do not work, who do not create anything, can be more terrible and destructive than the discipline and sacrifice of work and creation.

Is Gonzalo now free of the guilt which oppressed him and poisoned his leisure? He is no longer tortured by insomnia. He does not feel ashamed or humiliated before his friends. (One is a Spanish doctor who fought in the Civil War, the other a Frenchman who teaches mathematics at N. Y. U.) The editor of a South American magazine comes to see him.

He feels his power, has discovered his skills and gifts. At the same time, it is like watching a child lose his gaiety and innocence as he matures and assumes responsibility. Gonzalo paid dearly for his illusions of freedom. Henry [Miller]'s letters to me are burdened with guilt, talk of atonement. Even Henry, who always said he felt free of any feeling of gratitude or indebtedness. Even my father, who considered himself a freethinker, a man who did not believe in religion and therefore in guilt, allowed himself during his last days in Paris to resemble a breast-beating, atoning, religious maniac.

I watch Gonzalo work and a part of me is sad that he is not

free to enjoy, for both Gonzalo and Henry had an endless capacity for enjoyment. This was the secret of my acceptance of what seemed to others an exploitation of me.

Letter from Henry:

I had already seen the [Edmund] Wilson review*—several people sent me the clippings. It was well intentioned but inept and inadequate, wasn't it? I was furious, myself. So that did the trick! It's all so bloody spurious, what makes success here. The other night, after reading proofs of my new book with [James] Laughlin (*Sunday After the War*) because I had included in this book more pages about you, the diary, etc. (things you know) I went back to my essay *"Une Être Étoilique"*** and reread it. I had tears in my eyes. It is perhaps the best bit of writing I ever did. Even if no one person can possibly put in words all that may be said about the diary I feel that I made a very wonderful attempt, elliptically. (And how strange that George Orwell, the English writer, should have used my phrase "inside the whale" for his left-handed attack upon me!) I am thinking all the time only about how to get the diary launched. I have suggested it whenever and wherever possible. . . .

I must tell you that I am trying to raise a good sum of money—to live quietly for a year and finish what work I have on hand. I have had to waste a good deal of time these past two years to keep going. It doesn't bother me or hurt me—but it's a sheer waste. I am already receiving promises and half-promises of substantial aid. I think eventually I shall get much more than I asked for. In which case I shall be able to send you a substantial sum. And as I told you once, should you not want to bring out the diary yet, should you need the money for other purposes, why make what use of it you wish. I merely thought that the diary, the publishing of it, would be the best gift I could make you. It wouldn't even be a gift, because I am still digesting, assimilating, benefitting from all the tremendous gifts you made me. . . .

I still feel it is too bad that, with your enormous and truly "legendary" reputation, only glimpses of your great gift are seen. I urge you with all my heart to concentrate on the diary. The world will be bowled over when the real manifestation of your spirit begins, believe me. As I said before, rereading my own words about you I was so stirred that I was beside

* In *The New Yorker*, April 1, 1944—Ed.
** First published in *The Criterion*, London, 1937—Ed.

myself. It must be maddening to you. It is to me. How can they wait and wait and wait? I said to myself. And the more maddening because to help me, your own work has been neglected. But nobody wants more than I to redeem himself. . . .

I am living with nature more and more, and this Big Sur country (where I have been now for two months) is truly tremendous. There are only about twenty-five people on this mail route. Back from the coast over the mountains, there is an absolute emptiness. It is almost as forbidding as Tibet, and it fascinates me. I should like to go back in there and live for a time quite alone. But I would need a horse, and an axe and a few other things I have never used. I am a little terrified of it.

The other day I was offered a little house on a mountain—quite isolated—difficult to get to on foot (and I have only my feet to use) but I am taking it. I move in next week. My address remains the same. I shall have a taste of real solitude. Certainly I miss everything else—terribly. But I consider myself fortunate. And I am more and more at peace with myself. . . .

Will it surprise you if I say the only writer I care to rival, or surpass if possible, is Rimbaud? I am working feverishly to wind up all my autobiographical work, so that I may embark on a totally new venture in writing. The water colors helped me a lot, gave me courage. It's a strange story, too long to relate here.

Oh, yes, I must tell you that there is a writer named Wallace Fowlie who would like to get in touch with you. He is a Catholic writer, a friend of Maritain and others like him. He is a Professor at Yale and writes equally well in French and English, appears in two languages. He admires your work very much.

Also I had a letter from Larry Durrell the other day, from Cairo (or Alexandria) saying that he and Nancy had parted and that she and the child were now in Jerusalem. He asked me to send you his love. He seemed depressed—mostly about the war I gather.

I wrote a prophetic piece which will appear in the new book, and which nobody likes, apparently—called "Of Art and the Future." I would like to know what *you* think of it, when you see it. It is not a very bright picture, I must say. People do seem to insist on making the future bright, and yet anyone with half an eye can see the makings of the future right now. They expect miracles, but refuse to recognize the real miracles which take place. . . .

One last thing . . . you have undoubtedly your warmest admirer—of person and writing—in Jean Varda. He talks about you incessantly. Seems to have divined your whole being. . . . I do hope he will see you when he goes to New York this summer. I am sure you will like him. I know very well the collage he sent you, because I slept with that collage several weeks. It was I who inspired the transfer. Immediately I knew the title of it. I knew you must have it. It meant a great deal to me, this collage. Watch it in changing lights—specially very early morning light. Or with colored lights, if you use colored shades. . . .

Anyway, he is one of your great allies, one you didn't know about till recently. And there must be many more. You should have faith always, and more patience. You have the faith that moves mountains, where others are concerned, and yet when it comes to yourself that little grain of doubt which was implanted in you can corrode everything—and always when things are in your grasp. This is the only curse that has been put upon you, and you must fight it alone, or it will destroy everything you labored so triumphantly to build up. Don't resent my saying this! I am not saying it from some high and mighty seat. I have been quite crushed, believe me. But I seem to weather all storms. And the more I reflect on it the more I believe it is because I have always a kernel of faith left, and nothing destroys it, nothing can. But it is a faith in the whole large process, not in any one person, thing or idea. And my faith in you is indestructible.

I found the letter Jean Varda had written when he sent me his collage:

I take the liberty to send you a collage with a vain title: "Women Reconstructing the World." And if you should enjoy it, I would feel less indebted and wildly proud to have returned a small part of the joy I have received from the rivers of delectations which flow from your pen.

The first time you appeared to me after the reading of *Winter of Artifice,* you said to me: "It is undeniable that the source of all our miseries comes from our obstinacy in maintaining that Paradise is a garden. The psychoanalysts have added to the confusion by interpreting the floating dreams as a flight into space. The mystic is the only one who knows that all states of ecstasy are a state of floating in an ambiance more heavy than air. I say, but do not repeat it to anyone who is not ripe enough to receive it, Paradise is at the bottom of the sea. And I can also prove to you that angels are ships. They have no wings but large sails which they unfold noiselessly at night to cross Eternity."

As before being a painter I was a boat builder, your words made a deep impression on me.

The second time you appeared to me, always rigorously veiled (by water, as I realized later) you showed me a naked foot of hallucinating beauty which made me realize instantly that you belonged to the great lineage of tragic women: Cassandra, Clytemnestra, and Iseult. And you said: "And all art which is after all but an overflow of Paradise's surplus tends to only one thing: to recreate water. Think of Nijinsky, who forgot himself in space, think of Shankar who struggles slowly amidst algae, and Isadora who evoked a giant medusa. Think of the ballet exercises. The hand reproduces resistance to water. And what is painting but absolute transparency? It is art which is ecstasy, which is Paradise, and water."

Then I began to suspect that Anaïs Nin is a pseudonym and that in reality you are the great Amphitrite in person, and perhaps angry with me for revealing such a well hidden secret.

Olga only breaks down in my presence. Externally, she is a *femme du monde,* every hair in place, subdued, wearing tailored suits, her kimono a duplicate of her husband's, talking objectively about politics. But suddenly she calls me. She is in great pain from an ulcer. She is emotional, almost hysterical. When I arrive, she breaks into a wild confession. The stories in *Under a Glass Bell* renewed her contact with her young emotional self, the self who wrote poetry before she became involved in politics.

"It seemed more important to work in politics. To be of public service."

"But how can you determine what is of public service? You define it as adopting one political system rather than another, and converting everyone to it. But next month the system is proved corrupt, and disintegrates."

Olga felt she had deserted her poet self for a more altruistic occupation. Now her task was over. It was rendered futile by the turn of events. She is returning to an incomplete life, to an incomplete woman, to a half-created artist. This half-woman returns to haunt and harass her. Olga goes back to delve into waters too long stagnant while she served an impersonal cause. She had perceived the truth at the beginning, when she first read poetry to the workmen and inspired them. She exchanged this power for the clichés of political propaganda, mouthing others' words in the same mechanical way I mouthed the questions and answers of the catechism when I was a child:

"Who made the world?"

"God made the world."

Olga had given herself to a cause, a system: this system and cause had failed. While she gave herself, her own development on a deeper level was static.

When the system failed (historically), there was never a question that it may have failed because it was composed of incompleted human beings, human beings who had ceased to work on their individual development.

And it is this development which I believe will influence history from within, rather than systems. If enough individuals had worked at their own development, history would be formed as natural things are formed, organically, from the impulse of quality and maturity.

And now Olga was asking: "Where am I?"

Twenty years lost, from the time she first read her poems to the Russian workers, with her genuine flamboyant red hair and her husky voice, until now when she was aware of the collapse of the values she had served. She was back in time twenty years, back to the age of twenty-one. No longer the political journalist, no longer the woman of the world, but a woman in quest of her poetic self, trying to unlock the many doors she had closed upon this self. She had not only locked them, as she said, but she had lost the key.

I suggested the key lay in her ambivalence. She swings between attraction to my work and detraction of it. Spontaneous attraction ("The story of my soul is in your stories") and detraction—out of guilt, considering what I do contrary to the serving of a political cause.

"But poetry is a cause, too. It gives us strength and faith to go to battle, to endure. Don't you think your poems gave the workmen as much will to live as political slogans did?"

"Someone," I added, "has to supply the oxygen, to balance the horrors created, invented by politicians for their own glorification. You don't think men in politics are in it for the sake of humanity, do you?"

During the night, she dreamed Djuna Barnes and Anaïs Nin. She was seeking the lost poet, Olga. So it was me, now, who was serving a human being. While she served the revolution which had been her dream and her drama, I was preparing a world which would restore her, a vital world which does not crumble under systems, dictators, or power struggles.

"Every time our hope for a better world is based on a system, this system collapses, due to the corruptibility and imperfection of human beings. I believe we have to go back and work at the growth of human beings, so they will not need systems, but will know how to rule themselves. Now you have suffered the shock of disillusion in an ideology which has betrayed its ideals. It is a good time to return to the creation of yourself, not as a blind number in a group, but as an individual. Poetry is merely the language of our night-self, in which are imbedded the seeds of all we do and are in the day. We can only control it by knowing it. Better to make this journey back to what you had first intended, rather than to die of disillusion."

I gave her a copy of *Nightwood*. I gave her Jean Giraudoux' *Choix des Élues*, to help her re-enter the world of myth which alone makes the monstrosities of history bearable.

She had to return to an incomplete woman because the task she had undertaken had not matured her. When we blindly adopt a religion, a political system, a literary dogma, we become automatons. We cease to grow. When I first met Olga, she was writing a book about the first female captain of the Soviet merchant navy, Valentina Orlikova. A photograph of her had appeared, which all of us fell in love with. Short dark hair, regular features but fleshy and sensuous, beautiful dark eyes, clear-cut and stylized in her captain's uniform. She conveyed firmness and capability, without hardness or coldness. She became a symbol of woman's most secret wishes: to be able to be free and in command of her own destiny, responsible without loss of her womanliness.

We wanted to imitate Valentina Orlikova. We saw ourselves trim, efficient, capable captains of our ship and our own lives. It was not a desire to be a man, but to be free and capable of self direction and professional growth. I cut my hair short. This admiration for Valentina led to great misunderstandings. Gonzalo thought it was a revolution, and asserted he could never make love to a captain of a ship, a sniper, a lieutenant commander, no matter how beautiful she was.

Letter from Henry:

The patron came through. I am to get two hundred dollars a month for a year, unless in the meantime someone else steps in and wishes to aid me. Pay back when and how or if I like. So here is a hundred, and if nothing goes amiss you will get a hundred each month. This hundred, which was in addition to the two hundred, was to have gone for travelling expenses—to Mexico. But I am not going. I have the house (ten dollars a month, or free if I choose) and it suits me to the ground. I am alone and I am working. So I won't budge until I finish one book at least. Then I may think of Guatemala, where I am told the exchange is fifteen to one in our favor. In that way I can do more for all concerned with what comes to me. I don't count on good fortune (material fortune) to last very long—it's not in my destiny, I feel.

[Bern] Porter writes me that you have abandoned all thought of bringing out the diary here in America. . . .

Why don't you begin and trust in providence that money will be forthcoming to publish further editions? By the time you are ready to leave America you may have everything published but the difficult parts, which you can then complete in Europe. I am certain you will receive help.

I am living on the same scale as always. I have no big needs. But I am called on to help frequently now—and I do all I can. So, the more I get the more I will shell out. I am just a distributor.

I understand you are now writing a Proustian novel, so Porter says. Your two books from your own press are causing a stir everywhere. You should never have to hand-set type again. People should come to you, and they will, asking to let them do the work for you. Have faith.

I am tempted to inquire who my benefactor is. But perhaps it is better to remain ignorant. I know now that he is a painter and lives in California.

There is a small magazine in Berkeley—*Circle*. The young man who runs it, George T. Leite, is a Portuguese and a most well-meaning and intelligent boy. I saw him the other day when I was up that way. He thinks he may be able to *print* the magazine next issue (the first was mimeographed). He may also ask you to contribute something. He can't pay yet —he pays the entire cost of the magazine himself, works as a taxi driver, has wife and child. I think he has sent you a copy of it. You won't think much of it but I am going to help him get good writers and artists to make something of it. Dudley, I am told, received five thousand dollars to start his magazine. I doubt that he will make anything worth while of it. I am waiting for him to send me five hundred dollars before writing him again. He owes me that and more.

I will stay here in Big Sur until I finish *The Air-Conditioned Nightmare.*


In a mood for activity, I made changes in the studio, put away my sea shells, my collection of exotic shoes, to achieve more simplicity and clean lines. But what else can I do? Go back to the press as assistant printer, assistant paper cutter, assistant typesetter, under the wavering captainship of Gonzalo?

When I left Olga today, I became aware of an admiration for woman which is quite distinct from my admiration of man. I felt that woman suffers more in relationship, sacrifices more, cares more.

# [May, 1944]

Will the outer life become so strong that the inner one will disappear? I live less in the diary. The inner eye mirroring all is less active. The withdrawal to commune, to relieve, to ruminate, to conserve and interpret, is less frequent. Intense activity at the press. Forty more engravings to pull. Then home for a bath, dinner, friends, telephones, visitors. Hardly time to tell what is happening to me. Others' lives, others' happenings. The telephone here takes the place of letters.

Our psychoanalyst, Martha Jaeger, rebelling against her mother role, but too late. Martha unable to cast off her role because she looks the part physically: she is big and fat, full-bosomed, fleshy. She looks strong, ample, and nourishing. She radiates solidity, physicality. All of us have a maternal side, but it is not so obvious in our appearance. We pride ourselves in not even looking like wives, but more like mistresses. The *femme fatale* is our ideal in appearance! Martha helped to free us, and we cannot help her. She is aware of her husband's unfaithfulness and suffers. We all tried to make her beautiful. Frances Brown and I made her go to the hairdresser. We changed her old-fashioned, Middle-Western-school-teacher dresses. We made her diet. She has a good Greek-matron profile; a sweet voice. But that was all we could do. When we tried to take her into our life (of writers, sculptors, painters, poets, musicians), she did not fit into it. When we invited her to our parties, it often happened that several of us had been talking with her professionally, and so she could not escape her role. She was treated with deference, like the oracle and the wise adviser.

Once, she appeared quite handsome: hair nobly brushed back, setting off her regular features. She wore a small hairband with a veil. We were all very proud of our handiwork. But then she forgot about the veil and, plagued with a cold, she started to blow her nose through it.

Martha does not understand that I believe there is a time for analysis, and a time to live without it. Just as I think there is a time for passionate living, and a time for recording and interpreting.

For me, analysis is to be used only when necessary, like medicine. When I gained my orientation, turned my back on analysis, and went back into living, into writing, Martha wanted me to continue group discussions. I found such discussions sterile. I tried to explain: "Martha, I am an artist. I use analysis to orient myself, but once I have found my bearings, I take to my submarine again and plunge back into the deep, below the level of analysis, words, discussions. I am now in that realm, wherein living and writing have their source."

Martha insisted. I resisted. I incurred her queenly anger. She insisted I needed this kind of objectivity all the time. I maintained it was the wrong kind.

An odyssey from inner to outer life.

The inner chambers of the soul are like the photographer's darkroom. Like a laboratory. One cannot stay there all the time or it becomes the solitary cell of the neurotic. I know some who draw all their energy inward, coiled within themselves, and then all the senses—ears, eyes, touch—become atrophied. Communication stops. They shrivel.

Haitian friends told me the story of a couple haunted by a jealous, discarded lover. The couple believed that he lived with them, watched them, and waited for the moment to do them harm.

The witch doctor went through intricate voodoo rites to exorcise the jealous lover.

But the analyst goes so much further. He demonstrates that the haunting by the jealous lover is in our own minds; that we are possessed by the discarded lover only by way of guilt for deserting him; that it is this presence of the uneasy conscience, in the form of the ex-lover, which creates a fear of persecution or retaliation.

*But we are the authors of the ghost, and therefore we have the power to dissolve this presence which damages our present life.*

This is self-determination by insight, the opposite of fatalism. Character and ideas and emotional reactions can be altered. This is a subtler, a deeper way of becoming the captain of one's own ship.

Martha liberated me from my savior role by the simple expedient of pointing up my human and realistic limitations: what I could and what I could not do. The concept of the *miracle*, inherited from the Catholic religion, really made me believe I could help everyone, solve all the problems.

When Martha could not persuade me to join the discussion group, she resorted to a "banishment and excommunication" rite which ended my faith in her. She frightened me by using a graphologist to point to all the dangers in my own character still besetting me, awaiting me.

With this she destroyed her power as analyst.

She also exposed herself to the loss of our faith by confiding all the contradictions between her psychological wisdom and her personal life. Her seeking to redirect her life into channels not natural, and not genuine to her, to adopt our life and ways rather than seek her own, create her own world, made her a fallible human being, whom we loved, but could not rely on.

If her marriage should fail, she will need her work more than ever. Most of my talks with Frances are now filled with concern over Martha.

Notes on Caresse Crosby: Elizabeth Arden-pink. The inside of a Venus sea shell. Bedroom boudoir-pink. Bathroom full of pink negligees and chemises. The same colors on books, apartment rooms, garden grilles, letter box, writing paper. Max Ernst painted her as a petticoat. *Le boudoir disparu*. The motion, *mouvement perpetuel,* due to her saying "yes" to all life.

Caresse still saying "yes, yes"—the essence of her mobility and response. Carlyle's Yes and No man.

Rewrote story of Hans Reichel ["The Eye's Journey"] for *Dyn* magazine in Mexico City.

*Circle* magazine published my letter to Luise Rainer.

---

I must repay Samuel Goldberg's loan for printing the second edition of *Under a Glass Bell*. I owe money to Martha Jaeger, to the doctor, to the drugstore. Three hundred and sixty-five dollars to Thurema Sokol, who helped so generously with the moving of the press.

Work at the press at least eight hours a day. Went to the New School to see a Russian film about experiments on dogs: severing their heads, replacing them, seeing them dead, their hearts on a platter, and then revived. I was with Charles Duits and Frances. We were chilled at the prospects of science's control of life and death. We had a feeling of awe and sacrilege. Advance of science's power over death?

Henry sent a thousand dollars, the first large amount he ever earned, which helped me pay off debts; with the rest he bought a cottage in Big Sur.

Printed a thousand pages of *Under a Glass Bell*. Party at Moira's Saw Leo Lerman again. Conversations with him are similar to those with Conrad Moricand. A witty fencing, a skillful dodging, a game, peripheral and delightful. He is a past master at verbal fireworks. It is with Frances that I have deep and evolutional talks. We talk to understand ourselves and others, to interpret, to dissolve pain, to create counterpoisons to pain and disillusion. Tom Brown's silences and his inability to truly look at one, to allow one to read his eyes, his furtive exits, entrances, vanishings, make him seem ghostly.

Gonzalo's pride at mastering the new press: "I made it work, and without lessons either."

The Haitian Flag Dance in a big hall. One is carried back to the eighteenth century. The older Haitians are dressed formally: long dresses, gloves, fans, shawls, evening suits. They sit formally in chairs set against the walls.

They watch the younger people dance in a modern way. Then, when the time comes, they rise and dance a minuet as at the French court. Sedately and slowly, with dignity and stiffness. But without Albert Mangones, the dream of Haiti seems to have vanished.

Gonzalo and Ian Hugo worked on the cover, using the engraving press. Later, I separated the good from the bad pages with Thurema and Josephine Premice. Worked together gaily until midnight.

Made packages all day. Cut covers. Took books to bookbinder.

We printed a lithograph by Käthe Kollwitz for a book cover. Caresse Crosby came to see the press. Dinner with Jean Wahl, a teacher of philosophy who survived a concentration camp. This experience has left him dead in spirit. He is among us, but not with us. He is always dressed in black, in the shrunken style of French suits. It is as if no love or friendship can restore his life.

Every now and then I feel I should transform the diary, as Proust did in his life and memories. But the danger is that then some element is missing, what Martha finds missing from my novels: warmth and humanity. They were lost in the metamorphosis into myth, or fiction. How can I do this? Martha feels it will be a long time before people know enough about the unconscious to understand my writing. The truth is I get lost in the richness of the diary, and need to make great efforts to synthesize and organize it. I get lost in the abundance, and the labyrinth. I should begin slowly, gradually, and the themes may emerge later, by accretion.

Began to write a new book, *This Hunger*. Wrote portrait of Stella, in part inspired by Luise Rainer.

Henry sends me a visitor, Harry Herkovitz. He says "Anis," the way Henry did. He has been a sailor. He is dark, intense, lean, and wrote a strange story, influenced by Edgar Allan Poe, about ravens attacking a traveler. He tells me he asked Henry to leave him all his manuscripts and letters. But Henry evaded the issue. In our first talk he saw me as a composite of June,* myself, and the women in *House of Incest*. I realized he did not see me as I am, that he was seeking a myth. He was calling on an Anaïs as described by Henry, which bears no resemblance to reality.

Expansion, flowering. Frances says I am a very creative person in a relationship, but she has the same effect on me. I am working on the new book, and talking with Charles Duits, whose poetry I do not understand. He comments on my changeableness. Always a new person, always a different person. I have become adept at "unblocking" not only myself, but others.

Printed more engravings. Saw a Russian movie with Gonzalo. There was a time when every Russian film I saw paralyzed my work, but this time I did not feel arrested by the comparison. The contradiction was resolved. Every war and every revolution kills and maims emotions and sensibilities. Someone has to restore these currents. Someone has to resuscitate these people killed by massive doses of pain.

Harry said he could not feel the death of thousands he witnessed in China, but the death of one person affected him deeply. We are in danger of destroying feeling by the immensity of the horrors committed. I hold on to the protection of individual life.

As you mature, these paralyzing conflicts and choices cease to block you. They are resolved by a larger perspective.

* Henry Miller's second wife—Ed.

I see Charles Duits, Edmund Wilson, John Stroup, Harvey Breit. My only strength is the strength of wholeness, of total feeling. That is what I am writing with. Harry tells me he is the symbolic son of Henry. He was born in the same district of Brooklyn. But he is the adventurer, the seagoing man, the lean, dark, ardent Jew. He was writing about June and Henry as a study of illusion in love. I did not want to see him anymore. I want to be liberated from this past. He is plunging me back into the past. I told him so over the telephone. He pleaded. He wrote a love letter (to June, Anaïs, Sabina, Djuna, Alraune, Isolina, etc.). After two weeks, I let him visit again. Mona, June, Alraune had disappeared. I said: "Now it is Harry talking, not an imitation of Henry." He started his own book, not a book on Henry, June, etc. He is violent, primitive, and confused.

Gonzalo is the one who lives glued to the radio, who gives us all the news. A few days ago we celebrated the Allied landing in Normandy. What will happen now? We talk about it. It haunts our nights.

At the same time, because he only has *one* life, the one he shares with the present, in history, because he is not creating an antidote to the poisons of history, Gonzalo has no hope. He is crushed by events. He has no inner life to sustain and alchemize events.

I visited Martha and her husband at their mountain cabin. The quietness of the mountains, the still-life quality of their lives, the heavy eating, and the enclosure within their anxieties was torture. I had a feeling of oppression. I was listening to both their confessions. Martha was asking me to help her husband, and he was asking me to help her, but it would take years to reverse the process of their disharmony. "Martha does not live with her body. I am sensually starved," from him. And Martha, in her distress, wants to place her husband in my hands: "He can be influenced by you, I trust you." In the winter he had tried to commit suicide.

"Martha, when I was in trouble, I turned to a *doctor*. Why don't you and your husband do the same? A friend cannot help."

---

I came back to the madness of Harry. He lives with the life of Henry interwoven with his own and cannot disentangle them. He says: "Save me from the emptiness of June." (His June is a ballet dancer.) I refused. I said: "I won't combat the symbol of June again and again. You must do it alone. When you are free, come back to me." He has the word *destruction* on his lips.

This is a false drama, or a secondhand one. It stems from Henry's writing, from identification. He almost repeats Henry's words: "I want to write, I want to work, and she (the ballet dancer, replica of June) will not let me."

But I am not the same Anaïs. I cannot go on repeating the same drama. I am not going to sustain one half of Harry in his war against his other half.

"Once, in some dingy city, I lay on a couch and read Henry's description of your diary, and I felt: 'I must know this woman.' My fear was that you might have been trapped in Europe."

"But I am not the same woman, Harry."

He is young, and his hunger is immense. He lays his manuscripts on my knees when he comes, an offering. The pages are all horror, violence, terror, crime and punishment. It is an animal world. He seemed so gentle and soulful. What venomous fury in the writing. Lust, crime, madness. His writing full of flaws and falsities. The self-seeking of the instinct. The thwarted primitive.

"I was born in hunger and deprivation."

"But that is no reason to inflict this on others, devastate and shrivel the world until it is again as you first saw it."

Hunger has always tempted me, as a barren field tempts the sower. But this time I was able to resist. One can escape habitual patterns. Harry has a dream of love and work which requires my presence. I am supposed to be the answer to his hunger.

"I will not go to sea again, into war and danger, into suicide. I will stay and write," Harry says.

And then his "June" came to see me. She was not June at all! He had cast her as June. She was vulnerable, and loved Harry deeply. She was aware that he fictionalized her. She understood.

"Because I know he does that, I wanted to come and see if he had also invented you, and the overwhelming bond between you. I wanted to know if it was a delusion. If it is *real,* I will surrender, because you are good for his writing."

She looked at me so honestly, I could read everything: devotion, selflessness.

"I'm glad you came to me. Harry is a dreamer. He is still living Henry's life. There is no such bond between us. I responded at first to echoes from the past. But the real Harry I do not know. Perhaps because I am a writer, I can make him want to write. But you are completely different from June; I can see you are not destructive, and you have insight. I will help you. To begin with, there is no great love between us. It is an illusion he has. You are the woman in his life."

I never saw a woman show so clearly the effect of being delivered of pain. She sparkled with new faith and confidence.

"It is not I who stands in the way of Harry's love for you, but Harry himself who is filled with Henry's life and does not yet know who he is. The stronger spirit of Henry has filled him; he is filled with quotations and fiction. He is trying to live Henry's life. Your task will be to restore him to reality."

We embraced like sisters.

Letter to Henry:

I left without speaking to Harry about the wrongness of his taking from you. I feel I should no longer comment on these things. I always knew that the day you obtained what you wanted (a year of peace from the money problem, time to write) you would throw it all away on the wrong people. I am quite ready to give up my share but I know that this too will go to some weak or worthless person. Your last letter sounded sad. Your "protector" probably heard about your giving to Harry and others, keeping only $25. He may have felt badly that he was not really helping you. Your first thought should have been of your own work. This income which should and could have meant your freedom you handled so that today you write me you are relieved to no longer have it. Is it guilt that makes you unable to receive? But why do you give always to the wrong person? Futile words. We have discussed this often enough.

# [July, 1944]

Moira rented a big house in Amagansett and invited us all for a long weekend. Four days of calm, warmth.

I gave myself to the sea. The sea and the sun restore my strength, always.

But it was a painful moment when we all sat at the beach, suntanned, in brightly colored suits, hair flowing, gay, and a few yards behind us sat the philosopher, the professor from the Sorbonne who had been in a concentration camp. He wore the same black, tight, shrunken suit, a black hat and big dark glasses, black shoes and black socks. He was staying with the Zilkas, and we tried to welcome and befriend him. But we could not heal him, bring him back to life. He sat far from us, never undressed, and rarely joined us.

Bomb attempt on Hitler failed. Depression, discouragement. We had hoped for his death so often.

The second visit at Moira's became unbearable. She had invited Martha Jaeger, her husband, and Charles Duits. She said: "In this house everyone is free." But when we refused to go with her to a cocktail party, she was angry. She left us, saying: "There is very little food in the icebox. You will be sorry." We decided to sit around the kitchen table and spend the evening reading *Finnegans Wake* aloud. Charles read the banquet scene. We savored every word as if it were food. We found the sounds delectable. When Moira returned, she found us sitting contentedly, still reading, and not suffering from hunger.

When we return from the beach we ask: "Is there anything we can do?" Still in our bathing suits, we help in the kitchen. Only when Moira does not need us anymore do we shower and dress for dinner. Moira is proud of her cooking and likes to attend to the final touches herself. I washed my hair and put on a white dress. As I walked down the stairs Moira said: "Anaïs, it is your turn to take out the garbage."

"I'll change my dress."

"No, Anaïs," said Charles Duits. "I'll take the garbage out."

Moira introduced me to the Syrian poet Berthie Zilka. She will study writing in English with me, but we are to publish her poems in French.

We began work on Zilka's collection. Gonzalo designed a beautiful book. For the head of each poem James Woodward designed a delicate tracery, like a modern interpretation of Syrian designs.

U.S. troops have broken through at Saint-Lô.

I feel stronger for having recognized quickly the negative, the destructive, and for not allowing myself to be submerged or victimized by a fruitless combat against the confusion of Harry's mind: his wild statements, his inaccuracies, his erratic impulses. I was able to recognize them in time.

Seeking to break the friendship with Harry, I became more and more aware that he is disintegrated, chaotic, unbalanced. He says: "I want to read all the diaries. I want to know the secret of woman, to incorporate this knowledge into my writing. I feel I must know it. No other woman can give me the truth. Then I will possess knowledge." He spoke like a predatory invader. He complained: "Everything is locked to me. First you, and now the diary." The nakedness of his greed, audacity, and aggressiveness made me recoil.

"I asked Henry to leave me everything in his will. I am his son."

I finally said one day: "You cannot learn, love, or create by stealing. You have to create yourself first, and your work, and then bonds are born of this, genuine ones, and people exchange their treasures. You can't force things."

Liberation of France!
JOY. JOY. JOY. JOY. JOY. JOY. JOY. JOY. JOY.
Such joy, such happiness at the hope of war ending. Happiness in unison with the world. Delirious happiness.

At such times we are overwhelmed by a collective joy. We feel like shouting, demonstrating in the street. A joy you share with the whole world is almost too great for one human being. One is stunned before catastrophe, one is stunned by happiness, by peace, by the knowledge of millions of people free from pain and death.

For days we could not work. Then we returned to the press and finished Zilka's book. It has a red suede cover, to match the sensuous quality of the poems. She is a good poet, with new accents, new sensations which come from her Syrian background.

We dream of returning to France.

I would like to convert the diary into a long novel. From it I have already borrowed the themes of *Winter of Artifice* and *Under a Glass Bell*. I do want to dramatize the conflicts of woman. Conflict between maternal love and creation. Between romanticism and realism. Between expansion and sacrifice.

The conflicts of woman in present-day society. Theme of development of woman in her own terms, not as an imitation of man. This will become in the end the predominant theme of the novel: the effort of woman to find her own psychology, and her own significance, in contradiction to man-made psychology and interpretation. Woman finding her own language, and articulating her own feelings, discovering her own perceptions. Woman's role in the reconstruction of the world. The women who will appear in the novel: the masculine, objective one; the child woman of the world; the maternal woman; the sensation-seeker; the unconsciously dramatic one; the childish one; the cold, egotistical woman. And the healing, intuitive guide-woman. The evolution will be from subjectivity and neurosis to objectivity, expansion, fulfillment.

The physical as a symbol of the spiritual world. The people who keep old rags, old useless objects, who hoard, accumulate: are they also keepers and hoarders of old ideas, useless information, lovers of the past only, even in its form of detritus?

I suggested that in the ragpicker story. But I was never able to corroborate it. Helba is the only hoarder I know, and she of course ceased to grow early in her life.

I have the opposite obsession. In order to change skins, evolve into new cycles, I feel one has to learn to discard. If one changes internally, one should not continue to live with the same objects. They reflect one's mind and psyche of yesterday. I throw away what has no dynamic, living use. I keep nothing to remind me of the passage of time, deterioration, loss, shriveling.

Zilka's book had to be reprinted because Gonzalo took it to a "French" friend to proofread and this person did not know French! Zilka was deeply upset. I gave up rest and beach and returned to do the job again. Struggle to keep the press afloat. While I am working the electric company comes to turn off the electricity, and I have to pay the bill instantly. I work from ten to six o'clock, and Gonzalo from two to six.

A frightening episode. A man carrying some kind of badge, and papers as a special kind of guard, came to tell us we must pay him to be a night watchman of the press. He would put a sign on the door which would show everyone that he patrolled the district and kept an eye on the press. He said every shop in the neighborhood employed him, and that without him there would be burglarizing, etc. Gonzalo protested there was nothing worth stealing. "Who would steal a half-printed book, paper, type, or even engravings?" He argued. The man left. The next morning when I arrived, the picture window in front was shattered. The glass was scattered outside and inside. Anyone could have entered the press. I felt uneasy, as if there were some connection between the refusal to have a watchman and the breaking of the glass. When Gonzalo came, he was disturbed. We replaced the glass. The watchman called on us three days later. He said he had heard that we had had some trouble. This time Gonzalo explained that we were artists, not shopkeepers, that we had very little money to work with, that in fact we were in debt because we were still paying for a press, we owed the telephone company and the electric company, and the last job was not yet paid for.

Two days later, the window was broken again. This time we were desperate. We knew it was blackmail, but there was no way to defend ourselves. That night when Gonzalo went home, he was so depressed he stopped at the bar on the street floor of his building. And there was the watchman, in a friendly mood. He and Gonzalo drank together. They agreed on political questions. They fraternized. We were not bothered by him again. He even stamped his sign: "This place is patrolled by So-and-So" (some title he had invented for himself, I am sure).

Letter from England: J. M. Tambimuttu, poet-editor of *Poetry* magazine, suggests an English edition of *Winter of Artifice* and *Under a Glass Bell*. Letter from *Print* magazine: they cannot review *Winter of Artifice* because it is "improper"! Letter from Henry that he is coming to New York because his mother is ill.

Frances is the woman with the greatest inner depth, the most prolific unconscious. I will consider my whole trip to America worthwhile if I can give a person like Frances the power to exteriorize her richness, to live out her deepest self.

Wrote portrait of Stella, which is a composite of Luise Rainer and other characters. The novel is tentatively titled *This Hunger* and divided into two parts, "Bread" and "The Wafer." ("Bread" symbolic of physical hunger, "The Wafer" as an answer to metaphysical hunger.)

Trying to extract complete characters from the maze of the diary. Trying to construct a story. But a novel is the opposite of life. Discovery that characters are revealed in fragments, not all at once; and during our lifetime we rarely make a synthesis. I cannot work in the artificial form of the novel. I have to follow free associations from another source, to trace character not in its outward manifestations but in its underground life, in the development of its night life.

I am smothering under the weight of the press. I cannot arrest Gonzalo's destructiveness.

The way Pablo came one day was amusing. He introduced himself over the telephone: "I am in the Navy. I have been sitting in a bar for two hours, reading *Under a Glass Bell*. May I come to see you? A friend gave me your telephone number. I am only in New York for a day. I love *Under a Glass Bell*. I will only come for a moment, I promise. I am drunk on your stories and that is why I have the courage to call you." The voice was warm, elated, and young. I said: "Come for a moment. We are on our way out to dinner."

I only said this to leave a possibility of escape. As he walked up the stairs and I held the door open, I saw first of all an irresistible smile, a lithe figure, reddish-brown hair, freckles, laughing eyes. As soon as he came in I liked him. He stayed for dinner and for the whole evening, and we became friends. "At home, in Panama, my American father is a doctor. He married a Panamanian woman. Boys mature quicker there, and I was smoking and roaming the streets and visiting night clubs and whorehouses when I was fourteen. My first love was a married woman, a woman who loved me too much and was torn between freeing me and tying me to her. She felt it was her duty to send me away. I joined the Navy." He is now nineteen. All open and naturalness. But he has the very slender, very pliable hands of the feminine man. He is probably homosexual.

I received a telephone call from Harry Herkovitz. He said: "I am waiting downstairs with a gun. I'm going to kill you."

"You can't force people to love, Harry. I have been a good friend. Your girl loves you deeply, and that is rare to find."

"I'm going to kill you."

"I will call the police."

I hung up. I called the police station in our neighborhood. I explained what was happening. The answer was: "Lady, we can't do anything about a threat. We have to wait until he acts."

"You mean after I am shot?"

"Yes, lady. People get millions of threats every day. We can't do anything about that."

"But you are only two blocks away. Why can't you send someone to see if there is a young man with a gun waiting in front of 215 West Thirteenth Street? He has no right to carry a gun."

"We can't do that."

I stayed home all day. In the evening, I became restless. I called up a friend Harry does not know and asked him to come and see if Harry was still at the door. He came. Harry was gone.

A happy day at the press. Gonzalo received six hundred dollars to do a book. He bought himself much-needed glasses, shoes, pants. He bought me a handbag. He paid Ian Hugo fifty dollars for the engravings which will illustrate the book.

Frances was the only one to appreciate the subtle irony of all this. I do the heaviest part of the work and I let Gonzalo receive the compensations. I let him feel the sense of power in earning money and being able to make gifts to others. It may be an illusion I am nurturing, but it is an illusion which is creative, an illusion which has created a Gonzalo who is proud of himself, and who is making an effort, and who is freer of guilt. A day of pride and optimism and joy. Even if ten minutes later, after all these celebrations, I am at the press, working alone. Nevertheless it is true that Gonzalo has conquered his Indian laziness, his paralysis, his sense of failure and impotence.

Letter from Henry:

For some strange reason I have not been able to telephone you. I seem to feel you do not want to see me. I don't understand it myself. I am at a loss to say where to meet you as I am staying with Harry as there is no other place available, it's far from ideal. Now I am leaving for Bryn Mawr College. Should be back Monday. I'll be in New York (in and out as I have trips to make while I am here) until Thanksgiving. Then I return to the West Coast as my mother is recovering and may live another few years. I hope I get out of my present psychological morass about you the next few days. It may be only fear of hearing you reproach me. I wanted to see you first of all, and here I am writing you instead.

It was Henry who experienced hesitation at seeing me. He feels perhaps that when he made the choice to live in California, he was surrendering our friendship. He also developed guilt toward me when I broke down physically. He may have felt he had a share in overburdening me. Henry has never been able to face a situation like this openly. I would have been glad to see him. But perhaps this separation was good for both of us, and we did not want to witness or stress the finality of it.

When I have faith, I can live joyously. But there are times when I wonder if my faith is illusion, and at moments I feel too awakened, too aware. Did my faith in Henry make him strong enough to go on without me? Does one really create strength in others, or does one merely *become* that strength? Now I work at the press instead of being self-sustaining. If I left Gonzalo alone, would the press collapse? It is I who go there in time to receive the delivery of paper. It is I who pull the proofs for the exigent French client due at four o'clock. It is I who clean the machine left dirty by Gonzalo the night before. Gonzalo likes to design the books, to talk with the clients. As soon as there is a mountainous job, he leaves it to me. He arrives at three. If I am hurt or angry, he immediately flies off the handle. He says: "I'm an old anarchist. I cannot be disciplined." He slams the door and goes out boiling. Later he comes back. Is all this worthwhile?

Half an hour after I leave the press, Gonzalo telephones: "I'm still here. I can't find the book André Breton left with me. I'm worried. Did you see it?"

To calm my rebellions, he asserts his dependency. He dodges the shafts, avoids them with the marvelous self-protectiveness of the primitive. The nonprimitive, the aware, are not nearly as clever.

I buy my dresses secondhand at the thrift shop. As it is usually rich people who sell their clothes, there are some sumptuous items, like a black velvet opera cape, a red wool kimono with gold buttons.

Touched bottom again. Decided to liberate myself. I never go to the press until Gonzalo is there and calls me. Production slowed down.

We are never trapped unless we choose to be.

I began to write, out of despair (the press will fail). I saw art as a drug, the only drug left to me now that I am losing illusion.

I worked on Stella. Applied great care to the choice of language which suited her gestures, her rhythm, lightness, elusiveness.

Another poet came to the press, Lanny Baldwin. Frances Steloff introduced him to me at the Gotham Book Mart. He took me out to lunch. He was dressed like a businesman, with a collar so tight that it constricted his neck. Yet his poetry was surrealistic and free. He has humor and softness, moss-green eyes, and the hesitancies of an adolescent while he masters a mature job. He came to the press "to breathe."

Gonzalo designed a beautiful book of his poems, titled *Quinquivara*.

We went out together last night. French restaurant, French wine, long talk, and he read his new poems. He had been on the stage, and now had a good job, a comfortable home in Mount Kisco, two children. He began to behave like a true southern poet, in spite of his business suit.

On Sunday I wrote twenty-five pages. I have done portraits of Stella, Lillian, Hejda. The portraits are interiorized, and then moved outward. Frances dreamed that she looked for me in a little house by the sea, which had been inundated, but I was not drowned. The dream came after her reading about these women. Was it fear that I should go too deeply into the unconscious, and be drowned in it?

Writing intensely: on anxiety, on a bicycle ride symbolic of disharmony and mistiming in relationship. It was a memory of a summer in France. Gonzalo and Helba were staying at a beach several miles from Saint-Raphaël, where I was visiting my father. Gonzalo and I agreed that we would each bicycle half of the way, and meet at an outdoor café on the beach. But because he was never on time, because he was lazy, and because he bicycled slowly, it always ended with me arriving ahead of time, and he not at the rendezvous until it was almost time for me to be starting back.

Somehow this image seemed the only way to depict Lillian's temperament, active and dynamic, as against that of the man she loved, who was passive. I saw how Lillian's overactive role caused her the pain of not being able to mesh, to find the moment of contact. It seemed to me that this failed meeting told the whole story as it could not be told in hundreds of pages.

Thinking of what seems like a trivial fact: Moira did not sew back the button that had come off her blouse. From there to the French *"déboutonnage,"* which has a slight implication of exhibitionism. Unbuttoning. I thought of the oriental woman being too tightly bound and then unbinding herself to extremes.

For days I was haunted by the memory of mirrors in a garden. I had seen them in Paris at the Rothschilds' house, where I was invited to a concert. While I listened to music by a vehement Italian pianist, I saw out of the window three full-length mirrors in the garden, reflecting pool and lawn. It was an incongruous sight, enough to arrest attention at the time. But why did it stay in my memory, an indelible image? I decided to write about it, to describe it. While doing so, expanding on it (on the assumption that every image which imbeds itself so deeply in our memory must contain a meaningful key to our unconscious), I arrived at an interpretation of it. The mirror reflected nature. The mirror was art, and the book I am writing is concerned greatly with symbolism, and with the conflict between art and nature. Unconsciously I had arrived at a key to the book, an image which clarified my meaning. Woman as nature, the mirror, poetry and art. At times I describe nature as nature, at other times I use the mirror. The mirror is also an expression of fear. There is a taboo on truth, a fear of truth. The mirror allows us to contemplate nature while out of danger.

Through reflection, the story of the bicycle ride, which shows the absurd inequality (emotional or sexual) in the relationship, allows us to see it as ludicrous. We can laugh at her anxiety, a girl riding too fast, driven by the myth demon of anxiety: "I may arrive late, he may have waited and gone, he may think I am not coming." The naked garden in Paris, reflected in the three-faced mirror. People cannot bear the truth. They have placed mirrors where they can see bodies possessing each other (in all the assignation houses of Paris).

I asked a friend who was in Belgium if he could find any copies of *House of Incest* in Bruges, where it had originally been printed. The Gotham Book Mart has requests and is out of copies.

Letter from B. A., with the Canadian Army in Europe:

Dear Miss Nin: Well, I have had a lot of adventures searching for a copy of *House of Incest* but unfortunately drew a blank today. Soon after I got your card I started to make inquiries. I first found Desclee de Brouwer, a very large firm but they had a fire a few years ago at their warehouse and all their English books were burned. The manager said there might be copies at certain stores so I followed all these leads for a week or so. Then I met Dr. de Brouwer himself who suggested the Sainte Catherine Press, just outside of town here. So I tried them and sure enough, they had printed it. But all their English books were hidden from the Germans and they would have to search for them. Today I went back to see them and they haven't even a printer's copy. The only place I can try now is Paris.

The search was worth the trouble, though. I did meet at least twenty interesting families, one very beautiful girl, and drank three or four litres of fine cognac. I'm not finding it very hard to become Europeanized. When I wrote you last I had not read your books but I've finished them now and read some parts many times. I would be a very biased critic of this type of writing because it has been a weakness of mine for so long. I thought Virginia Woolf had gone as far as anyone in portraying delicate human emotions, but you've gone a head above her. Her emotions are always too refined. She never gets any earth or good wholesome sensuality into her work and you have got both. This style of yours gives you wonderful scope for going beyond even D. H. Lawrence at his best in the portrayal of the unusual and delicate human relationships. It is at once very erotic and very beautifully disarming prose. There have been enough bedpans and undisguised Freud in fiction lately. It's time someone came along and got the same effect in a more subtle and beautiful manner. Good luck with your next book and I hope it puts you where you belong.

A letter like this annuls the indifference of the critics. There were only two reviews of the first edition of *Winter of Artifice,* and three of *Under a Glass Bell.*

# [January, 1945]

I am learning to create characters. I can do this up to a point. I begin inspired by reality, by Frances, Thurema, Luise, etc. But no sooner have I gone beyond the literal portrait, and created fictional characters, than I am faced by a limitation. I do not know the contents of their minds, all their feelings and thoughts, and I am forced to draw from my own supply. I pass some of my own substance, consciousness, into them. They are no longer any one person. They are composites. If the landscape of their lives is restrictive, I expand it with my own travels. But they are not really me. I cannot accept the limitations of the faithful portrait, or the often static pause in others' lives, their sudden stratifications, or even worse, their obsessional repetitions of patterns. So I have to go beyond reality. To reach infinite and limitless possibilities. I am aware of my technical inadequacies. I am guided only by a vision of character infinite in depth and change, in timelessness, and in space.

Heard about Henry's marriage to Janina Lepska, and wrote him a warm letter of celebration. I met a friend of Lepska's, Miriam Kreiselman, who told me a great deal about her. She has a doctorate in philosophy, is attractive, young, and very intelligent. Henry sent me a surprise gift of a check.

Letter to Henry:

Yes, I saw Varda, at parties. Loved him. See him as you do, a free, lusty and joyous man, a poet but a real man, very youthful, and his love of women is a relief after so much disparaging I see around me. He turns them into myths, poems, collages, delights of all kinds.

Letter from Leonard W.:

Dear Miss Nin: This letter is mostly an expression of reverence mixed with a little awe, and quite a bit of appreciation. I first saw your name in a dedication of Henry Miller's and it was Wallace Fowlie who urged me to read your stories and lent me *Under a Glass Bell*. . . . I honestly found everyone of the stories very good, especially *"Je Suis le Plus Malade des Surréalistes"* and "Birth." One of the things which struck me most was the poetic quality of every phrase, each if changed in any way would be ruined, it seems, and the beautiful images evoked, as in the labyrinth. I was a bit worried when I read in the preface that you considered destroying them. It make one think: What had she written before that might actually have been destroyed and what will the succeeding book be like? I haven't yet been able to find *Winter of Artifice*, so I have only to hope that the change is for the best, as of course, it probably is. If you have any copies left of any or all your books and if you are willing to part with them, I will feel really honored if you will allow me to buy some from you. For even if I have read a particularly good book many times, nothing gives me greater pleasure than to own a copy. I also wish I had a book printed so that I would be able to offer you a copy in gratitude. It is really too soon for me to start analyzing why I like your stories so much, or what it is in them that attracts me so, but one thing I know is this. After the emotional storm of *Une Saison en Enfer,* and *Les Chants du Maldoror,* it is pleasant and somewhat of a relief to sail more leisurely in the quieter waters of *Under a Glass Bell,* although I must confess, often my anchor finds no bottom even there. Upon re-reading I find that the above is not a particularly felicitous metaphor, but it serves. Another thing I admire very much and would like to cultivate in my own work is the unity of each story. Each is as structurally perfect as the Ferris wheel in "The Mohican," and yet the pulse of life is felt along the entire periphery. Well, I have said enough. I hope I have managed to convey some part of the deep admiration and appreciation I feel for your work.

I answered and mailed him a copy of *Winter of Artifice*.

### Letter from Leonard W.:

I received your wonderful letter and this afternoon the book. I am now on the fifteenth reading of the letter, and each time I get the same feeling of elation that I did at first. As for *Winter of Artifice,* I can only echo the words of Rebecca West, Edmund Wilson and Henry Miller. However, here is how it struck me. The whole music metaphor in *Winter of Artifice* was a superb thing in itself. I liked very much all of "The Voice." The orchestra symbols are very interesting. I have been hearing many provocative things lately about your diary. I hope sincerely you can either publish it yourself or find someone who will. I promise you I shall send you the money for the book I received as soon as I pay a slight debt to Henry Miller for a painting. I showed Mr. Fowlie what you said about his article in the *Kenyon Review* and he was indeed pleased. We will both see you soon, I hope. As regard to my work, which you show such a kind interest in, I am working on a short story now. You see, everything I had written before I took Mr. Fowlie's course in contemporary French authors had been so much in the romantic schoolboy vein that I have rejected it all. As a matter of fact, I can say without exaggeration that an entirely new world was revealed to me when I swallowed my first mouthful of Baudelaire, Rimbaud, Miller, André Gide, Verlaine, Proust and boundless others. . . . So I am just beginning to write. And from all present indications it will be months and years before the influence of this new order of literature has assumed its proper proportion in my life. But I talk too long of me. I am quite overwhelmed when I read a letter like yours regarding cooperation between the artist and the public. Relatively unknown and unsung men like Miller, George Leite in California, yourself, who raise money for destitute authors, encourage one another, overwhelm me with humility. I think I would rather be one of your numbers than a Somerset Maugham or a Booth Tarkington. Sometimes I feel like consecrating myself to the task of becoming a millionaire, so that I might provide grants or funds for a publishing company, the kind that would publish the volumes of Anaïs Nin's journals in vellum and gold ink. Well, I have taken enough of your time I am afraid. Thank you again for the book and the letters and even more for your warm interest. I cannot close without re-iterating my admiration for your technique which I can't quite define yet and for the beautiful and fearless flow of symbols, the one merging into the other in perfect metamorphosis, like the themes of Stravinsky's "Petrouchka."

A snowstorm. I was working on *This Hunger*, when my typewriter broke down. I went out into the snow with it to get it repaired. When I came back, I did not feel like writing the continuation of Djuna's life at the orphan asylum and her hunger. I felt like writing about snow. I wrote every image, every sensation, every fantasy I had experienced during my walk. The snowstorm had thrown me back into the past, into my innocent adolescence, surrounded by desires, at sixteen, intimidated, tense. I compared my adolescence with the frozen adolescence of others around me today. They all fused: snow, the frost of fear, the ice of virginity, purity, innocence, and always the sudden danger of melting. I wrote myself out. And when I was finished, I realized I had described Djuna's adolescence, and the adolescent contractions of other adolescents. I had written thirty-eight pages on the snow in women and men, on Djuna and the asylum, her hunger.

*Town and Country* magazine had published a photograph of me dressed fashionably by Henry La Pensée. The photographer heard me describe the four women of my next book and wanted to experiment with a photograph in which I would dress differently for each character, and then as myself, Anaïs, the novelist, in the center. I assembled the clothes which seemed to fit Lillian, Djuna, Stella, Hejda. For Lillian I chose the evening suit altered to fit me (when we all wanted to imitate the woman captain, Valentina), with a more severe shirtwaist. I dressed my hair severely, and what did I see in the mirror? A resemblance to my father, who wore his hair long in the back, as artists of his time did. This amused me, and appealed to my love of disguises. Then I dressed as Hejda, oriental, with a veil across the face. Stella, of course, was soft and feminine, pliant; and the novelist in the center was dressed simply, and looked up naturally between her "characters." All this was done in a playful, surrealist mood. The photographer made a collage. But *Town and Country* was not amused. Nothing came of it. The photographer gave me the photograph.

Days of feverish inspiration, a flood of spontaneous writing. Onrush of associations, of impromptu anecdotes, utter freedom. What has happened is that I have touched off such a deep level of unconscious life that the women lose their separate and distinct traits and flow into one another. As if I were writing about the night life of woman and it became all one. The boundaries, distinctions, are erased; on that subconscious level, people are the same: emotions, instincts, dreams. As I lose my grip on construction, on realism, I seem to gain another kind of reality. I emerged today with thirty-eight pages on the snow woman, adolescence, the virgin woman, interwoven with the story told to me by Frances of her life in the orphan asylum.

The beauty of this moment is in my freedom. My abundance of love able to live itself out, to keep everyone in a state of romance, to make each hour, each evening, each moment yield up its fullness. To disperse and dispense tenderness, attentiveness, joy in living.

Twenty years ago Elsa De Brun lived in Forest Hills, where I took the train to go to work. She saw me walking toward the station and she said to herself: "If ever I am in trouble, this is the woman I will go to." And twenty years later she was in trouble and sought me out. She had bought a bad sketch of me made by a Village artist. She had collected all my books and photographs. Her first question, even before she talked about herself, was how did I feel about woman. I answered: "I feel great warmth and lively friendship, but never sexual desire. I once had a desire for June, which was never lived out."

Our life is composed greatly from dreams, from the unconscious, and they must be brought into connection with action. They must be woven together. It is not because I love complexity that I have tried to gather together all the elements. Frances called it symphonic, a vast gathering together. This is the way we live. She did speak against ornamentation. When will I write a quartet? But the unconscious does produce these great intricacies, multiple levels and facets. I listen to music as never before, bathe in it. My symphonic writing puzzles those I love and trust. But I have had only the desire that writing should become music and penetrate the senses directly. For this, poetry is necessary. The unconscious speaks only the language of symbol. That is my language.

Frances responds to the direct statement I make about woman in the preface. But that is the writing of the intelligence. It is not the writing of emotion and the senses, which I seek. I want meaning to enter the body by some other route, not the mind. I am not writing with the mind. Frances likes it when my mind appears to explain. I like it best when I am submerged in symphony, and when the world in my head becomes a world of images and music. Writing has for too long been without magical power. In me everything was married, love and the body, heaven and hell, dream and action. No analytical dismemberment or separation of elements. As a woman, I shall put together all that was divided and give new birth to everything that was killed.

Edmund Wilson invited me for lunch. I felt his distress, received his confession. Even though not an intimate friend, Wilson senses my sympathy and turns toward it. He is lonely and lost. He is going to France as a war correspondent. He asks me to accompany him while he buys his uniform, his sleeping bag. We talk. He tells me about his suffering with Mary McCarthy.

I rewrote the snow passage and then that of the yielding of woman.

The book is taking shape. The women have been divided into elements: Djuna, perception; Stella, blind suffering; Sabina, the free woman; Lillian, the one who seeks liberation in aggression.

The nearness of the Russians to Berlin—ninety miles—is the feverish theme of all our talks and interest. A terrifying moment for the world.

I feel the spring. I enjoy Pablo's gaiety, Charles Duits' poetry. I am writing, loving, and choose to believe the letters I receive rather than the sour reviewers.

The bell rang unexpectedly. At the door stands a most beautiful man of seventeen, tall, slender, blond, with deep-blue eyes, long lashes, a transparent skin like a *jeune fille en fleur*, a great seriousness in his bearing, a shyness, an innocence, a purity. It all radiates from him as he stands there and says: "I am Leonard W."

He was born in Manila of American parents, spent four years in Manila, four years in China, then America. But the early uprootings created loneliness. He has incredibly slender hands. His eyes are long, slanted, almost oriental when he is dreaming, but intense and hypnotic when he examines you. The curiously blue shadows over them when he looks down, blue shadows of a celestial blue. He destroyed his diary, his adolescence, when he came home from college. He brings me a story he wrote, his water colors, and leaves them with me to be blessed, he said. I am rich indeed with young men's dreams and worship. They create a world so distinct from the harsh, purely intellectual, unemotional and unimaginative world of people like Edmund Wilson, editors of *Partisan Review,* etc.

I had spoken of Leonard's hypnotic eyes. So many blue eyes look diluted, as if painted by a water colorist, but his are intense, like the deepest part of the ocean in some prestorm mood. And last night when he came, he told us that he could hypnotize people. Pablo offered himself for the experiment. He lay on the couch and Leonard, in a deep, rich, tranquil voice, talked to him monotonously until he fell asleep. Leonard told Pablo: "You are now two years old." Pablo said in Spanish: *"Agua."*

Leonard: "Now you are three years old."

Pablo said: "Nanny."

Leonard: "Now you are four years old."

Pablo sat up and sang a little song in an unknown language. At age five he said: "I broke a vase," and went to stand at the corner of the room, face to the wall, for punishment. At seven he asked for paper and pencil and drew the face of a little girl with a boarded-up mouth. Leonard offered him a cigarette which he smoked awkwardly, making a wry face and coughing.

"You are now at home, in Panama. What do you want to do?"

Pablo: "Lie on the sand, in the sun, or swim."

"Now you are in New York. What do you want to do?"

"Write and paint," said Pablo.

Leonard asked him to sing a song like Sablon. Pablo did. Then to sing the same song in an operatic way. Pablo did. And he did this with open eyes but a fixed, empty glance, and a childlike expression of complete submission. He was told to act drunk. He stumbled about. Then Leonard gave his final order: "When you awaken, you will not see Anaïs. You will not see Anaïs until I snap my fingers."

Pablo awakened. Leonard had given me a letter to hand to him. Pablo saw the letter but not me. Then he tried to sit on the chair where I was sitting. When I touched his hair, he brushed my hand away as if it were an invisible insect. We were all half-anxious, half-amused, half-fearful of Leonard's power. Leonard was smiling, firm and dominant. The beauty of his face was astonishing, its paleness, the fine, clear, lean lines of the cheekbone, the very full sensuous mouth, the boy's hair, tousled, falling over his eyes, the very image of what mystics or poets should look like.

Another evening of hypnotism. This time for Luise Rainer and Frances. Leonard hypnotized Pablo. Told him that he was Roosevelt and must make a speech. Pablo was sitting on the couch. He did not move. We thought the hypnosis had failed. But when Leonard repeated his order, Pablo said: "I need help to rise." Roosevelt. A chill ran down our spines. Then with help he did get up, and he made a very Roosevelt-like speech. Then Leonard told him he would not see Luise Rainer when he awakened. And

Pablo did not see her. When it was time to leave, Leonard had still not snapped his finger, saying: "Now you can see Luise." Pablo was standing by the door on his way out. Luise had gone into the kitchen for a glass of water. The kitchen light was behind her. Her shadow appeared on the white wall by the entrance. Pablo saw this shadow, but not her, and was disturbed. The next day he said he would not submit to hypnosis again, that it frightened him, this loss of his will, and being controlled by Leonard to such an extent. He was afraid it would affect his will, or influence him into acts he did not wish to enter into.

Letter from Henry:

George Leite showed me your wonderful letter about *Circle* magazine and other things, since it contained a message for me. At the same time I had a letter from Wallace Fowlie saying he had plucked up enough courage to visit you (more courage than I had). No, I knew you had not left for Europe yet. I hear about you all the time, from this one, and that. I would have seen you in New York but I had a feeling you did not want to see me. Now that the ice is broken perhaps we can write one another again. For the moment I don't know what to say. Just glad to know you're alive and in good spirits. I am surprised about your change of plans. Somehow I expect still more changes. Did you know that Maurice Kahane is still carrying on in Paris? He changed his name during the war to Girodias. I get letters from soldiers in Paris telling me all our books are prominently displayed in the shops and selling well, yours, [Michael] Fraenkel's, Durrell's and mine. Will we ever get royalties from them I wonder. I'm eager to see your new work. George Leite is going to show me whatever you send. Durrell always asks about you. Do write when you can. I miss you.

Wallace Fowlie, at Yale, read *Under a Glass Bell*. This started a correspondence between us. I loved the way Fowlie wrote about the poets, like a poet and not an academician. His interpretations were inspiring.

When Fowlie came to see me I found a quiet, small man, dressed in a dark suit, with soft hands. Somehow, he seemed muted, self-effacing, impersonal. His love of Henry Miller's writing did not seem compatible with the first impression I had.

We talked about literature, mostly. Fowlie speaks perfect French. In fact that Anglo-Saxon, prudish appearance and the perfect knowledge of French and French literature seemed like one more paradox. I liked him and believed we would have a good friendship.

Leonard and I sat in Washington Square talking over his rebellion against his family. They sound abnormally rigid. I took him to the press. He wanted to help. He looks exhausted after the sessions of hypnosis, as if he had made love.

"Can you make someone fall in love with you?"

"That would be a poor kind of love."

Later Leonard said: "If I had a place to stay, I would leave home."

Tom and Frances Brown offered him a small room next to their apartment, with a separate door. I offered him food and pocket money. He has only two months of freedom before he goes into the army, and would like to live as he feels for this precious period.

"I feel I know what I want now, not only from reading books and knowing you, but from sharing your life, the spontaneity of Pablo, the vitality of Josephine, the gay creative atmosphere, the other friends, and the warmth."

"Do you feel emotionally ready to cut yourself off from your family?"

"They are not my real spiritual family. You are."

Sunday afternoon we went to Pelham Bay, to look for a houseboat for Pablo. I dressed in Pablo's sailor suit and beret. Saturday evening we had a party, a warm, lively, joyous evening, with Josephine singing and drumming and making us all sing and drum and dance. Luise Rainer came; Frances; Tony Smith, a mystical architect, and his actress-wife, Lawrence. Others brought friends. At the end of the evening Leonard hypnotized Marshall, another beautiful young man, who had come with a harp player. When Marshall returns to age one, two, three, etc., we find it comical. But we are afraid to let Leonard try: "And before that, further back." Suppose Marshall remained a baby, did not return? He has huge green eyes, a golden tan skin, soft features. And all of them are full of invention. Leonard and Pablo fought a duel with two metal measuring tapes. The tapes would at times remain stiff like swords, and then unexpectedly and absurdly collapse just at the moment of victory.

Leonard sculpted a metal bird of paradise and we hung it from a thread in the middle of the room. At the slightest wave of air it spins, seems to be flying. He also painted scenes with fluorescent paints which only show in the dark, so at night the studio appears to be an exotic jungle. Pablo brought a hamster whose hair he had dyed blue.

After the party Leonard talked about his dramas at home.

He wanted to know why we were all willing to help him.

"I think it's an act of faith in you," I said. "We all believe in you. You belong with us."

"When I grow up, I will be able to do the same for others."

"Yes, of course." His saying: "When I grow up" made me aware of his youth. When he leaves, he places his delicate, sensitive, soft-skinned hands in mine as if he would leave them there, in a shelter.

Sunday was the critical day for him. His father wanted him to go to work with him downtown on Monday morning. His father owns an oil company. Leonard said he first had to go to Yale to collect his belongings.

Monday morning he appeared at my door with his valise.

"Your real life is beginning."

"I feel I have gained more than I have lost."

We went together to Frances' apartment on Charles Street. We tidied the guest room. And then the dream began. Leonard eating with us, sharing all our evenings, sharing books, music, my friends, playing chess with Tom, smiling at times like a child, at others like an old soul, talking about transmigration, making sketches of me, eager to harmonize with all our activities. (His family found him cold, stubborn.)

I began to see him as Jakob Wassermann's Caspar Hauser, because of his innocence and sudden insights. He has intuitions about people which are those of an old soul. There is no trace of his upper-class, sheltered, narrow life. He is an adventurer in spirit, has spiritual courage. He reads everything, absorbs, evaluates. His body alone is bound.

He dreamed that his father and mother came to take him back and that he rebelled.

At times he is inarticulate, confused. Or at other times withdrawn and separate.

Leonard pastes a small piece of mirror between my eyes: "Your third eye." He pastes silver paper over my toe nails. When I tell Frances how I see Leonard, she says with her usual wisdom: "The future Leonard."

Fascinating to watch in Leonard the oscillations between adolescence and manhood. He wears a white scarf and walks through shabby streets as if he did not see them. He got drunk for the first time at Frances'. He wanted me to open the diary and show him what I had written about him.

"The diary would be destroyed if I opened it. To be able to tell the truth I have to maintain the mystery."

"I will hypnotize you, make you open the 'safe, and read them all."

In three weeks he has to go to war. His mother seeks an interview. She talks badly about decadent artists, and he passes judgment on her. His father calls him to discuss his "future.".

Pablo and Leonard painted a tapestry which hangs over my bed. They decorate bottles, make collages and drawings. I come back from the hard work at the press, from pressing debts, talk of Helba's illness, and I find them all at work. I make tea and honeybutter.

Leonard's father had come to Tom's and Frances' apartment to see the kind of place his son was living in. He set a detective to watch my life. He took my books to a lawyer, and the lawyer admitted there was nothing in either book to incite a young man to break with his parents. He said at worst they were "bizarre," but nothing the law could attack. And the other book, Lautréamont's *Maldoror,* well he was a writer who had been dead for a hundred years and could not be sued. He tried to harm Wallace Fowlie and complained to the college about the books Fowlie had given Leonard to read. Power against spirit. Frances' husband, Tom, the coolest one, was delegated to talk to Leonard's father. He gained his confidence. Lightning was averted for a time.

When Leonard is happy he hugs me so tightly that I said: "You're flattening me into a wafer."

"The better to commune with, my dear."

He opens and reads all my letters.

Lanny Baldwin is another who, while enjoying the writing, enjoying the character of Lillian, tells me over the telephone, referring to all that is missing around Lillian: "We will get down to brass tacks." When he came, we did not get down to brass tacks. He climbed to my stratosphere.

Frances gives me a small velvet hat with a trailing feather, the latest fashion. Pablo repainted the feather a more vivid pink. I wear this dashing hat when we go to the theater or ballet.

After Leonard's father visited Frances' and Tom's apartment to see the kind of people his son was staying with, we expected him also to come to my studio. I climbed a ladder and took down the colored bird of paradise. But he did not come.

He sent a detective instead to question me.

The detective found the studio occupied by Pablo and Leonard, both painting on the same canvas a luxuriant jungle with exotic birds and flowers à la Rousseau. Pablo's hamster was chewing lettuce in his cage. Fresh engravings lay drying between blotters. I was typing my new book. His comment: "Not much to report."

We went to the ballet and sat up in the balcony, far too much to one side, while downstairs Leonard's father's box yawned empty.

Joaquin's "Quintet for Piano and Strings" was played at the Museum of Modern Art.

In my brother's music there is always a sense of space, air, as if the lyrical experience had been distilled into a light essence and become transparent. The color gold is always a part of it. Emotion is contained, but always clear and strong.

Joaquin's piano recitals and his compositions are a permanent motif in my life, confirming my convictions that music is the highest of the arts.

When he was five years old, a spirited and restless child no one could tame, he would spend hours absolutely still on the staircase of our home in Brussels, listening to the musicians rehearsing. That was the sign of his vocation. We both listened. I can still hear the lines of Bach which were most often repeated. Joaquin became a musician, and in me music was channeled into writing.

In New York, in the brownstone on Seventy-fifth Street, he studied piano with an eccentric old maid, Emilia Quintero, whom I often described in my childhood diary. She kept a white silk scarf of Sarasate's as others keep a memento of a saint. She had loved him secretly and hopelessly. Some of this love was transferred to the handsome Joaquin.

His music was always there. In Richmond Hill he practiced every hour he did not spend in school. In Paris he practiced all day, in spite of delicate health. In Louveciennes he had his studio in a large, beautiful attic room. There was not only the practicing, but even in childhood there were moments of improvisation, the forerunners of his later compositions.

In Paris we had adjoining apartments. He was studying piano with Paul Braud at the Schola Cantorum, and privately with Alfred Cortot and Ricardo Vinez. He studied harmony, counterpoint, and fugue with Jean and Noel Gallon of the Paris Conservatory. He studied musical composition with Paul Dukas at the Paris Conservatory, and privately with Manuel de Falla in Granada, Spain.

I heard him study and compose by the hour. In Louveciennes, when he grew weary of the discipline, he would visit my mother in her apartment, and then me at my typewriter, and ask "Tu m'aime?"

Satisfied and recharged, he would go back to work. He drew his strength from his love, never from hatred, and later it was his capacity for love, understanding, and forgiveness which kept the family from estrangements. He was always trying to reunite and reconstruct the family unit. He never took sides, judged, or turned a hostile back on anyone.

He gave concerts in Spain, France, Switzerland, Italy, Belgium, Denmark, England, the United States, Canada, and Cuba.

He is proud and modest, unassuming and yet uncompromising, unable to cripple a rival, push anyone aside, or assert himself.

When he whistles, it means he is standing by his piano writing down his compositions, correcting his scores.

Once, in Paris, he destroyed one movement of a quintet whose motif I loved. He commented it was too romantic. Perhaps I heard in it the wistful adolescent parting from adolescent sorrows. Perhaps he had, musically, very good reasons for casting it off, to reach a more austere modernism. But I felt the loss as emotional, and its disappearance as a part of Joaquin himself that he was shedding for more rigorous standards. It coincided with the burning of his diaries. Ten years later, during a period of psychoanalysis, I came out singing the entire melodic theme, I who am not a musician and who cannot read music. This proved to me how deeply his music penetrated an unconscious universe. Even when apparently forgotten, lost, this fragment had remained imbedded in me.

In my father there was a distinct faithfulness to Spanish folklore. Spain was recognizable in the themes he embroidered on and harmonized for concert use. With Joaquin something else happened, which brought his music into the realm of modern universal compositions. The Spanish themes became transformed into something more abstract, more unconscious, not the cliché Spain. He modernized the colors, the fervors, the richness of Spain into daring abstractions. It was a far more complex and subtle Spain. There was a tension between simplicity, the single line, and the highly evolved complexities of colors and tones. The intricacies, like the Moorish lacework of Granada, were always unified into the single wistful chant of "cante Jondo."

I spoke of the color gold. There is always a crystalline quality, the transparencies of truth, a strange faculty for musical sincerity which never reaches a common, explicit statement. The composition always spirals away deftly from a familiar statement. It appeals to a third ear, an unborn ear, the ears of today, more intricate but always true: he has a perfect pitch of the soul.

He explores constantly for daring juxtapositions, daring multiplicities, and superimpositions. He achieves radiations, luminosities, and sparkle. The human being and the composer are one. The sources are good humor, generosity, hidden sorrows he does not burden others with, gray days and joyous days, back-breaking labor and early morning whistling.

Joaquin never slides into anger, caricature, or emptiness, or into any of the artifices and pretensions of some of his contemporaries.

I am sure that listening to his music directed my choice of words, my search for rhythm, my ear for tonalities, my use of the unconscious as a many-voiced symphony. I am sure he is the orchestra conductor who quietly and modestly indicates the major theme of the diary; words similar to music which can penetrate the feelings and bypass the mind. His music, far from being in the background of my life, was in the foreground. It was he as a musician who accomplished what I dreamed of, and I followed as well as I could with the inferior power of words. The ear is purer than the eye, which reads only relative meaning into words. Whereas the distillation of experience into pure sound, a state of music, is timeless and absolute.

As a human being, he is the strongest influence in my life, for it is not the failed relationships which influence our life—they influence our death. With Joaquin I had the model of the best relationship I had throughout childhood and adolescence. True, I had to take care of him; he was five years younger. True, it was he who lived out the wildness, the freedom, the independence, while I had to become responsible for his safety, his well-being. But in return he gave the greatest responsiveness and tenderness. He was loving and loyal. We never quarreled. Once, when I lost some money given to me for marketing (when we had little enough), he offered to take the blame. He was ten years old. He set the pattern for the many little brothers I was to have, whose life I must watch over but who return an immense care and tenderness. He never passed judgment, he was never critical. Our lives were different, but we kept an immense respect for each other.

Just as Joaquin's discarded composition had sunk into my unconscious and disappeared for ten years, to be remembered then clearly and completely, I was startled to find that a book read ten years ago in France, Leon Pierre Quint on Proust, had so deeply influenced my attitude toward writing that today what I have written about the craft seems taken from it. Of all the books written about Proust, none have come to the level and beauty of this one. It is the only book Proust might have read without pain. There is not one false note in it. Quint was a writer on the same level as Proust, could comment on and describe him like a twin, as if Proust himself had stood away from his work and clarified it. He is as refined, as subtle, as accurate, and as penetrating in writing of Proust's life and work as Proust was in his analysis of people. Usually the critic is a lesser writer and a lesser psychological interpreter. He diminishes the work in order to allow himself and others like him to enter the world of the novelist.

Leon Pierre Quint was never translated. He should have been.

Here are some of my favorite excerpts:

Proust's philosophy of instability, mobility, flow and continuity . . .

Our unconscious is the supreme reality of our inner life.

All the personages of Proust are painted in large incomplete frescoes, like the statues of Rodin which leave room for mystery. The fragments that are missing correspond to the evolution of the character and those that are carefully wrought are powerful enough to suggest his life in the past and in the present.

How is it that the critics did not understand that each time a writer discovers a new subject for study, bourgeois morality is alarmed, that each time the writer enters an unexplored domain he appears sacrilegious. Yet the very existence of art depends on its exploration of the parts of life which have not yet been opened, even on its creation of new modes of life.

A particular trait of his vision of people, which was to become more intensely developed with time, was telescopic. It brought people very close to him, limiting the width of his field, but giving him perception into all their complexities.

And these:

He knew that when our wishes were fulfilled it is never at the time or in the circumstances which would have given the greatest pleasure. It should have happened as soon as the wish was made. When he heard one of his friends say: "I would love to have this or that" he would get it for him immediately, not at Christmas or New Year. He remembered that a pleasure too long awaited is a lost pleasure.

His novel, as he said himself, is real because nothing is more real than the contents of the self; but it is not realistic.

If Proust's phrases are not crystal clear and logical it is because our psychological life is confused and intelligence penetrates into it through dark corridors with many labyrinthian turns.

The memory of our conscious intelligent self could give him information into past events but emptied of all emotional content which is reconstructed by associative memory.


Talking about his own emotional imprisonment, Lanny Baldwin says: "Emotions choke me, push the tears right behind my eyes, strangle me. It comes like a wave of ecstasy."

"The difference between us is that I ride on this wave when it comes, I never deny it."

In a world that is destroying itself with hatred, I persist in loving, and those who love me are concerned at my defeats.

As soon as he visits his family, Leonard becomes sad, dead, eclipsed. As soon as he comes to see me, it is a reprieve from death in life.

His mother asked him: "Would I like Anaïs Nin?"

He answered: "You are poles apart."


For the novel: Use iron lung as a symbol of one person breathing through another, living through transfusion of oxygen. Dependence of Djuna on Jay. Any dependence causes anxiety. Because one is living through another and fears the loss of the other. For Lillian it was not her throat, her senses, her life, but all the tasting, touching was done by way of Jay. When he welcomed friends, was at ease in groups, accepted and included all of life, undifferentiated, then she experienced this openness, this total absence of retraction through him. In herself she carried a mechanism which interfered with deep intakes of life and people. Her critical faculty would pass judgment, evaluate, reject, limit. Jay never limited his time or energy. When the time came, he fell asleep. But Lillian felt she had to forestall such a surrender, because it was public. She had to foresee when her energy would fail, and so she lived by the clock. At twelve she should leave. Even if the evening was just beginning to flower, she had to cut the cord, resist the demands of others, assert a solitary gesture of determination, the opposite of surrender to the current life. Jay permitted himself to be consumed. He was more rested even when he slept less, by his relaxed abandon, than Lillian was from her exertion of control.

Never understood until now why I had to make myself poor enough in Paris to go to the pawnshop. It was because all my friends went there, and I wanted to reach the same level of poverty and denial, to descend with them into the ordeal of parting from loved objects, losing everything. I was never as emotionally united with all of them as when I, too, sat on the hard bench and waited, watching people's eloquent faces, the story of objects, the atmosphere of dispossession and sacrifice.

In describing relationships, rhythm is important: lax or tense; unilateral or multilateral; crystallized or expanded; fixed or mobile; accelerated or slowed down. When deprived of one sense, reliance on others, those who see best, or hear best, or remember best. There is also the vital matter of distance. People do not live in the present always, at one with it. They live at all kinds and manners of distance from it, as difficult to measure as the course of planets. Fears and traumas make their journeys slanted, peripheral, uneven, evasive.

I, myself, concentrated so much on my sixth sense that I developed this vision which sees beyond facts, the better to find sensations and divinations. It is possible I never learned the names of birds in order to discover the bird of peace, the bird of paradise, the bird of the soul, the bird of desire. It is possible I avoided learning the names of composers and their music the better to close my eyes and listen to the mystery of all music as an ocean. It may be I have not learned dates in history in order to reach the essence of timelessness. It may be I never learned geography the better to map my own routes and discover my own lands. The unknown was my compass. The unknown was my encyclopedia. The unnamed was my science and progress.

Leonard is with his family during the last days before he goes into the army. Put away his belongings, records, the box with the phosphorescent paints, the sheets of copper, scissors, the colored glass, the copper plates, prints, poems, notes, sketches.

Tom had been telling Leonard that all has been written, that intellectual development has killed literature, but I tell him of all that is left to be done. "If the intellect has killed writing, then let the other kind of writing, emotional, kill the intellect."

He telephoned: "I'm at the induction office and taking the train for Fort Dix at six." An hour later, he appeared. He had fainted when he was given an injection.

To send such fragile, not-yet-men into war. His body is vulnerable. It has not yet gained its full strength. He is tall and underweight. He has the neck and ears of a fourteen-year-old.

Of all the elements which stay in my memory, the most vivid is his curious luminosity. Why does it appear in children and adolescents, and then vanish? Is it the presence of the spirit? Is it that the skin, the flesh, is still transparent, not dense and opaque?

My concern is that now Leonard will close. I saw him expand and contract, expand and withdraw. To protect his vulnerability.

Formal German surrender signed. The war in Europe is over. A date to remember: May 8, 1945.

I correspond with Wolfgang Paalen, editor and publisher of *Dyn* magazine in Mexico. He accepted a story of mine, "The Eye's Journey," the one based on Hans Reichel. I found a surrealist passage in the magazine I liked and wrote a fan letter to the author, a man called "Givor," care of Paalen. But Paalen had written it himself, under a pen name, and he did not know whether to be pleased or jealous of this other self which had attracted my praise. His wife Alice is a painter.

I met her today at an exhibition. She is striking in appearance. Tall, dark-haired, sunburned, she looks like a Mexican-Indian woman. But she was born in France, in Brittany.

Her smile and her expression are dazzling, dazzling with spirit, wit, life.

She has some trouble with her hip or leg, which makes her limp.

Her paintings are completely drawn from subterranean worlds, while her descriptions of Mexico are violent with color, drama, and joy.

Wonderful to hear about the sun, about the jungle and rivers, about the colors, the costumes, the habits, the smile in dark faces, the smell of herbs and the grinding of corn, about Mexico's history, its past, the painters who live there and paint with such power. It is a different Mexico from that of D. H. Lawrence. For him, it was strange. For Alice it is familiar, sparkling with gaiety and life, even in poverty.

I developed a longing, which was coupled with the fear that by suffering from the coldness and malice of New York, I would become, in the end, like the people who wrote without feeling, all calluses, bitterness, cynicism.

Added to Alice Paalen's description of Mexico was Pablo's description of Panama. The warmth of climate was wedded to warmth of behavior. The sun was linked to generosity of being.

Letter from Henry:

Went to bed last night with an excellent idea about your diary. Suddenly I sat up in bed and asked myself why had we never thought of Maurice Girodias as a publisher for the diary? Why should you have to do this gargantuan task yourself. It's absurd. . . .

What do you think? Should I write to him at length? I had an idea that when printing each volume he could bring out a small de luxe edition by facsimile process which would establish the authenticity of the work and be a handsome product at the same time. Many of your friends would like to have these.

Robert Laffont has a review called *Magazin du Spectacle* in which he published my "Scenario" from *House of Incest*. *Max and the White*

*Phagocites* will be out in French any day now with my essay on the diary. That should help you. So do think it over.

Long ago I had discussed with Dr. Otto Rank what he called "the Double," which is another expression of our need to project a part of ourselves onto others. Dr. Esther Harding talked about this most clearly one evening. I took notes.

We play a *persona* role to the world.

The acceptance of this social role delivers us to the demands of the collective, and makes us a stranger to our own reality.

The consequent split in the personality may find the ego in agreement with general community expectations, while the repressed shadow turns dissenter.

Failure to acknowledge this dark alter ego creates the tendency to project it onto someone in the immediate environment, the mirror-opposite to one's self.

This redeems the masked self from total annihilation.

Dr. Harding dwelt at length upon the need for acceptance of the shadow in human relationships. The denial of evil on the part of the ego becomes heavily compensated by a dark "psychic atmosphere."

Dr. Harding portrayed this shadow mechanism as a necessary defense against the unknown, since to take up in consciousness the undomesticated patterns of the psyche is to drive one's self into rebellion against society. But one can grow in psychic stature only in proportion as one assimilates the consequences of self-acceptance. The shadow should be a part of the conscious personality.

I do not remember if Rank and I discussed the haunting problem of my sense of responsibility for Henry and Gonzalo. At least I do not believe I was aware of it until this statement by Dr. Harding made me realize why I felt so utterly responsible for their lives. They acted out for me all that I refused myself the freedom to act out. They were both totally irresponsible, rebellious, anarchic, and lived only for their own freedom of action. As all their freedoms were unacceptable to me, and I felt overresponsible for the care of others (beginning with my deserted mother, my abandoned brothers, and so on), I lived this out through them. And I was there to prevent them from suffering the consequences.

Frances and I spent an hour trying to detect and disentangle when the analyst Martha Jaeger is objective and when not. Now that she has shown that she confuses her personal feelings with analysis, I am afraid she will not do us any good. Frances will now have to be watching for mistakes.

Frances visited and I showed her Leonard's water colors. She thought them very fine technically, and beautiful, but withdrawn. When Leonard complains he cannot express feeling, I write him:

Expressing feeling is linked directly with creation. My telling all to the diary helped me in this. You find yourself in a barren environment and tend to withdraw. This will be bad for you as an artist, writer, or painter. In this ability to tap the sources of feeling and imagination lies the secret of abundance. In withdrawing there is danger of sterility or withering. Try to write in your diary to keep that little flame burning. Expand, open, speak, name, describe, exclaim, paint, caricature, dance, jump in your writing. We are here as writers to say everything. Speak for your moods, make your muteness and silence eloquent. The drawings you sent are a closed face upon the world.

Alice Paalen came, Charles Duits, Pablo, and a young man who had been at Michigan University studying Japanese. He told me how intensive the studying was, how intensive the training. Duits and Pablo tried to put on the same comic dueling with the metal tape measure, but, symbolically, it has become limp and without any electrical stiffening. As if this quality came from Leonard himself. Alice Paalen smells of sandalwood and wears a Hindu shawl. She talks interestingly about Picasso, whose mistress she was at one time, and who delighted in withholding pleasure from women.

Madame Chareau is translating the stories from *Under a Glass*

*Bell.* I relearn my vanishing French. She commented on how indirectly and subtly I said things. She realized only much later all that I had implied by describing the way Moricand held himself, with a young girl's shy gesture of covering her sex with her hand.

I am pulling the woodcuts in color by hand, not by machine. I tack the rice paper to a wooden frame, and press by hand on the hand-inked block, as in the old Chinese method.

Edmund Wilson writes from England, rather wistfully, referring to a possible divorce from Mary McCarthy. The first time I read *The Company She Keeps* I felt it was a feat of intellectual hardness, a true piece of granite and self-hatred, and hatred of sensuality.

Caresse was here last night and explained that she received too many poems and needed short stories, or articles of substantial length, for her "Portfolio." She came with the mulatto painter Beardon, who showed us his latest colored drawings à la Rouault— heavy black lines, intense colors, but with a very personal mobility and dynamism. She is exhibiting his paintings in her Washington gallery.

Letter to Henry:

The copy of Pierre Mabille's *Miroir du Merveilleux* was loaned to me by Tanguy, or Yves *qui Tangent,* as I call him, so I cannot send it to you. I tried to find a copy and if I ever do I will let you know.

David Moore came, a tall, pale, tubercular young man, interesting, difficult, and I believe on a quest of a discovery of you. I was amazed that Michael Fraenkel spent an afternoon convincing him that *Tropic of Cancer* would not have been written but for Michael Fraenkel's books and influence. I was amazed at the falsity of this (and I could not take it seriously) knowing Fraenkel, but even more when I heard that Fraenkel wrote an essay on this to which you wholly assented. I can hardly believe this when I think of Fraenkel's ideology as the very opposite of yours, his small stature as a writer, and his overintellectualizations which you never espoused. Is this true? Incidentally, he told Moore that after my book on Lawrence my talent became perverted and that I did nothing ever since.

I have seen Fraenkel around the Village, and once when I was at the movies, watching Eisenstein's film on Mexico, he put his cadaverous hand on my shoulder, like the very hand of death itself. I have carefully avoided him. Moore I believe is worth your interest and I hope his work on you will satisfy you. I know you are overloaded with mail so I will not forward his thirteen-page letter, mostly about you.

You ask about the press. I am still and always on the verge of losing it, and after I print this new book I will be forced to give it up.

Charles Duits and other friends whom Leonard has subtly driven away, gather around me again. My friendship with Frances had deepened because we share the friendship of Leonard.

This week I was battered. First by Martha Jaeger not understanding the novel; then by Frances seeking to develop the realist in me, after admitting my intense focusing on the inner life uncovered an imaginative, inventive, dream-rich world; then by Leonard writing me that my letters were elusive, evanescent, almost invisible, like the Chinese paper I write them on.

This is an example of what happens to me constantly and depresses me: C. L. Baldwin read *Under a Glass Bell* before meeting me, was fascinated, and wanted to meet me. Then immediately, as if I were a balloon or a kite, he started pulling at the string to bring me down to reality. Baldwin said the stories were intoxicating, then he adds: "I want to see you write simply and directly, as when you describe Jay. Writing that can be smelled and touched, warm and human. Not fantasy. Your fantasy in *Under a Glass Bell* makes me uneasy. When I yield to it I feel I am losing my sanity. I feel secure in reality, in the country, working in my garden."

The great beauty of my life is that I live out what others only dream about, talk about, analyze. I want to go on living the uncensored dream, the free unconscious.

I make my concession to reality. I work at the press for eight hours. Then I come home and work on the novel.

Perhaps my illusion (that Leonard will become what I imagined) is not illusion, but intuition. Intuition of potentials, of the future, of the not-yet-born.

What my friends do mind is that I relate to one side of themselves (their intimate, secret self) and I flee from the other. Frances and I have marvelous interchanges, but I run away when her friends come to play poker, or argue harshly about writers and politics. I take the best of Martha's wisdom, and elude her "real" life.

## [June, 1945]

Work. Work. Work. Pasting the beautiful series of five of Ian Hugo's colored woodblocks for *This Hunger* into a special portfolio with a preface written by hand by me forty times. We turned out a beautiful limited edition of forty copies and it is selling quickly. Now we can pay for the linotype, and buy paper. Work. The press. Talks with Frances. Light dinners because of the heat.

Poor Pablo, starved for love, not lucky, overabundant in his warmth, and pitted against paltry natures. He is so alive.

Frances says: "You are Leonard's anima."

"You would have been a better one. Leonard said you were more of a happy medium than I, more intellectual."

"But you release the creative imagination."

Pablo's place is a small room with two windows opening on an old elm tree. The room is so small that it seems to be built as part of the tree, a tree house. The tree fills the room with its greenness, with its whispers of silk.

The story of Caspar Hauser is a story far more beautiful than that of Christ. It is the story of innocence, of a dreamer destroyed by the world. First the child is imprisoned. Then he is abandoned to strangers. Power, intrigue, evil cynicism join to murder him. Never was the ugliness of the world more clearly depicted. Caspar Hauser died at seventeen. Leonard could die at seventeen, eighteen, killed in battle in the Far East.

I read Rilke's *Letters to a Young Poet*. "An emotion is pure whenever it takes up your whole being."

What is it that attracts me to the young? When I am with mature people I feel their rigidities, their tight crystallizations. They have become, at least in my eyes, like the statues of the famous. Achieved. Final.

Leonard is concerned about how little he has to give me.

I write him:

I like to live always at the beginnings of life, not at their end. We all lose some of our faith under the oppression of mad leaders, insane history, pathologic cruelties of daily life. I am by nature always beginning and believing and so I find your company more fruitful than that of, say, Edmund Wilson, who asserts his opinions, beliefs, and knowledge as the ultimate verity. Older people fall into rigid patterns. Curiosity, risk, exploration are forgotten by them. You have not yet discovered that you have a lot to give, and that the more you give the more riches you will find in yourself. It amazed me that you felt that each time you write a story you gave away one of your dreams and you felt the poorer for it. But then you have not thought that this dream is planted in others, others begin to live it too, it is shared, it is the beginning of friendship and love. How was this world made which you enjoyed, the friends around me you loved? They came because I first gave away my stories. They came to respond, and to replenish the source. Pablo heard *Under a Glass Bell* tolling for the fiesta and arrived with his own stories. You must not fear, hold back, count or be a miser with your thoughts and feelings. It is also true that creation comes from an overflow, so you have to learn to intake, to imbibe, to nourish yourself and not be afraid of fullness. The fullness is like a tidal wave which then carries you, sweeps you into experience and into writing. Permit yourself to flow and overflow, allow for the rise in temperature, all the expansions and intensifications. Something is always born of excess: great art was born of great terrors, great loneliness, great inhibitions, instabilities, and it always balances them. If it seems to you that I move in a world of certitudes, you, *par contre,* must benefit from the great privilege of youth, which is that you move in a world of mysteries. But both must be ruled by faith.

Frances and I play psychological chess games. Frances would like me to be more of a realist. She is the one who incited me to print the *Under a Glass Bell* stories. What I leave out of my work I leave out, discard, and overlook in life as well, because I do not think it is important. It weighs people down, and kills vision and spiritual perceptions. Too much upholstery. We are limited enough as it is without weighing ourselves down with facts which do not inspire, nourish, or liberate us. Frances admits that by being almost exclusively interested in her inner voyages, which are immensely rich, fecund, that particular inner world gained in vividness. Everything else to me are obstacles, interferences, clutterings, inessentials. America suffers from too much realism, too much Dreiserism, too many Hemingways and Thomas Wolfes. My passion is for freedom from contingencies, from statistics, from literalness, from photographic descriptions. After this talk, Frances dreamed of me as a gypsy, a nomad, but one driven by a spiritual quest.

I read Eliot to please Frances. He has an orderly and formal mind. I do not like his Victorian morality. A new philosophy will come out of our psychological development. We will know that good and evil are not separate elements, but are interactive in the same person, dialectically, at different periods, and in different circumstances, changing aspects. Therefore, when Eliot speaks against Lawrence's characters, he speaks as a Puritan of this "amorality." Lawrence brought to the surface the entire unconscious, without selectivity or control, showing the contradictory impulses as such. Of course, admitting the strong power of guilt, psychoanalysis admits conscience and a religious censorship within ourselves. The important task of literature is to free man, not to censor him, and that is why Puritanism was the most destructive and evil force which ever oppressed people and their literature: it created hypocrisy, perversion, fears, sterility. There was a book written on how Puritanism destroyed the universal grandeur of American literature for the world, blighting Emerson, Whitman, and others as incomplete forces. The value of Henry Miller is not at all in spiritual or moral qualities, but in his shattering of Puritan crystallizations. He was a liberating force. There are many ways to be free. One of them is to transcend reality by imagination, as I try to do.

I am collecting notes on writing for a lecture I have to give in the fall.

I prefer Wallace Fowlie to Eliot, because he proceeds by these sudden illuminations, leaving out all the inessentials. When he writes about the poets, I live his illuminated phrases in which so much knowledge is telescoped.

I find Eliot "*déséchant*." I feel the prime morality of literature should be to teach how to live, expand physically and mentally, how to experience, see, hear, feel, and give birth simultaneously to the soul and the body. I still feel Fowlie is more inspiring, more contagious, vibrant, highlighting deeper realms.

Sold eighteen portfolios to museums and galleries.

First page proofs of *This Hunger*.

Walking down Thirteenth Street I remembered the French postman so much loved by the surrealists. Just a humble, small, anonymous postman, walking for thirty years along the same route in the South of France, and one day he said to himself: "How can one keep from going mad with monotony, walking the same route for thirty years? By dreaming." And he built this amazing castle, stone by stone, a real fantasy, exteriorized by patient hard labor. There were photographs of it in the old *Minotaure*. I wondered how many years I would walk between the press and the studio, along the same street. Would I ever walk through the streets of the faraway cities I want to see?

Josephine Premice is becoming quite famous and successful. She is singing at Café Society. I went to hear her. She always embraces me shouting: "My sister!"

Dali appeared at a lecture in a diver's suit. At first I laughed at the absurdity, as everyone did, then I realized the deep significance of it. The artist finds his way into the most secret, the deepest, and most unconscious self, where lies the real source of creation. Often I think of us as the earth itself, full of hidden treasures, gold, precious stones, fire, metals, or of the riches at the bottom of the sea, all subterranean and having to be brought to the surface. We could also wear a miner's suit.

Saw several of Maya Deren's films. Truly unconscious dream material, better in some ways than the early surrealist movies because there are no artificial effects, just a simple following of the threads of fantasy. Good camera finesse. Went with Frances and Tom.

*Meshes of the Afternoon:* "A film concerned with the inner realities of an individual and with the way in which the subconscious will develop an apparently casual occurrence into a critical emotional experience."

*At Land:* "A film in the nature of an inverted Odyssey, where the Universe assumes the initiative of movement and confronts the individual with a continuous fluidity toward which, as a constant identity, he seeks to relate himself."

I see the influence of Cocteau, except that she will not resort to any symbolism or artifice to present the dream. The dream resembles realism. The objects are not altered, there is no mystery. There is nothing to indicate that one is dreaming or free-associating. A curious prosaic quality imposed upon the imagination.

A Chekhov-play day. Olga drove us to Port Jefferson, on Long Island, where a Russian colony congregates. First we called on Vassily Vassilinoff, then on Tatiana Nabukova, then on Nikolai Vaharoff, then Gregory Psnikov Guriananoff, and we all gathered on a small, placid, Long Island beach. Everybody talking at once about God, death, war, dreams, music, literature, heroism, with the most incredible fantasy and enthusiasm. I remembered Olga's own words once: "In my family we did everything with enthusiasm. We even *died* with enthusiam." And she mimed someone rising from a death bed and greeting the invisible death with the elation of a lover. In and out of the water we popped, writers, singers. Someone asked when Nabukova was going home; if So-and-So was returning to Paris, to the same old pension; how Tatiana was returning to Moscow; how Olga may go back to Poland.

There are many signs pointing to an accelerated war and a quick ending.

The only one who can open Pandora's box with impunity is the artist. Because when he has emptied the box of one illusion, he can create another and replenish it with new material. He can put back into the box the worlds he created and the discoveries he made. No one can live with only a clinical, psychological, or historical vision of the world. There must be a capacity to recreate, renovate, renew. Martha continues to analyze in place of feeling, analyze instead of living sensually, unconsciously. The same after my talks with Rank: too much lucidity creates a desert, and one has to find water again, to replant, reseed.

Frances seeks to clarify the difference between creative intuition and illusion. She fears that many of my intuitions are illusions, and then later they turn out to be correct. She feels it is my illusions which cause me anguish. But intuition can cause anguish, too, because you have it and cannot prove it to anyone else, and you are alone with it, and everyone else says it is not so. Analysis, too, can disintegrate. It has a dual role. But I see clearly now that both are necessary: to live passionately and blindly, to take risks; and then to interpret later, in order to rescue one's self from disaster if it turns out to be an illusion rather than a creative intuition.

Baldwin obeys only his fears, ambivalences. He seeks safety. He has been attracted to our world, and he is afraid of it.

I see my writing as an early presentiment of the imprisonment to which human beings are subjected. It was my means of evasion, burrowing my way out to freedom.

The novel is false. I rebel against it while I write it. Composites are false. Sabina, the woman of passion; Lillian, the woman of instinct but inhibited; Djuna, the woman of the psyche; Hejda, the woman of oriental obliqueness and new freedom; Stella, the actress living by osmosis.

Frances said with amazement: "In the end, you always write the truth. People think it is fantasy, but it is psychologically absolutely real. That's what people did not see. You discard realism, but not reality."

A summer night. Windows and the door to the porch open. The noises of the city clear and sharp. The foghorns from the river gay and short. The metal bird is revolving up under the ceiling, the tapestry painted by Leonard and Pablo flowering in the dark. All the lights are out.

A moment of peace.

The rest is work. Work at the press, work on *This Hunger,* correcting proofs.

Leonard said before leaving: "I will have seventeen months of training and study and then they will send me to Japan."

There is an analogy between the bombardment of the atom and the bombardment of the personality by the method of analysis, the dismemberment, separation of the elements of the psyche which may release new energies. I believe scientific principles can be applied to the life of the psyche.

I must study scientific principles as symbolic ways of making the workings of the psyche clear. The time has come to give the psyche a concrete symbolism. I feel there is a connection between what takes place within us and what takes place outside. Just as scientists stripped away the layers of matter to get at the heart of the atom, the analyst has stripped away the layers of the personality to get at the core of the psyche.

Have I found the secret of joy? I remember reading Georges Bernanos' *La Joie*. I did not read it as he wished it to be read, for his descriptions of the states of ecstasy experienced by the girl were based on religious ecstasy, and that was not what I was seeking. But the way he described it, being a poet, was such an absolute state of joy invading the senses, possessing the whole body, that I retained that but sought the source of it elsewhere. Joy appears now in little things. The big themes remain tragic. But a leaf fluttered in through the window this morning, as if supported by the rays of the sun, a bird settled on the fire escape, joy in the taste of the coffee, joy accompanied me as I walked to the press. The secret of joy is the mastery of pain.

David Moore. A purity and austerity of face, black wavy hair which he wears in a slightly Spanish fashion. Sudden smiles. Tension. Romanticism. He has recently separated from his wife. And all he found instead is a muse! We have elaborate and intricate talks: he is too aware, too mental. But I recognize the fear, disguised in complexities.

He does not take the place of Leonard, who was drugged by dreams. But I will no longer practice this insane murder of the present in which the romantic neurotic is so skilled.

The neurotic says: "I will not enjoy, I will not breathe, I will not love, unless I can reach this particular dream, person, state, place . . ." Henry enjoyed the present, by not caring. I do care, yet I will not die of it. The interchangeable friends, identities have ceased to count fatally. David Moore is a continuation of Leonard, Pablo, Charles Duits, the poets ever present in one form or another, demanding a legendary woman with all her veils and myths to create with.

But last night David Moore the poet was suddenly eclipsed by the preacher. In the course of our talk he revealed that his father was Irish, and loved women and drink. "And I like neither," said David. Aside from his marriage, he has had no experience with women. "I am a Puritan. I think that at bottom, all women are whores." The Irish wit and charm vanished. "You are good for me." I did not say: "But you are not good for me. You kill my naturalness and joy."

"You make me lose a certain order," he said.

"I only had one playmate in my father's house," he said. "It was George. George was an Irish pixie, an invisible personage. He was small, and always laughing, and hiding everywhere. Do you hear him now? He is out on the porch, making rustling sounds. He is a kind of wind blowing all around me." He does not understand the unconscious, and what he does not understand he is against. He also loves a fight. In company he assumes a haughty, pedantic pose. He only has confidence in his intellect. Why do people have confidence in their little conscious world, and such fear of the much deeper and larger one below consciousness? I pretend not to hear his indirect confessions of love.

At the press everything is difficult. Problems created by Gonzalo never keeping his word, never finishing books on time, never paying his bills. But this is balanced by the life in the studio, which has been taken over by Pablo, Charles, Josephine, Marshall. They distract me, cheer me, like a household of adolescents. When I arrive from work there is a mobile hanging from the doorknob. But like children, too, they exert their tyrannies. They have established a court, a form of mock trial, and I have to listen to the reasons why Baldwin and David Moore must be excluded from the circle. Baldwin is too conventional, starchy. He is the man in the business suit with a brief case. True, he has written poetry, but he does not behave like a poet. David is arrogant and pedantic, and if they cannot obtain a banishment from me, then, when the unwanted visitor comes, they act so much as if they owned the studio, were settled there in full possession, by either painting the furniture or changing the arrangements, that the unwanted visitor feels like a stranger.

Leonard writes: "Every dream of mine cast into a story and put on paper and made public is one less dream for myself and of them I have few enough."

I answered him:

Many writers have felt as you do. Maurice de Guérin carried this dislike of giving his intimate thoughts to such an extreme that he wrote them down in a secret journal which was published only after his death by his sister. Amiel wrote a diary and nothing else. Rilke complains of this in his *Letters to a Young Poet,* which I will send you later. I will go as far as to say that writing of enigmatic poetry is an expression of this reluctance—here one is clothed in the symbols, protected by the mystery from being completely exposed to the world. But there is another aspect to this. To write means to give all. No withholding is possible. The best writers are those who give all. However, there is the choice of clothing: fiction, symbolism, poetry, etc. I agree with you that a dream given is no longer yours, but it is also true that the more dreams you give, the more you exercise the production of dreams to fill the void, and this faculty grows stronger as you make demands upon it. It is like love. The more you spend of it, the more you stir new sources, new energies. To hold back is an activity which withers, inhibits, and ultimately kills the seeds. When you first surrender your dream, you may feel poor. But the instinct, like that of nature, is to replenish, refecundate. I have found this to be true. The more I write, the more I give, the more I love, the stronger grows the source. The writer is exposing himself in any form, ultimately, as we do in love, but it is a risk we must take.

I do remember, at your age, my paralyzing timidity, which prevented me from writing anything but the diary, in which I felt safe from either prying or judging eyes. And then don't forget that dreams beget dreams. If I had not given up my dream of the houseboat, written a story, and thus given up my secret, my own private possession, the story would not have been read by a boy of seventeen at Yale, and he would not have come to present me with a dream of Caspar Hauser. I know you said you would not read it because he died at the end. And you are afraid of death. But Caspar Hauser was no poet, and in the poet, the child, the adolescent, never dies. Remember Fowlie saying in every poet there is a man, a woman, and a child. It is out of the child's unimpaired receptivity, undamaged senses, that the poet receives his constant responsiveness and inspiration. Throw your dream into space like a kite, and you do not know what it will bring back, a new life, a new friend, a new love, a new country.

Letter to Leonard:

Wallace Fowlie writes to Miller that his admiration for me was unchanged but that, nevertheless, I was a *femme fatale* for the poets. That he feared my spell, and particularly for you.

I finally refused to meet Marshall Field. I have a prejudice against people with money. I have known so many, and none have escaped the corruption of power. In this I am a purist. I love people motivated by love and not by power. If you have money and power, and are motivated by love, you give it all away.

I was happy yesterday because Olga sent my books to the French critic Leon Pierre Quint, who wrote the remarkable study of Proust, and who guided my taste when I first arrived in France.

I attended the wedding of Luise Rainer and Robert Knittel. It was very formal and I did not enjoy it, but they seemed very happy and I am glad she is saved from a difficult life as an actress.

As I can only write well about what I feel, I have had to find a way to relate what I see and feel to the book, rather than the other way around. The way Otto Rank conducted analysis helped me find a form for the book.

Not easy to achieve freedom without chaos. While Leonard was here I observed and responded to what I called the transparencies and phosphorescences of adolescence, described them, and let them take their place in the book. Rank did not believe in going back. He felt the same drama would manifest itself in the present; all one needed to do was to examine the present. So in the present I was experiencing a conflict between the openness of the young, their curiosity, exploration, receptivity, playfulness, nimbleness, as against the heavy, opaque, solid, immovable mass of maturity I meet at parties. On this theme of hardening of the arteries of feeling I have done forty pages for the new book. In spite of the press, visitors, correspondence.

An atom bomb dropped on Hiroshima. A horror to stun the world. Unbelievable barbarism.

One summer afternoon in Amagansett, we were all walking back from a long exploration of the beach. It was toward the end of the afternoon.

From afar, we observed what seemed to be a body being rolled by the waves toward the shore. Two men were watching it. When it rolled at their feet, the body would stand up, and soon after run into the waves and begin again. As we came nearer we were puzzled. It was a woman. She had abundant long hair which floated as she let herself be rolled by the waves. She had to do this several times for the young man who was filming. We watched for a while, exchanged smiles, and walked on.

Later we found out this was Maya Deren and her husband,

Sasha Hammid. He had worked with John Steinbeck and Herbert Kline on the film *The Forgotten Village*. She was making another surrealist film. We became friends. Maya invited us to come and see the film when it was finished. We arrived at her studio in the Village, a vast place on the top floor. It was filled with exotic objects: drums, masks, statuettes, recordings, cameras, lights, screens, costumes. The bathroom and a large bedroom were in the back. The film was original. It was a dream. It had many strange effects which reminded me of Cocteau. Friends had acted in it whom we recognized. And we recognized the scene by the sea-shore. Maya had a fascinating face. She was a Russian Jewess. Under the wealth of curly, wild hair, which she allowed to frame her face in a halo, she had pale-blue eyes, and a primitive face. The mouth was wide and fleshy, the nose with a touch of South-Sea-islander fullness. When Sasha filmed her, as he loved her and found her beautiful, he caught a moment when Maya appeared behind a glass window, and, softened by the glass, she created a truly Botticelli effect. The round face, the round halo of hair, the eyes wide apart.

She had a strong will and influence, which we all felt. We were also hypnotized by film-making. Although that first day we did not agree with her "theories," we were captivated by the images. She denied all symbolic meaning (the knife, the faceless figure, the flower, etc.). Her father was a psychiatrist and she had developed a rebellion against all psychological interpretations. She did not acknowledge any link with the surrealists or with Cocteau. We did not insist. That evening, after the film, we danced, we played records. Maya was enchanted with Pablo, with Marshall, with David. She was planning her next film and looking at all of us through the eyes of a director.

Second bomb dropped on Nagasaki. This is savagery on such a scale that I cannot believe it.

Japan surrendered. It seems unbelievable that we can go on living, loving, working, in a world so monstrous, and this because we do not know how to curb the savagery of war, how to control history. That is why I hate history, because it makes man feel helpless in the strangle hold of hatred. More wars. More wars. More destruction. More horrible ways to destroy human beings. What can we do? Because we feel we have no say in all this, we turn away. Those who talk politics all day and all night have not solved anything.

Wrote pages on attributes of a lover (*Ladders to Fire*), Sabina and the fire ladder ("from the very first Jay hated her"), began Djuna and her city (pawnshop, whorehouse for the blind in Paris, Rue Dolent), and the chapter I call "Bread and the Wafer."

I am still extracting essences, not giving the experience itself, the incident, because I am distilling the diary. What was once told directly and humanly has to be transformed into the myth. One sees the transformation of reality, but not the reality. Ten years ago I was already writing about emotional algebra.

When writing fiction, in contrast to the diary, I may start slowly at the beginning, intending to tell the whole story. The first thing that happens is that my pace becomes rapid, my rhythm breathless, and I skip the obvious, the solid, to produce this condensation, this quintessence, and emotional relativity. Whenever I hear an explanation of relativity, I feel there is an equivalent in psychological reality. Why does the poet use symbolism in his tales? Why does the natural storyteller take his time and deal in a direct way with untransformed events?

I cannot answer this yet, except that untransformed reality weighs heavily and oppresses the spirit, kills our hope that we *may* transform, alter, change, evolve. That it is the proof of what the imagination can do which gives us our love of life, hope, joy. Truth and reality are at the basis of all I write. I can always bring forth proofs of the incident which inspired the character or place, but in order to capture emotion, the reality of how we feel or see the world, I have to go beyond appearance, and then it takes on the quality of a dream; but it is not a dream, it is the way our interior life is lived. For example, the interior monologue we all practice never resembles the way we talk. Will everything I write have to be translated, as when one reads a dream and seeks its meaning? That is why I never get this immediate response I need so much to sustain my work. The poet gets it. The fact that something is called a poem seems to establish a certain way of reading it. If I do get a response, it is a delayed one. The writing has an aftereffect. It penetrates in a more mysterious way, and gets retranslated into action, or familiar life. The abstract is restored to naturalism.

David Moore inspired the page on the black moth at the end of the book. He appears at the party as a zombi, dead in life. Two or three times when he was visiting me, a black moth took up its abode in the studio.

Begin printing *This Hunger.*

As a diversion, Marshall took me to see *On the Town,* which I loved. The only musical I ever really enjoyed. Modern, witty, fast tempo, airy dancing.

*Under a Glass Bell* is being translated for Cuba's avant-garde review *Origines.*

Today, after printing heavily and hard, I felt the machine giving me back strength. I felt the lead, so heavy to carry, giving me back power. I left the work elated.

A fabulous week in our history, a new world beginning, the end of the war! Tremendous changes. So much rejoicing. Clamors and celebrations.

Yet we all know war is the cancerous disease of power. I think it was Cocteau who said: "I am not interested in history. I am interested in civilization." History and politics are merely the record of the power-evil. We celebrate peace. Yet we pay no attention to the ways of curing aggression in human beings. And when one sees in psychoanalysis hostility disappearing as people conquer their fears, one wonders if the cure is not there. We do not pay attention, because we only pay attention to headlines and the press.

———

Edmund Wilson is back from Europe. He is separated from Mary McCarthy. He seems lonely. He portrays himself as a man who has suffered because he loves clever women and "clever women are impossibly neurotic."

As I sat waiting for him at Longchamps, the most banal of all restaurants, I felt that the orange walls were as beautiful as fruit, and the noises and the lights of the summer gay and wonderful.

David I am safe from, from his death-dealing rays. Those who cannot live fully often become destroyers of life.

Neurosis is a kind of death by absence. One bitter man can infect the whole community. Those who suffer from inner disturbances are contagious.

Marshall was one of the young men who was there when Leonard dominated the group, so he was never described. He is twenty-two, Russian-Jewish, has large green eyes, a skin which appears slightly sunburned; his dark hair is alive and shining. He is talented in several fields, designing, writing lyrics for songs, and he is working for *Esquire*. He is soft, lax, expressive, warm. He entered into and contributed to all the imaginative, lyric evenings we had: Haitian evenings; an evening with an Irish harp-player, at which his friend sang movingly; another evening with a banjo-player singing humorous American folk songs. Each visitor bringing something new.

I received a letter from Marshall:

It is the deepest time of night. I have been sending you all my dreams. Don't you begin to suspect all this mystery? The labyrinth in which I enclose each idea. I simply love you in a terrible way. Terrible in a cockeyed reversal of all moralities, yet it makes the average morality an embodiment of the seven cardinal virtues. As a consequence, we must not see each other for a long time. If you feel you have something to say write to me care of *Esquire*.

A letter from Leonard:

I have made a discovery about myself. When anyone expresses feeling toward me I can accept it but I cannot give it back. I cannot respond to it. I am better able to have friendships with cold people. I am really like Tom. Perhaps it is because of my father who never expresses emotion. He always said one must keep feelings locked inside of one's heart. I am a *roman à clef*.

Edmund Wilson gave me the manuscript of *Memoirs of Hecate County* to read. The publisher expects trouble and is not very happy. Wilson may have to come out in the open and fight against censorship for all of us.

The tragic aspect of love appears only when one tries to fit a boundless love into a limited one. All around me I find that one love is not enough, two are not enough. The women I know seek to add one love to another, and then when that does not fill their needs, they become the *grandes amoureuses* of the world.

Now we enter the night of woman's life, chaos and the mystery of woman. We enter the deepest, most hidden realm of all, a region unacknowledged, where all women melt into one, and only in that moment of hopeless struggle to free one's self of one absolute love are all women melted into one. At one moment in the novel this happens, too. It is in the night life, in the unconscious, that this resemblance takes place; often, as in Lillian, not lived out; denied, as in Djuna, abstracted by insight; in Sabina lived out blindly.

Yesterday I printed the one hundred and eighty-fourth page, the last of the de luxe edition of *This Hunger*. Then I came home, rested, bathed, and dressed for Marshall, descendant of the famous Rabbi Barer. He is intelligent, imaginative, and quick-witted. We went dancing with Estelle and another young man.

Somehow all the young men began to be woven together while I wrote "Bread and the Wafer." The title also came from Frances' saying I had no respect for bread. Then the contrast between daily bread and the symbolic wafer dispensed at Mass, which has a purely symbolic nourishment, appeared to me as descriptive of these gifted, often brilliant, imaginative, and magical young men, who are not nourishing to the woman, only to the artist.

I react against the plain, the one-dimensional men. I will not name them. I meet them everywhere, prosaic, down-to-earth, always talking of politics, never for one moment in the world of music or pleasure, never free of the weight of daily problems, never joyous, never elated, made of either concrete and steel or like work horses, indifferent to their bodies, obsessed with power.

In reacting away from their lugubrious and enslaved world, I fall into a magic world of illusion. In "Bread and the Wafer" I describe it as a ballet. It is a study of the evasive, elusive, unsubstantial adolescents. Because of fear, they proceed by oscillation. I was caught in their charm, their tenderness, their games. They peopled the world with delight, and were helpless when the mature world dictated to them: "Go to war. Earn your living." I see the demands of reality corrupting their dream and Caspar Hauser's innocence. Soon they will be heavy, joyless, obsessed men, like their fathers.

A tragic sense of life means one's obsession with an ideal, not a primitive, natural life. When was it I set such ideals for myself and made my life so difficult? Why did I struggle against the chaos and destructiveness of Henry's life, rather than participate joyously in his irresponsibilities, his using of others? Why did I struggle against Gonzalo's inertia, fatalism, destructiveness, rather than follow along and become equally lazy, casual, free? I never yielded to their way of life. I withdrew into my own. I have withstood the obsession with politics because I do not believe any system will make man less cruel or less greedy. He has to do this himself, individually.

We finished printing the regular edition of *This Hunger*. I fell into a suicidal depression. Had to face criticism of my book. Diana Trilling assumed because I had studied psychology I was writing case histories. The best way I can describe this criticism is that they only see what I have left out, but not what I have put in.

"Stella is not real. We never see her going to the icebox for a snack."

"How can you dwell on such neurotic characters at a time like this when only war and politics really matter?"

Edmund Wilson took me out to dinner. Then he wanted me to see his house. He drove me to an impasse in the East Nineties. A street lined with old-fashioned English brick houses. Pointed slate roofs, ivy and trees, but all of them so narrow and bleak; the windows long and narrow. He had forgotten his key, so we entered through the basement. The place had an air of devastation. "Mary took away all the furniture." We entered the parlor, a deep and narrow room. In the middle of the empty room stood two rocking chairs. On the walls, a series of Hogarth prints. I was chilled by the barrenness and the homeliness of everything. His description of Mary McCarthy sounds like mine of Lillian in *This Hunger*.

We sat on the rocking chairs (the surrealists would have appreciated that) and talked about Mary, about Hogarth, about Greek art. There is a paradox in Edmund Wilson which interested me. Contrary to his academic, formal, classical work, and the cold intellectual criticism, he himself is fervent, irrational, lustful, violent.

His house, his books, his pictures, were like those of my father. The bourgeois and the classical formal world.

He wanted me to help him reconstruct his life, to help him choose a couch, wanted to talk with me. But I wanted to leave.

When he talked about my work he had more to say about the flaws of *Winter of Artifice* and little about the achievement. Yet in the same breath he admitted the book had guided him in his relationship with his daughter! He also admitted that although my character Lillian never drank or went to the icebox, she did remind him of Mary McCarthy. "I marked many passages which describe Mary. I must be severe with you. *This Hunger* has no form. It is not concrete enough. But what amazing insights! Marvelous insights!"

His was a world of power and certitudes, solidities and aggressiveness. Strength and willfulness.

A break in the world of subtleties, muteness, evasions of adolescence. The young, who do not court, seize, who melt into you and away, like mirages. Toward Wilson I act as they do. Elusive.

The inadequacies of my children leave me at the mercy of the father. They abandon me to the father! The words they cannot say, the acts they cannot do, the page they cannot write, the book they cannot grasp—children of silence, delinquent children, luminous children, will I be overwhelmed by the power of the father?

Wilson, if he ever tastes of me, will be eating a substance not good for him, some phosphorescent matter which illuminates the soul and does not answer to lust. Unpossessable, for we are children of the albatross and our luminosity is a poison!

Strange, the world he cannot possess, the woman he cannot possess, because he has no real access to her. I have more affinities with those adolescents with no surplus of flesh around their soul, with their eclipses. Edmund Wilson's reality holds terror for me, nameless dangers.

But Wilson clings. He has a book for me. He has a review of *This Hunger.*

Edmund Wilson in *The New Yorker:*

There is not much expert craftsmanship in *This Hunger* by Anaïs Nin but it is a more important book than either Marquand or Isherwood because it explores a new realm of material. Even Isherwood can do little more than add to an already long series another lucid and well-turned irony of the bourgeois world on the eve of war. But Anaïs Nin is one of those women writers who have lately been trying to put into words a new feminine point of view, who deal with the conflicts created for women by living half in a man-controlled world against which they cannot help rebelling, half in a world which they have made for themselves but which they cannot find completely satisfactory. *This Hunger* is the first installment of what is evidently to be a long novel. It deals particularly, says the author in her foreword, "with the aspect of destruction in woman. . . . Man appears only partially in this first volume, because for the woman at war with herself, he can only appear thus, not as an entity."

This volume is, therefore, quite different from the author's last book, *Under a Glass Bell,* which was a collection of prose poems and poetic character sketches, each of which limited itself to presenting an image or a mood. The episodes of *This Hunger* are somewhat less satisfactory as writing than the pieces in *Under a Glass Bell,* but Anaïs Nin is attempting something more original and more complex. The new book consists of three sections, each of which presents a woman in her closest emotional relationship with men and with other women. These three groups have as yet no interconnections, and it is impossible to judge the author's project on the basis of this beginning. It is probable that when the various sets of characters shall have been made to react on one another, a larger design will appear and give these earlier chapters new value.

In the meantime, it does seem, however, as if Anaïs Nin, not yet expert in fiction, has not fully been able to exploit her material, which is constantly suggesting possibilities for dramatic contrast and surprise that the author has done little to realize—though the first section, the simplest and shortest, does complete a dramatic cycle. There is, for example, a movie actress, a masochistic and tied-up girl, who becomes envious and resentful of her screen personality because it represents a woman who is free, and always loved and in love. It is impossible to say that someone else would have handled this theme more effectively, because it is probably the kind of thing only Anaïs Nin would have thought of, but one feels that it is a brilliant idea which ought to have had a more striking presentation. The narrative, too, a little lacks movement. The influence of D. H. Lawrence, about whom Anaïs Nin wrote her first book, has perhaps been impeding her here. Like Sherwood Anderson, she seems to have caught from Lawrence a repetitious and a solemn hieratic tone which though a natural enough contagion for Anderson, should not be inevitable in the case of Anaïs Nin. She has, at her best, a very personal and human voice, and is instinctively, I do believe, the kind of writer who does not rely upon the impact of verbiage but cares about the right word, and who has no business blurring, as she sometimes does, the climaxes of her paragraphs.

The surface of *This Hunger* is thus a little uneven. There are passages where the psychological insights find their appropriate expression in clear language and vivid images, as in the pages that describe the self-doubt that is always compelling the movie actress to make more and more exacting demands of her lovers; and there are moments when little set pieces, as fragile and strange as those in *Under a Glass Bell* partly emerge from the background of psychological exposition—such as the golden salon with crystal lamps from which one of the heroines walks out into a garden where a light rain has washed the faces of the leaves and where she finds herself confronted by three full-length mirrors placed as casually as in a boudoir. But these pieces are not planted or prepared for so that they function in a general theme. They stand out with special life and color from a background where the outline of the characters seems rather dim, and where the description of relationships—when it falls into the Lawrence formula—seems sometimes a little abstract. Yet behind the whole thing is a vision of the vicissitudes of passion and friendship in a world in which men and women have become semi-independent of one another that makes *This Hunger* always a revelatory document.

Once one has used such words as "passion" and "friendship," one realizes how far Anaïs Nin has gone in breaking up these clichés that we use for the dynamics of emotion. Though she owes something to Freud, as she does to Lawrence, she has worked out her own system of dynamics, and gives us a picture, quite distinct from that of any other writer, of the confusions that result to our emotions from the uncertainty of our capacity to identify the kind of love that we tend to imagine with our actual sexual contacts, and of the ambivalent attractions and repulsions that are so hard on contemporary nerves.

Interesting though *This Hunger* is and charming though *Under a Glass Bell* was, I feel sure that Anaïs Nin has still hardly begun to get out of her intelligence and talent the writing that they ought to produce. This new book, like the one before it, has been published by Anaïs Nin herself. Anaïs Nin is at present a special cult, when she ought to have a general public.

### Diana Trilling in *The Nation:*

. . . The volume contains three stories, connected by the fact that each of them is about a gravely maladjusted woman hungering for affection. The first, Hejda, is about an Oriental girl who emerges from her veils to become something of an exhibitionist. The second, Stella, is about a movie star unable to love because of her excessive need to be reassured that she is loved. The third and most complicated, bearing the names of two women, Lillian and Djuna, is mostly about Lillian, a woman of conspicuous energy, confused—as far as I can make out—between the need to protect and her need to be protected.

I refer to the three pieces as stories. Actually, however, while Miss Nin's narrative borrows the manner of fiction, they are much more like case histories than like short fiction of any sort.

Miss Nin's characters have many of the conventional appurtenances of fictional life: they have been born, presumably they live and will die; they look a certain way; they have friends, money, sexual relationships, even children. But they exist for the author only as the sum of their clinically significant emotional responses; we are made aware only of such activities, physical surroundings, and encounters with other people as Miss Nin conceives to be relevant to their psychic health.

Every writer establishes a role for herself in her books, and Miss Nin's role is psychoanalyst to her group of typical women. Her sole concern with her characters—I had almost said patients—is with the formation and expression of their symptoms, and what goes on in the rest of their lives she rigorously ignores.

For instance, we are told of Hejda that, having been born in the Orient, her face was veiled during her early years, but we are not told the name of the country of her birth; or in connection with Lillian, Miss Nin suddenly mentions a husband and children, but because neither husband nor children influence Lillian's emotional development Miss Nin doesn't consider it pertinent to tell us anything about them. So much abstraction of her characters from the context of their real lives, together with so much specific detail when it suits Miss Nin's purpose to be specific, gives a certain surrealist quality to her stories. But her approach is not properly described as surrealist, since, in the instance of each woman Miss Nin is primarily concerned to lay out a case.

The method of *This Hunger* is, as I say, the method of the clinical history, but with two important differences—one, that Miss Nin relies for effect not only on her clinical observations and conclusions, but also on her literary skill; and two, that whereas it is the intention of the writer of a case history only to add to our clinical knowledge, and if any wider comment is present it is present only by happy accident, it is the first intention of Miss Nin to make a full-sized literary comment upon life. And yet I find *This Hunger* both less good reading and less enlightening about life in general than many simon-pure case studies. Nor is this because I object—though I do—to the dominant poetical tone of Miss Nin's prose. Nor is it because I reject—though I do—the major implications of Miss Nin's stories, but because *This Hunger* is inferior to a good psychoanalytical case. . . .

. . . I keep wondering why a book like *This Hunger* could not receive commercial publication in these days when nothing sells like the sick psyche.

———

Wilson talked about his marriage.

"With Mary it was war. Even sex was a belligerent affair. It could never happen naturally and joyfully, in a relaxed way. There had to be some play-acting. There had to be a battle."

Scrutinizing me, he added: "You are a friend of man's, aren't you? You don't demolish him?"

"If you demolish a man, you lose a lover," I said.

"I hear you are surrounded by very young men."

"They come to me. I like the adolescent world, yes, because they are still vulnerable and open. They are a relief from tight, closed, hard, harsh worlds. One of them was born May eighth, on your birthday."

The contrast between Leonard and Edmund Wilson amused me.

Edmund Wilson saying: "I hate young writers. I hate them." And I had a vision of Leonard, tall, lean, almost transparently thin, skin like a sea shell, pale and faintly roseate, the shining smile, not coarsened yet, not toughened yet, no self-assertion yet; retreats, retrograde evasions. Wilson arrogant, sure of himself. Even in his empty house I had the feeling that he was born in the English tradition of letters, nourished by libraries, formulas, and classical scholarship.

I ran away, and the only reason I consented to see him again was that when I left he ran out to get me a taxi, and because my leaving was so precipitate he felt it was a desertion and shouted a most untypical cry: "Don't desert me. Don't leave me alone."

The next day I had a cold. Edmund Wilson sent flowers, and a set of Jane Austen, with a note. He was hoping I would learn how to write a novel from reading her!

But I am not an imitator of past styles.

Meanwhile, he reread *Winter of Artifice,* and when I was well he came to see me.

His face was red and flushed from weather or from drink. The five flights were hard on him, yet he made no preparatory speech. He was so directly affected by the book that he stood in the middle of the studio and blurted out: "You realize, of course, that the father is right, in *Winter of Artifice,* and the daughter completely in the wrong."

"Yes, of course, you would feel that. You identify with the father, the classicist, and you imagine we have the same conflict."

"I would love to be married to you, and I would teach you to write."

If for days I had been depressed to realize the evanescence, the unsubstantiality of the adolescent world, suddenly I realized in Edmund Wilson the full tyranny of the father, the wall of misunderstanding and lack of intuition of the father.

He appeared to me as an oppressing figure. I do not remember what I answered. I have never felt it worthwhile to argue with the enemy.

But my illusion of the adolescent world satisfying me was gone. I carry a deeper hunger, which adolescents cannot fulfill. They can only distract me from deeper troubles.

The money Gonzalo received for printing a book is gone. He gave the last three hundred dollars to a salesman who came to sell him a bigger and better press which we do not need and cannot afford. He gave the money without a receipt. The machine would come straight from the factory. It never came. I was faced with a realization that Gonzalo can never deal with realities, that he is weighed with debts, and will ultimately destroy the press.

This hunger is what I recognized in Frances and wrote about, and which both of us alchemized into a giving to others what we wanted so much ourselves: uncritical and deep love, passion, help in creation, faith, loyalty.

The fiction writer, the artist, sometimes expresses what entered the consciousness of others. Strange that in the middle of plenty, of many friends, of activities, of achievements, I should carry about a book called *This Hunger*.

In Leonard I loved the innocence of Caspar Hauser. Caspar Hauser could only love a memory or a dream of a mother, divined behind a door, a mother he did not even see, a mother he could not find again.

If Edmund Wilson is *reality,* and my art world and the young artists who fit into it, illusion, then reality is far more destructive.

In order to escape the world of the man—Edmund Wilson—I disguised the woman in myself to be allowed to re-enter the world of the poet, the dreamer, the child. To live once more in the house of innocence and escape the mature world, which only thinks of power. A grim, cold, gray world.

I went out with Edmund Wilson again. He said: "The first time I saw you, years ago at the Gotham, you were wearing a little cape and hood. I thought you were the most exquisite woman I had ever seen. I was so enthusiastic that I went and told Mary McCarthy. As I took my marriage very seriously and it was the first time I had praised another woman so much, Mary was very irritated. When we began to be estranged, to quarrel, among other things she accused me of being in love with you. I had tried to see you again. I found out that Paul Rosenfeld saw you. He arranged a cocktail party, remember?"

I did remember, and I remembered that when I saw Edmund Wilson there, I thought he looked like the burghers in the Dutch paintings, too solid. I paid little attention to him.

"We did not talk very much," said Edmund Wilson. "Then Frances Steloff put *Under a Glass Bell* in my hands. I had not liked your work before. It was too ethereal, too elusive. But I liked *Under a Glass Bell.* I did not do it justice."

In contrast to the luminous adolescents, here was a strong, determined, palpable, positive man. Unable to enter my heart.

I prefer my dreams.

For all these people, there is no reality in my work only because the reality they know is that of sweat, the present surroundings, politics, ugliness of war, belligerent relationships.

Talked with Maya Deren. What a fighter she is for her films, for her ideas. She defends and explains her work. She is stronger than I am. She takes her films around and is willing to enter the arena. I have not done that. I was completely overwhelmed when Frances' friends talked to me one evening and argued in favor of the realistic novel. I began to realize they did not accept or understand abstraction, timelessness, my effort to transcend class, history, time, race, in order to reach emotional dramas which lie *behind* that. It *is* visionary writing. How do you argue about that?

I came home and wrote about realism and reality. Realism was not reality. Reality was how we felt and saw events, not events as they appeared objectively, because we are not objective.

Behind, always behind masochism lies sadism. Behind indirectness does not lie feminity, but a crippled, fearful self who does not dare. Behind my romanticism lies a primitive woman with primitive hungers.

I examine Djuna's goodness, and mine, too. What lies behind that? The whole obsession in my fiction is to uncover the disguises. There is an indirect power and a more subtle form of destructiveness. Rock bottom. Bitter truth. The faces of others change in my eyes. My own changes as I seek lucidity and honesty. I face my fear of the ugliness in which my friends have been born, in which they feel at ease, as Henry did, and which they have no desire to banish or transform. We all live in a web of subterfuges and transmutations.

My greatest problem here, in a polemic-loving America, is my dislike of polemics, of belligerence, of battle. Even intellectually, I do not like wrestling matches, I do not like talk marathons, I do not like arguments, or struggles to convert others. I seek harmony. If it is not there, I move away.

The face of Leonard has changed, too, with his letters. The bareness of the letters, the inexpressiveness. His letters were immensely disillusioning. Parsimonious, cool, and another self from the one which warmed itself in my presence. No more Caspar Hauser. That was a romantic concept of his vulnerability!

Why is it I developed no fangs? All these years, I spent no time growing defenses.

I did not think I would have to defend my work, too. The

winter lies coiled outside of the window, bright and cruel. The new book is on the table. Not wholly loved or accepted.

Maya Deren asked us to act in her new film. We went very early to Central Park, to the very place where I played as a child. She had erected a Maypole, and we danced around it. Pablo, Marshall, Frank Westbrook, the ballet dancer. At first I had the small role of a mystery woman in a black cape who was everywhere. Then Maya gave me more and more to do. Dancing, etc.

I have divided the world into two hostile camps:

| World of the Artist | World of Reality |
|---|---|
| Joy | Greed |
| | Power |
| Creation | War |
| | Self-interest |
| Freedom | Corruption |
| | Dullness |
| Altruism | Hypocrisy |

I have a hostility toward authority, money, the organization of the world.

At Edmund Wilson's I dislike the dismal, joyless house of the father, his power in the literary world, the solidity of his environment, his good manners, his taste for classical literature. I remembered that many years ago, when we read Wilson in Paris, I disagreed with his saying that Joyce had invented the contents of *Ulysses'* unconscious, since no unconscious ever contained so many allusions and associations.

He does not understand my way of life.

He does not understand that I refrain from firing up his neurosis: "I am a very quarrelsome man."

Sometimes I suspect that I see him just to prove to myself I could never live in what others call the "mature" world. I always experience a desire to postpone my visits with Wilson. While he confines himself to admiring me as a woman, we are safe. He is not the man creating the future. He is tradition.

He is crystallized and inflexible. He tells me that he has always loved two contrasting types of women, one destructive, one kind and creative.

To me he seemed to have this hardening of the arteries I find in men of achievement. The florid skin, the satiated flesh, the solidity of the earth, and its heaviness. He is didactic; he has conventional ideas about form and style; he has scholarship. He is all brown: brown earth, brown thought, brown writing. His descriptions of life with Mary McCarthy sound like Jakob Wasserman's character Ganna in *Doctor Kerkhoven*.

Father, man, critic, enemy of the artist.

"You are a woman who does not destroy man."

That may be true, but he is a man who would destroy me.


The conflict in my life is the conflict in my novels: opposition of an ugly reality to a marvelous intuition or dream of other worlds. Not permitting the human to destroy illusion. Opposing the artist to the world of authority, power, and destructiveness.

I write like a medium. I fear criticism because I fear it will destroy my spontaneity. I fear restrictions. I live by impulse and improvisation, and want to write the same way.

I set up Edmund Wilson as a symbol of the man's world, the critic who wants to direct my writing. You see how a man behaves? Beneath his interest, tyranny. Men of power use their power. The artists I live with have no power in the world. They are the dreamers, who create beauty.

He is a force, a force of certitudes and convictions.

It is not Wilson but my image of reality I see in him. Force, authority, power. They are uncreative. I have a right to elude them.

I set out on an errand, a full-grown woman, and this is what happened to me. I, weighing about one hundred and thirteen pounds, five feet one inch tall, wearing a womanly black coat, womanly shoes with high heels, a womanly black dress, walking along Eighteenth Street with a package for the Railway Express Agency.

From the left and from the right emerged giant trucks. The street was lined with truck garages, and the trucks were starting out for the day's deliveries, all of them red, with huge red-and-silver noses, shining fireman-red bodies, wheels as tall as I. Backing out of the garages, making a wall around me, parked on the curbs, so that my entire vision of the street was one of massive accumulation of red trucks, huge wheels turning slowly. And suddenly I was no longer a woman walking firmly, assuredly, down Eighteenth Street. Somewhere I had stepped through a mirror and some force had waved a hand and made me smaller. I was small. The trucks were immense. The mechanically opening iron doors were immense. The wheels were crushing. I was small, helpless, hopeless. My dress was not the curved, body-formed dress of a woman. My coat was not tall and long. My feet felt small and fragile. I felt diminished, reduced to nothingness. I felt lost, fearful, diminutive. I could not remember what the accumulation of years had formed and contributed toward my maturity. In one instant this maturity was lost, discarded. A child emerged and stood in its place, a child afraid, threatened on every side by giant trucks directed blindly by men sitting so high above me they could not see me. The wheels did not see me as they turned upon me, did not feel me, I had no density or weight. I do not remember why Alice in Wonderland was changed, or how she became smaller than her original size. But I knew that my smallness was a great shock to me. I was small, and the city gigantic, and the trucks overwhelming, and the garage doors made for giants.

My first thought was: Now I understand my love for the adolescents, for Leonard, for Pablo, Marshall, and Charles Duits. Why was it not clear before? Pablo, nineteen, saying everything with his body; Leonard, nineteen, wrapped still in the mists of adolescence, the trailing mists one sees around planets as yet far from the earth; Marshall, twenty, warm, and bright, active like mercury; and Charles Duits, composed of the crystals of finite poetry, not melting, but sending signals of distress from amethyst eyes. I was not with them because I wanted to protect and guide them, but because I feel as they do, act and think as they do. And all the time I was pretending to be the wise mother or the clear-sighted muse, was pretending to be a mature and stable woman, I was wearing my mother's clothes and they were too large for me, for my role. All they revealed was my true substance, which made me understand how they feel, and therefore know their needs. And on that morning I was even smaller and more frightened than they were. I was completely lowered and diminished.

The presence of the young lightens the world and changes it from an oppressive, definitive, solidified one to a fluid, potentially marvelous, malleable, variable, as-yet-to-be-created world. I call them the transparent children. When Wilson disparages the pleasure I take in their company, as if they were not the proper companions for a mature woman, I see in him what alienates me from maturity and draws me to the future. Above all, there is the absence of joy. For example, in food Wilson is a glutton, and in *Hecate County* the realism of sex is not joyous. There is a heaviness throughout, and a prosaic quality. It is a world of ideas and traditions already set. I once objected to the story of the biblical laws engraved on stone. (Unchangeable!) So Edmund Wilson's life, words, and writing are on stone. And I return to my transparent world, where the young say spontaneous things, act by their dreams, seek their fantasies to be fulfilled.

I had to face my fear of appearing in public. I agreed to appear at a Young Men's Hebrew Association poetry reading.

I awakened in the morning, thinking: "This is my birthday." I was calm all day. I made myself as attractive as possible. I wore my black tailored suit with a fuchsia-colored blouse. Frances came with me. My heart began to beat wildly. I did not remain seated at the table, as Parker Tyler did. I stood up. The lights were strong. At first I was frightened. Then I read my short lecture, and a passage from *This Hunger*: "She talked to the child inside of her." I also read "Ragtime." The audience applauded. I could not tell what people felt. But I felt what I was reading as if I had just written it. The applause was warm and spontaneous. I signed books. I felt elated to have mastered my fear, to have communicated with those who read me. To have come out of my shell. Frances said I read well and that people were moved.

Afterward we went to Maya Deren's studio. I danced wildly with Pablo. The image of an opaque world one cannot change, as against a transparent one through which one sees the spirit and possibilities of change and creation. Dream of the transparent children, the light in them. I saw transparent shoes and wanted them. I love crystal. I love transparence.

On the mastery of shyness. How can knowing about one's fear change anything? The greatest of all my fears was facing an unknown public. I dreaded the ordeal. An ordeal to come out of my circle of friends, in which I felt secure. I investigated the cause of this and talked it over in analysis.

As children, we are made to feel we will only be loved if we are good (in the parent's terms). As soon as we begin to affirm our real selves, parents begin to reject us. We grow up with the idea that if we are ourselves we will be rejected. So, as artists, in our work we express our real self. But we keep the fear of not being loved for this real self. And timidity and shyness are the symptoms. A timidity we can overcome with those who understand and accept us. Now when I have to face the world with my real self exposed in the writing, there is a crisis. Am I going to be accepted, approved, loved, or punished and rejected? Hence the fear. Last night I took this chance and won.

––––––

Wilson's writing never gathers up oxygen and flies into space. It always follows earthy gravitation and rolls downward. He is conventional, uninspired.

I am aware that it is I who choose my characters. Then I make up a story. You see, Wilson represents maturity, and that means lust, power, self-interest, worldly aims; whereas in the world of the artist and the young there is disinterestedness, and a purity.

When one tells a story in the form of a parable, a myth, a fantasy, people have to do the unraveling of the meaning, as when you bring a dream to the analyst and he has to interpret it. But I find that readers want me to do the unraveling. That would be like writing a poem and then its analysis.

Leo Lerman tells me that in Maya's film I looked like Shelley, transparent. When you focus on a key word, a theme word, it seems at times as if everyone uses it. Leo Lerman and I often have whimsical and completely free talks over the telephone. He told me he had walked into a glass window.

I said: "I am sure you could do that, walk right through unharmed."

"Why do you say that? The glass shattered and I was not harmed."

"Because you have a gift for transforming reality, for flying above the dangers, walking through glass."

In Edmund Wilson I sought reconciliation with the father. Or was I seeking to conquer the father? Once more, to be able to say: He does not understand. One moment he thinks I am Ondine, that I have never loved or suffered; another moment he thinks my bohemian life must be absolutely amoral, decadent.

As soon as he says something unsubtle, I withdraw. I never argue. I inhabit the unconscious, and I will always write from that realm, deeper and deeper, until I reach the collective unconscious of woman.

"You do not live in reality. Political reality."

"Does your political reality make you understand human beings?"

When he says "reality" I see gray mornings, war, cruelty, exploitative booksellers who do not pay for the books we labored over, money problems, the critical father (Wilson), the aggressive mother (Lillian). Man the father is gross, heavy, not loving. The sons, the boys, the young artists are beautiful, delicate, subtle, tender, imaginative. I choose my personages to prove my point.

There is a paradox in the dreamed life. I dream a houseboat, find it, live the dream as I wished. But at times the dreamed life, if it does not fulfill itself in reality, becomes a tragic trap. Is it true we choose our personages, our friends, according to the unconscious pattern we wish to prove? It is impossible to gain understanding from the father, from the church, from banks, governments, leaders. Don Quixote and the windmills? I do not think I am tilting at impossible enemies. Wilson is the enemy of what I stand for, write, seek, love. He is invested with an unquestioned authority over writers. He is a dictator up there on his *New Yorker* throne.

People bow to the name and do not question his judgments.

Meanwhile, leaving Maya Deren's studio, Marshall takes my hand and says: "Let's run. If we run fast enough, we will not see the ugliness of New York."

Charles Duits is the most intelligent, the most cohesive, cultured, and developed of the adolescents. Leonard is intuitive by fits and starts, often confused, immature, with sudden illuminations. Marshall is more experienced in life, more emotional and free. Pablo is all emotion, a carnival of gay affection, physical expansiveness, violence. Leonard is still a nebula, clouded, misty, dim, sleepwalking. Marshall is more accessible to human feelings. All of them elusive, subtle, close to me. But they have created a luminous prison. They shut out other visitors, make fun of overserious or ponderous people, drive away academicians, famous, successful people, people of achievement, persecuting the banal, the trite, the ordinary as the ultimate crime.

Frances feels that the time I spend with them is wasted, but I feel it is rich, richer than the time spent with Wilson. I feel inspired, moved. They understand me better. They have the exigent idealism of the young. They demand much, and make sure you never yield or sell out. To please them one must remain unadulterated, uncorrupted by reality. How well they recognize the first step toward concession.

The analogy between the artist and the child is that both live in a world of their own making. This world soon enters into conflict with the outside world. Both the artist and the child create an inner world ruled by their fantasies or dreams. They do not understand the world of money, or the pursuit of power. They create without commercial intent. They rebel against existing conditions. They cannot be deceived. The realistic world for them is ruled by conscious compromises, self-betrayals, selling out.

Dream of Edmund Wilson as a Roman emperor, wearing purple hair. (Judge?)

There is a link between the playing in adolescent worlds and art. Rank wrote about this. Play and imagination. Fowlie wrote somewhere, too, that the poet was the one in whom the child's sensitivity survived in the adult, and that it was from this source that he wrote poetry.

I always assumed I lived close to the young in order to protect them, or to guide them, but I think now it was also that I feel as they do, I think and act as they do. All the time I watched Pablo dancing, I was a dancer; and all the times Marshall painted glittering exotic fish, I was one of them; I was Leonard's nebulousness and his infrequent appearances in reality, his timid stories and complete eclipses, his muteness and inarticulateness, which I still practice when I am in an unharmonious, unpropitious atmosphere. A roomful of people I cannot feel close to, and I become Leonard. I also practice some of Charles Duits' constant flights from triteness in writing, his dreamer's intolerance and exigencies.

Noguchi's studio in Macdougal Alley, one of the loveliest places in New York. The houses are small, the street of cobblestones, there are gas lanterns. It is an echo of English or French streets. At the closed end is a wall with trees behind. The houses and studios are each different in shape and decoration. It is intimate and mysterious.

He showed me the diminutive models of his major works. They seem like a city of abstract sculptures. When I asked him if he loved the miniature models, he answered: "I feel greater tenderness for them. They belong to me. They are human and possessable; they are near; they lie in the hollow of my hand. The major work is so large. It is cut off from me. It goes to big buildings, to the Museum of Modern Art. It will be admired, but it is not mine any longer. I love this universe of small statues. . . ."

A small world. A new world. Where and when have I seen before this opposition of the large and the small, of the strong and delicate? At the beginning. In childhood, houses, parents, cities loom enormous. And under certain stresses, certain violent events, losses, separations, one experiences the world in the emotional size of Alice in Wonderland. One has a feeling of being smaller than events call for.

More and more resemblances between psychoanalysis and the procedure of the novelist. He must be a psychologist, able to reconstruct a character from a fragment, to distinguish between distortion and verity.

While I live surrounded in my leisure hours by the adolescents, I see also that they are parallels to my two brothers, younger than I. We are three in our house, hiding under the dining room table, as in a small Indian tent. The cover is green and has long fringes. We are three in a world of enormous angers. With my brothers, I feel a closer bond than that to the parents who create our world, changes, disruptions, without our having a say in them. The young men are those who cannot destroy me. But Edmund Wilson can, either by a destructive review or by indifference.

In maturity, the child is known and amalgamated to the man or woman, integrated with the adult. But a child who has not received enough mothering or fathering will later seek the child in others, and give to them what he lacked.

Wilson had said: "If I were married to you, I would bully you, force you, want you absorbed in me, and you could not develop. I can see how a woman like you needs her freedom to grow."

Slaying dragons again. The big dean of the critics, the conventional, traditional critic, who cannot possibly understand. Had I thought that through knowing me, he would understand my work?

He believes I am not destructive. Perhaps not. But when he says: "You bring out the best in me," I am not able to say that he does the same for me.

So I went into the habitat of the father, the enemy. To win him?

Reread the Tibetan *Book of the Dead*. I feel that the states of consciousness described did not take place after death, that the *bardos* happened during the lifetime. What has happened in our time is that body and soul do not travel together. They were rent asunder by Christianity, and so the passages become dangerous, they are incompletely achieved, and anxiety sets in, due to achieving neither life nor death, metaphysical or sensual fulfillment. I feel that what I have described very often in the diary, and in the story "The Labyrinth," are *bardo* states. Why did the Tibetans think we achieved this cyclical and circular journey only after death?

I named this diary volume "The Transparent Children." For days I followed an association of images stemming from a dream about a transparent child, a transparent pair of shoes I wanted, my general love of transparency, and Leo Lerman saying I appeared transparent in Maya Deren's film. And back along this route to the world of the artist, the child, walking always together and trying to understand each other, because the child influenced our adult life. Beside me lies Wilson's review, too heavy and opaque to seize me, weighed down by conventionalities. The story of Caspar Hauser has a relation to this. The child is imprisoned for fifteen years in darkness, through the intrigue of a powerful adult world (royalty here stands for power). Then he is freed, accidentally, in a strange city. His honesty, his direct statements, his acts seem so strange to the adult world. They adopt him, and at the same time seek to convert him to their ways. They feel he is different. He keeps a diary. He destroys the diary because he feels they are trying to violate his secrets. He has a dream (or a recollection) of another world. It is a dream of a castle. Behind the door stands his beautiful mother. He wants to return to this castle and find his mother behind the closed door. The woman who could have loved him and saved his life did not dare transgress the barrier of age. He died because he was unprotected.

Last night we were excavating the Maya Deren mystery. We all sit in a circle and wonder why we do exactly what she commands us to do. We are subject to her will, her strong personality, yet at the same time we do not trust or love her wholly. We recognize her talent. We talk of rebellion, of being forced, of tyranny, but we bow to her projects, make sacrifices.

A quotation from Wilson on Joyce:

Just as Joyce in *Ulysses* laid the Odyssey under requisition to help provide a structure for his material—material which once it had begun to gush from the rock of Joyce's sealed personality at the blow of Aaron's rod of free associations, threatened to rise and submerge the artist, like the flood which the sorcerer's apprentice let loose by his bedevilled broom . . .

Whoever has studied psychoanalysis knows that there is no need to look for a classical myth outside to contain the free association. The structure lies at the core of free association and has to be searched for, like the opening of the labyrinth. A precise and architectural form emerges at the end, when all the images have been explored and related to experience, when the link has been made between the association and its origin. In other words, it is an invisible structure at first, and only when fully explored will it yield its own pattern.

Richard Wright has moved into the Village, and came to see me. Tennessee Williams sent me tickets for his new play.

At the home of the owners of the Kleeman Gallery, I saw one

of the five extant copies of Shelley's *Diary*, which he wrote alternating with Mary, so that the entries are now by one, now by the other. The original is in London.

An evening at Sonya Sekula's home. Her paintings are beautiful. Vivid and full of fantasy.

A farewell party for André Breton, who will deliver a lecture in Haiti. His new wife seems most interesting, a sensitive international type, whose origin one can no longer guess. Esteban Frances, the Spanish surrealist painter, very lively and humorous, and his beautiful Mexican wife; Helion, the French painter, with a dazzling orange tie and mussed hair; Pegine Vail, with her hair down over her shoulders, and a turquoise comb; Peggy Guggenheim, with two miniature dogs and her clown face; Noguchi, with his startled, wistful air, tired from watching the moving of his big rose marble figure to the Museum of Modern Art; Madame Saint-Exupéry, with the consumed look of a woman who has lived, loved, taken drugs, lost her husband to his passion for air and space, now living with Denis de Rougemont. Sonya's mother beaming lovingly on this crowd; her father, *grand homme d'affaires,* peeking in, smiling, and vanishing. Frederick Kiesler, the modern architect, kissing ladies' hands. But as he is four feet tall, it makes a woman feel like the Statue of Liberty.

Publishers are calling me. I am supposed to see Random House, Harper's, and Pascal Covici, of Viking. I am both happy and sad. I do not like their world, their values. I want to keep my sincerity. It means a harder battle, not like the one with my small press, my debts, overwork, but one against values I do not believe in. I have to keep my world intact. My lunch with Covici was interesting. We laughed, and he was ready to sign a contract if I agreed to change from a wafer into bread.

After my lunch with Harper's, I realized the most difficult part of my life is starting now. The struggle with money and the press is nothing compared with the more subtle struggle against accepting money for compromising. Harper's began today, like Mephistopheles with Faust: "Yes, we absolutely want you. You have great talent. But do you think the next book might be . . . more of a novel . . . according to orthodox forms?"

"No," I said. "It will be done in my own way."

"It is strange," the editor admitted. "Publishers think they can tell the writer what the public wants, and then along comes someone who does something different, like you, and it is very obvious the public wants you."

"It is a question of sincerity," I said. "If you would let the writer be himself, then naturally his experience answers a real need, not a spurious one."

Kimon Friar asked me to attend his lecture on love at the Y.M.H.A. so I went yesterday. I was in a depressed mood. I wore a black dress with long sleeves half-covering the hands, and a small heart-shaped black hat, with a pearl edging, shaped like Mary Stuart's hat. Kimon lectured at the head of a long table. At the foot of the table, one chair was empty. I took it. Maya Deren sat a few chairs away. Next to me sat a handsome young lieutenant. During a pause I leaned over to speak with Maya. She said: "You look dramatic."

I said: "I feel like Mary Stuart, who will soon be beheaded."

The lieutenant leaned over and introduced himself: "I am Warrant Officer Gore Vidal. I am a descendant of Troubador Vidal." Later he admitted that he had guessed who I was. He is luminous and manly. Near the earth. He is not nebulous, but clear and bright, a contrast to Leonard. He talks. He is active, alert, poised. He is tall, slender, cool eyes and sensual mouth. Kimon was lecturing on Plato's symposium of love. When it was finished, Vidal and I talked a little more. He is twenty years old, and the youngest editor at E. P. Dutton. His own novel is appearing in the spring. He knows *Under a Glass Bell*. He asked when he might visit me.

Mr. Covici of the Viking Press took me to lunch. An intelligent Romanian, who also came to America at the age of eleven.

I told him my work was like those distant planets which have a nebula and slowly approach the earth, and when they do there will be an explosion.

"That's just what I want," said Mr. Covici, "collision with the earth. I want you more earthy."

"You'll have to wait for that," I said.

"Oh," he groaned, "can't you write a novel like everybody else, with a beginning and an end?"

"No."

"I admit you are evolving your own form."

The defenses people build up become in themselves the trap. I think what I love about the young is that they have not yet created disguises and masks.

The fear of this, which I saw happening to everyone around me, also created the diary. The real Anaïs is in the diary. Even the destructive Anaïs who refuses to destroy in life. I do not harm Wilson, who is for the moment a man in trouble, but I do make his portrait in the colors I do not like; the brown of philosophy, the gray ashes of scholarship, the dreary traditions.

Gore Vidal's first visit to the studio caught us in a humorous moment, for when he arrived a group of us (Frances, Marshall, Jean Garrigue, Duits, Pablo) were enacting a wake for Matta. Poor Matta.

"Did he die?" asked Gore Vidal.

"No," I said. "But he married a millionairess, and we are seriously concerned as to what will happen to him as a painter."

Gore Vidal comes from a wealthy family, so this conversation must have astounded him.

He came another time, alone. He tells me he will one day be president of the United States. He identifies with Richard the Second, the king-poet. He is full of pride, conceals his sensitiveness, and oscillates between hardness and softness. He is dual. He is capable of feeling, but I sense a distortion in his vision.

He has great assurance in the world, talks easily, is a public figure, shines. He can do clever take-offs, imitate public figures.

He walks in easily, he is no dream-laden adolescent. His eyes are hazel; clear, open, mocking.

His grandfather was Senator Gore. His mother left his father when Gore was ten, to marry someone else. "She is Latin-looking, vivacious, handsome, beloved of many."

With all that, he is lonely. In the Aleutians he suffered frostbite. This freezing seems to cling to him. He has something of the frozen adolescent who has not yet melted with trust, passion. He is tight. "In the army I lived like a monk. I wrote my novel."

When he brings me the novel, I am startled by the muted tone, the cool, detached words. It is writing I do not admire. The once-frozen young man is not as lifeless as the writing. Action, no feeling.

Am I wrong to think there is a potential warmth in him? Is the writing a disguise, a mask? Another Hemingway to come?

Rather than engage in a belligerent friendship with Edmund Wilson, I broke with him. I do not want to live again and again the father-and-daughter drama.

I broke gently, and he was sad.

Gore said: "I do not want to be involved, ever. I live detached from my present life. At home our relationships are casual. My father married a young model. I like casual relationships. When you are involved you get hurt."

My father's desertion created the opposite reaction in me. I was always seeking new closeness, greater closeness.

But he does not like the artist life, and he represents my father's values. He takes me to luxurious restaurants to eat caviar and drink champagne, or to Charles à la Pomme Soufflé.

*This Hunger* will soon be out of print. I get a flood of letters.

Gore is at Mitchell Field. He comes in on weekends. He comes to see me. We had a fine talk. He read to me from *Richard II.* He complained of an arthritic hand. I said: "It's a psychic cramp, from writing about an ordinary character when you yourself are not an ordinary character." I tease him. Touched upon his depressions. Then Marshall arrived with a Welshman and his harp. He sang ballads in a beautiful voice. Charles Duits came, and Pablo. The evening was airy and magical.

When Gore telephones, he says: "This is Troubador Vidal."

Gonzalo tells me there is a romantic-looking girl who sits near the press, reading *Under a Glass Bell,* and wants to know me. But at the same time, she is frightened, so he suggested she meet me when I lecture at the Mills School. At the end of the lecture, she appeared. I recognized her. She was like a ghost of a younger me, a dreaming woman, with very soft, burning eyes, long hair streaming over her shoulders, ready at any moment to vanish if the atmosphere was not propitious.

I could have said: "You are the romantic Anaïs I am trying to conquer. You are a figure out of the past." But so they come, out of the stories, out of the novels, magnetized by affinities, by similar characters. And I could not dispel her. I loved her. She did not say a word. She merely stared at me, and then handed me a music box mechanism, without its box. She finally told me in a whisper that she always carries it in her pocket and listens to it in the street. She wound it up for me, and placed it against my ear, as if we were alone and not in a busy school hall, filled with bustling students and professors waiting for me. A strand of her long hair had caught in the mechanism and it seemed as if the music came from it.

She came to see me, blue eyes dissolved in moisture, slender, orphaned child of poverty, speaking softly and exaltedly. Pleading, hurt, vulnerable, breathless. Her voice touches the heart. She came because she felt lost. I had found the words which made her life clearer. She talks as I write, as if I had created a language for her feelings. She walks out of my books and confronts me. She is without strength and without defenses, as I was when I first met Henry and Gonzalo.

Her name is Sherry Martinelli. She lives with a painter, Enrique Zanarte. She tells me: "Enrique says I am mad, because sometimes I ask him: 'Are you feeling blue or purple today?' as I believe our moods have colors. Also, I prefer to break a dish after I eat, rather than wash it. Do you think there might be, somewhere, a man who feels as I do? When we went to the zoo together, I was angry because he loved the rhinoceros, who has a carapace against feeling, whereas I liked the kangaroo, who carries its young as I would like to carry my three-year-old daughter with me all the time."

She is twenty-seven, but she belongs with Pablo, Marshall, and Charles Duits. "There are phrases one picks up in the street and lives with." She is pure poetry walking and breathing, inside and outside of my books, so I feel I am not lying, I am not inventing, I am not far from the truth. "Oh God, all the books one reads which don't bring you near the truth. Only yours, Anaïs."

Her eyes become immense when she asks questions. Blue, with the pupil very dark and dilated. She looks mischievous and fragile. She wears rough, ugly clothes, like an orphan. She is part Jewish, part Irish. Her voice sings, changes: low, gay, sad, heavy, trailing, dreaming.

Edmund Wilson came with orchids, kissed my hand and said: "Why did you desert me?"

My love-starved children. Demanding. Never enough. Endless needs.

Josephine was in love with her cousin, who was several shades paler than she, and her father and mother worried constantly that she would succumb to him. Josephine treated my studio as her second home. She jokingly called me her sister, and we talked a great deal about everything. But about her cousin we did not talk. He came to the parties. He was well-dressed. He had a good job. He spoke beautiful French. But Josephine's *joie de vivre* was so powerful that a love sorrow would not show through all the sparkle. With the children, she was the favorite. They responded to her gaiety and energy. They were all a little in love with her. She taught us to dance. We admired her prancing, the proud firmness of her back, her strong legs, her humor.

The anxiety of the parents communicated itself to me. If Josephine and her cousin were lovers, and he did not marry her, then she would be hurt. I thought of a plan to discover the truth. When we were all acting in a charade, which we loved to do, I asked her to make all the sounds known to a woman making love.

Josephine lay on the carpet and gave such a vivid, such a complete scale of the sounds of love's delight that it would have taken a whole chapter by Richard Burton to describe them. The coo of dreamy delight, the response in vibrations to the finger notations, the sound of delight at proximity, the cry of simultaneous courtship. The echoes of the other cries: the answer, the bird calls, the tear cry when pleasure strikes like lightning. She knew all of them.

When she was finished and we laughed and complimented her, and tried some that were less expert than her own, for her voice had a range none of ours had, she looked at me. And she knew then that I knew her secret. But I never knew at what moment Josephine was hurt, because although she never married her cousin, Josephine never shed tears about past loves. She was always speeding ahead to love anew.

I forgot to tell the story of my tea bath. In the summer I felt ashamed not to be sun-tanned, so I bought a pound of tea and bathed in it. Josephine came in, and when she found out what I was doing, she laughed uncontrollably. We both laughed at the irony of it.

My friendship with Leo Lerman is a telephone friendship. Over the telephone he talks of flowers, and he shows his storyteller's gift. His tales, already fictionalized by his heightened personality, delight me. I hear them more clearly than at parties. Like the tales of Moricand, they are intended to charm without revealing anything of the storyteller. I am certain Leo conceals a tragic life, stubbornly disguised in frivolity.

This morning, late, he called: "Guess what I am doing? We are sitting here reading *Under a Glass Bell.*"

"Who is we?"

"Truman Capote."

"Do you like the stories?"

"We love them. He loves them."

Leo Lerman re-created for me a part of his childhood which was so vivid that I felt I had known it. It is a Russian background, and perhaps Russian literature prepared me for it. The entire family emigrated, a tribe. The grandfather was a *melamed,* spiritual and severe, rigid, wisdom and punishments meted out equally. Each member of the family as clear as a Chekhov character. Aunts, cousins, brothers, sisters. The hierarchic figure of the grandfather was dominant, but the one I loved best was the mother, who had brought from Russia a love of cut glass. Love, I said. It was not love, but a passion. Her greatest pleasure was to dress up and visit all the Third Avenue antique shops, searching for cut-glass salad bowls, or glasses, saltcellars, water jugs, tea cups. To her it was like a search for diamonds. Whatever tragedy took place at home, illness, Leo's own fragile health, material problems, family dramas, Leo's mother healed herself with cut glass. The pinch of poverty, religion, and the luxuries of ritual, none could diminish her passion for cut glass. She frequented auctions. She was so fearful of being condemned by her husband that she brought her trophies home in ordinary brown shopping bags.

The house in which they lived was in a quarter of Russian immigrants, talking their own language, Russian-Yiddish, so complete a universe that Leo did not want to go to school and learn English. But eventually the members of the family went their own ways, carried away by job opportunities in other cities. When the time came to move out definitely to become a part of American life, rather than remain an island of Russian *melamed* learning, Leo's mother was still collecting cut glass. The house was full of cut glass. The closets were full of cut glass. Some cut with more refinement and grace than others, but always casting those magical kaleidoscopic light rays which make cut glass a fascination to the eye. The light refracted through each piece was a vibration of magic. The house was dispersed, the family was dispersed, but Leo's mother was still buying cut glass. Objects from the past. They were her entrance to a dream.

I gave a party. Mrs. Mary Louise Aswell had invited Truman Capote. When the bell rang I went to the door. I saw a small, slender young man, with hair over his eyes, extending the softest and most boneless hand I had ever held, like a baby's nestling in mine.

He was painfully timid. He looked as if he wanted to hide, or as if, as I had so often done myself, he were looking for the exit. Timidity always arouses my own. He seemed fragile and easily wounded. He seemed, above all, the most childlike of all the young I had around me. I had read only one story of his, delicately written, tender.

After this meeting we met at parties, at Leo Lerman's, and we never talked. We met at the wrong moment. I had too many childlike people around me. I hungered for a mature, full-grown artist! But his work entranced me. His power to dream, his subtlety of style, his imagination. Above all, his sensitivity.

Maya has stopped working on her film, temporarily. We all live on pins and needles for fear of catastrophe, a quarrel or anything else that will spoil it, as she has a need to seduce everyone, from Duits to Marshall to Pablo, and even me. We all live breathlessly, hoping she will find someone to pacify her so that filming may go on. We may have to draw lots: Now *you*, Number Nine, go to Maya and make love to her and make her happy, for the sake of the film.

I will probably sign a contract with Dutton since they may take me on unconditionally, because of Gore Vidal.

*This Hunger* is sold out.

Sonya told me Breton said I was one of the "illuminated women," and asked to have some of my work translated for him.

To please Mr. Covici of the Viking Press, to write as others do: Marshall Barer is twenty-four years old, he weighs one hundred and twenty-six pounds, his height is five feet ten inches, and he was born February nineteenth. He came one evening, brought by Kim Hoffman, and immediately started to tell me stories.

There was a man who could put his hand through glass, who could walk through a mirror, whose only concern was that the wonderful sensation of walking through glass did not last long enough. One day, a newspaper reporter wrote, during a public visit to a big observatory, after the inauguration of a new giant telescope, it was discovered that one visitor was missing. When the guard returned to the telescope, he found a man's suit of clothes neatly folded next to it. No identification papers.

Marshall danced with Josephine, as nimble and malleable as she is. He courted her away from Pablo. Leonard and Pablo were jealous of him. When he telephoned, there was a mute protest from them.

His presence was elating. I liked the airy, gusty way he comes in, his brightness and alertness. The last visit, late afternoon, he had been reading Elizabeth Bowen, so he was in a mood for a high tea, for polished shoes, and dainty housekeeping. As it happened, Millicent had given the apartment a spring cleaning, I was making tea with care and trimmings, and all was set to match Elizabeth Bowen's book but the shoes. Marshall asked for shoe polish and cleaned his shoes.

In our studio life, whoever starts a game, a mood, a theater act, we all fall in.

Marshall's body is completely lax, loose. When he lies down, he seems to spill onto the couch, no rigidities. He never sits on chairs, but on the rug. Marshall reads on the rug.

Gore came.

We slide easily into a sincere, warm talk. He dropped his armor, his defenses. "I don't like women. They are either silly, giggly, like the girls in my set I'm expected to marry, or they are harsh and strident masculine intellectuals. You are neither."

Intellectually he knows everything. Psychologically he knows the meaning of his mother abandoning him when he was ten, to remarry and have other children. The insecurity which followed the second break he made, at nineteen, after a quarrel with his mother. His admiration, attachment, hatred, and criticalness. Nor is it pity, he says. He is proud that she is beautiful and loved, yet he condemns her possessiveness, her chaos, her willfulness, and revolts against it. He knows this. But he does not know why he cannot love.

His face, as the afternoon light changed, became clearer. The frown between his eyes disappeared. He was a child thrust out too soon, into a world of very famous, assertive, successful, power personalities. His mother confesses her life to him. He moves among men and women of achievement. He was cheated of a carefree childhood, of a happy adolescence. He was rushed into sophistication and into experience with the surface of himself, but the deeper self was secret and lonely.

"My demon is pride and arrogance," he said. "One you will never see."

I receive from him gentleness and trust. He first asked me not to write down what he would say. He carries his father's diplomatic brief case with his own poems and novel in it. He carries his responsibilities seriously, is careful not to let his one-night encounters know his name, his family. As future president of the United States, he protects his reputation, entrusts me with state secrets to lighten his solitude. Later he wants to write it all down, as we want to explore his secret labyrinth together, to find the secret of his ambivalence. To explore. Yet life has taken charge to alter the situation again. He, the lonely one, has trusted woman for the first time, and we start the journey of our friendship, as badly loved children who raised themselves, both stronger and weaker by it.

He suffers the consequences of his wartime frostbite, great

malaises and neuritis. He suffers from black depressions. He is nearsighted. A boy without age, who talks like an old man. My other children do not accept him, understand him.

While all the society mothers are looking for him for their cocktails, dances, we may be talking quietly somewhere in a restaurant, a night club. A debutante wrote him: "Why are you so detached?" Gore attends the functions, bows, dances, leaves. Dear mothers and debutantes, can you give this boy back his childhood, his mother, his security, the warmth and understanding he needed then? Can you answer his thoughts, dialogue with his brightness, keep pace with his intelligence?

He came at four and left at midnight. He made me laugh with the most amazingly well acted pastiches of Roosevelt, Churchill, a southern senator, a petition at the House of Commons. He has a sense of satire.

He is very much concerned with establishing a contrast between Pablo, Marshall, and Charles, as adolescents not yet successful, not yet matured, and himself, already mature in his roles as writer, editor, etc.

"I give you the true Gore."

And then: "I'm coming Wednesday. Send the children away."

Wednesday I met Gore at a restaurant. He had news for me. Dutton had had an editorial conference, was offering an advance of one thousand dollars, and a contract for all the novels. We celebrated. He tells me I must finish the new book, *Ladders to Fire*, in two months. I am not sure I can do it, with the work at the press, the visitors.

Gore thinks I live a fantasy, that I see things that are not there, that I am inventing a world.

Gore's visits on Sunday now a habit. He brings his dreams written out, his early novel to show me: the one he wrote at seventeen, *Williwaw*.

I enjoy his quick responses. He never eludes. He holds his ground, answers, responds. He is firm and quick-witted. He has an intelligent awareness, is attentive and alert, and observant.

Part of the great fascination of Gore's age, and the children's, is the mystery of what they will become. One is watching growth. Unlike Wilson, who sits determined and formed, with opinions, judgments.

Already set, in these young men one sees the ambivalences and conflicts. Is the illumination which surrounds them that of hope? They are still tender, still vulnerable, still struggling.

Gore said: "I belong nowhere. I do not feel American. I do not feel at home in any world. I pass casually through all of them. I take no sides."

The writing I do has created a world which draws into it the people I want to live with, who want to live in my world. One can make a world out of paper and ink and words. They make good constructions, habitable refuges, with overdoses of oxygen.

"I think, dear Gore, that you choose to write about ordinary people in an ordinary world to mask the extraordinary you and the out-of-the-ordinary world in which you live, which is like mine. I feel in you imagination, poetry, intuition of worlds you do not trust because they are linked with your emotions and sensibilities. And you have to work far removed from that territory of feeling where danger lies."

To find the poet in Gore was more difficult. Leonard looked like a poet and a dreamer. Gore looks warm, near and realistic. But there it is, another inarticulate poet, a secret dreamer.

The direction of Gore's writing distresses me. But at twenty did I know my direction? At twenty I imitated D. H. Lawrence.

My never glorifying the famous, the achieved, powerful figures restores to Gore a sense of his individual value. I am not awed by success.

I do respond when he tells me about his worship of Amelia Earhart, and how shocked he was by her death. She was a friend of the family. Gore's father financed her fatal trip.

Gore has a feeling of power. He feels he can accomplish whatever he wishes. He has clarity and decisiveness. He is capable of leadership. This on the conscious, willful level. In the emotional realm, imagination and intuition are there, but not trusted. It may be that he associates them with softer and more feminine qualities he does not wish to develop in himself.

Gore's three evenings. One with a writer: a drinking bout. One escorting a debutante to the Victory Ball, and feeling stifled and bored. The third evening with me. He brings me a poem, two pages of childhood recollections, the fourth chapter of his novel, his physical troubles from the war, talks about his mother, his father, his childhood. Complains of a feeling of split, of unreality. Talks of death. Reveals the mystic. Obsessed, as Leonard was, by the circles.

Sunday. Midnight. Gore is sitting at the foot of the couch writing his play on the werewolf.

He said: "We met just at the right moment."

He reads my new book and likes it. He tells me his father read *This Hunger* and saw himself in Jay.

"But I won't let you meet him. He would like you too well, and you might like him too well. You might get along too well."

"Not better than you and I."

"It is so good to be oneself without poses," he said.

Why do I not have this trust in Wilson? Why did I never talk with Wilson like this? Because Wilson is the critic, and would pass judgment on me as he did on my work? Because he would not understand? Why did I never trust him, and yet trust Gore?

In the world of Wilson there was no magic and no poetry. No sweet delights of intimacy, admission of doubts. The mystifications and surprises of the young. The mysteries. Always a shadowy labyrinth. There was in Wilson a harsh absolutism and literalness. A spade is a spade is a spade. Oh no, a spade can be a symbol of something other than what it was built for, can carry a message, represent a hundred other things.

Gore says about my continuation of *This Hunger* into *Ladders to Fire:* "You have expanded in depth, now expand in width."

He finished his play and brought it as a Christmas present. It was intense and strong. "I've never written this way, impulsively, directly, and without plan." He was pale. Worn. I let him read my pages on adolescence and snow and the timidities of adolescent love.

Gore wanted to know when I would make his portrait. "I made it in the diary when you gave me permission."

"I gave you permission because I knew you would do it anyway."

He asked if he could read it.

I let him.

I was uneasy, anxious about unmasking him.

"I didn't mind being unmasked by you," said Gore.

The end of *Ladders to Fire* brings two worlds into opposition: nature and neurosis. The external world, the salon, the garden, the mirrors, and the reflections of them in the mirror. The sense of unreality in the neurotic comes when he is looking at the reflections of his life, when he is not at one with it.

Gore says his feeling about writing is changing. He wants color, magic. He is aware of the conventional mask of his first novel.

His hidden self is emerging. His imagination is manifesting itself in the play. He is no longer dying. There is a warm flush on his cheeks, and warmth in his voice. The frown has vanished.

He mocks his world, but draws strength from being in the *Social Register*, from his friends' high positions, from the power of his father and mother. He needs his class privileges. I was saddened by his vanity, his display of position. He was partly dependent on wordly attributes. Terribly in need of glorification. I saw his persona in the world. It was another Gore.

In one of his letters, Leonard quoted Eliot: "A shadow falls between my feelings and fulfilment."

He came for a short visit. We visited Noguchi together. We went to the Museum of Modern Art. Air and light between the interstices of his fears. Fire and light, magic, distance, loss, shadows. I understand the adolescents and their perfect dance around the rim of their own dreams and desires. They play on the rim of my life.

———

## Horoscope of Gore:

Neptune, making for high illusions, upsets his Venusian life. He is not satisfied with power. He does not trust Neptune, because of childhood experiences. He is the kind of person who responds to softness by aggressiveness. Might be stimulated, disturbed, by a Piscean-Neptune type of person. Could be the deepest experience for him, because it reaches a deeper level of consciousness. What balances him is the power to rebel against authority. Without this it would be a one-sided horoscope. Emotional rebellions offset the power-loving side. Mystical unconscious. Through the emotions depth will be in proportion to his yielding to his emotions, not through brilliancy of the intellect.

# [January, 1946]

Gore dispersed the group around me, and then asked if he could bring his friends down. I imagined them slick, hard, cynical, and I was uneasy. But when they came, they were not as I had feared. Elizabeth Talbot-Martin, a talented *diseuse,* charming, clever, and direct. The TV producer Stanley Haggart, big, handsome, warm, giving a feeling of generosity and intuition. Woody Parrish-Martin, imaginative, a dark, smiling raconteur from the South.

They knew and admired my stories. Stanley read my handwriting: "You are a kind of heroine, struggling against the ordinary, struggling to transcend your pattern. You seek to live on a higher plane. You seek the extraordinary. By great lovingness you transform everything. At the moment there is a deep depression which may affect your writing. You seek to tell the truth, but enveloped in magic."

These were the friends with whom Gore had planned to buy a brownstone on Eighty-fifth Street, which Stanley would rebuild and decorate.

Edmund Wilson said: "I've given up the idea of absorbing you. You're too strong a personality."

"Why should you want to absorb anyone?"

I began to space our meetings. I did not enjoy them; they were a strain. I was not natural with him. He grew resentful. I knew that as a critic he would punish me sooner or later, either by destructive faultfinding or by silence.

I always maintained to Olga that a change of system would not cure mankind of war and greed. That the only solution was each man working upon himself, his individual discipline against hostility, prejudice and distortion of others, where the evil begins. We often argued about this. Now she is disillusioned by the political turn of events, the work to which she has given twenty-seven years of her life. She said: "Anaïs, you were born with a deeper vision. You went into deeper worlds, and they have not failed you. You have found fundamental truths. I went into external worlds of action, and was betrayed by them. I have lost my faith. I have built nothing. All because of my fear of the inner world. You had the great courage to seek the truth and to write the truth. I want to do something deeper, and I can't. I'm afraid."

This came after she had attacked *This Hunger* for being merely a study in pathology, saying she could not review it for the magazine *Soviet Russia* because it was not constructive but decadent.

After she had said all this to me, she wept for two hours. "I knew I had attacked my own conscience, my own soul. Oh, Anaïs, how you have gone about quietly and with such courage, saying things I would fear to say."

Each system begins pure and is corrupted by human nature, and there is no cure but to confront human nature itself, by knowledge of it. The psychologists are doing the only constructive work in the world.

I denied having been born with a bigger vision:

"We are all born with a bigger vision, with a knowledge of two worlds. A shock threw me back into interior worlds, where I found strength and depth. But you were courageous in the exterior world. You faced it, and I feared it: the political, international life of wealth and power. I do not feel at home in it. I flee from it. I am not sure whether it was courage which sent me exploring underground, or fear."

Friday I wrote at one sitting the first ten pages of the party scene in the new book, *Ladders to Fire*. I found a new way to deal with neurotic vision, a symbolic theater representation of what takes place in our vision. It is an interior party, the one I describe as the most unattended because each guest experienced only interferences with the reality of it. I fused symbols and externals. I was inspired by the dance style of Martha Graham. The placing of the characters, the symbolic enacting, the suggestiveness.

Saturday I wrote five more pages.

Yesterday five more, on Djuna's absence from the party. It is a study of absence. Realistic parties are always described as if everyone were there, but neurosis and dreaming remove one from the present. It was not an easy thing to describe.

My greatest inspiration comes from the work of other artists: the subtle, suggestive, mysterious world of Martha Graham; the modern painters; modern music, which accepts discordance; sculpture; and dress design.

Five minutes after returning to New York, Gore telephoned me to meet him at Charles Restaurant. He disregards my other engagements. It was to celebrate his coming out of the army. He was in civilian clothes, looking more slender, more youthful, and more vulnerable.

He said: "I feel as if I were coming home. In Washington I felt lost. You have cast a spell on me. What I once accepted, I now do not like. I found my grandfather, the senator, boring."

We sat at the Ruban Bleu. We drank and talked. He told me his mother said to him: "No one will ever love you as I do."

He had wanted his mother to die.

I was moved at the change in Gore, a young man who lived in the most external and superficial of all worlds—that he should be capable of giving himself to a dream, an unusual friendship.

I wrote on Djuna's flight from the party. The real wonders of life lie in the depths. Exploring the depths for truths is the real wonder which the child and the artist know: magic and power lie in truth.

When Diana Trilling complains that Lillian and her husband and children are unreal, and not thoroughly or substantially treated, she does not understand that if I spent four hundred pages building the house, the everyday life, the details which would make it "realistic," I would meanwhile fail to describe how Lillian *felt*, the *unreality* to her of her marriage, home, and children. How can one spend the length of a novel making something real which appears unreal to the central character? I made it plain that Lillian did not feel them; that when she went first of all to the kitchen to see Nanny, the servant for whom the home was real, she sought to come closer to her home and children through Nanny, because for Lillian the connections were broken. When Nanny leaves, the home collapses.

Diana Trilling failed to understand that.

How easy it is to do what Steinbeck does, to take people suffering physical hunger, physical poverty, whose troubles are direct, concrete, simple. His world is simple to tell. I take a far more unexplored world, that of neurosis, and I want to picture the drama which the psychologist struggles with every day: a world of diffused vision, broken connections, symbolic dramas in which the psychic vision creates totally different and elusive problems. To picture Lillian's family as she experiences, feels, and sees it. To dramatize vividly the inner drama, as clearly as Martha Graham pictures jealousy, torment, fear.

I am writing not about objective reality, which is photographic, but as people see and *feel* reality, their reality. I can bring clarity to these feelings. All the world, alas, cannot be analyzed, which it needs to be, but modern literature has a task to fulfill. Novels of the past dealt either with classic objectivity, or accepted the subjective irrational but never clarified it. To write about human beings struggling for food is wonderful. But it is also necessary to become aware of our collective neurosis, to explore it, to seek to bring back into the world the one who has detached himself from it and is suffering from alienation. The neurotic is deprived of his human world. It can be restored to him. Without this work no history will ever progress. Everything which stemmed and developed and grew from Freud, or even in opposition to him, would have been more useful than Marx. For the world cannot feel the poverty or hunger of others when it is neurotic, self-centered, or self-contained. *Those who have a vision into the neurotic world are those who are getting at the roots of aggression, war, hostilities, and prejudice.* So in the end, a neurotic restored to his human life may become a true humanist.

———

I introduced Gore to *Harper's Bazaar* with a portion of his new novel. Also to *Town and Country*.

Marshall came one day with a costume he had bought in a thrift shop. Leo Lerman was giving a party in which the women were to go dressed in the fashion of the twenties. Marshall had a stringy, weepy, flat-chested, waistless beaded dress, a cloche hat which sank to my ears like a chamber pot, make-up for a clown, a circle of red on the cheek. I put on the outfit, took one look in the mirror, and refused to wear it. Marshall had spent thirty-five dollars (there was also a red feather boa) and was very hurt by my refusal. I explained to him as well as I could: "When my father told me I was homely, I spent the rest of my life repairing that as well as I could, worked at improving myself. Why should I go to a party looking like an awkward clown?"

Marshall did not agree. I told Leo Lerman I would not go in costume. He pleaded I should come anyway. The women looked freakish, as they were intended to. I could not even recognize them!

But Marshall and I are still estranged.

Gore fights battles with threatening forces, faces critics, is vulnerable. Like all writers, he dreams of total acceptance, unanimous love. A dream. Someone said they preferred his first novel, *Williwaw*, to the second, *In a Yellow Wood*. When he hears this over the telephone, he comes out pale. It matters to him what others think.

I remind him that first one has to ask: Who is the person who made the statement? Why? Is it someone whose opinion is valuable?

He urges me to battle Diana Trilling.

"The best attack is to continue to work. To do better and better work, that is where to put my energy. I cannot make Trilling more subtle or more understanding."

Gonzalo and I still walk along the streets together. We still sit at coffee shops. But we are no longer walking the streets of the present but those of the past. These are echoes of a deep association, its human echoes. We are sitting at extensions in time of our Paris cafés. It is the old friendship which guides our steps, which orders the drinks, guides our talk. It is the old friendship which makes pale gestures with familiar warmth. The spark is no longer there. Lingering echoes. The streets of a nine-year-old devotion are still richly peopled. He still has lusty stories to tell me, even if I do not hear them as vividly or record them in the diary; he is still full of Indian humor, malice, roguishness. But they are all tributaries from the past, echoes, reverberations, mellow and evaporating before more vivid moments with other friends.

Gore has such a desperate need to assert himself.

His first novel is dedicated to his mother, Nina. His play is dedicated to me.

I can tell him what I was once told by Otto Rank: "Be careful not to enter the world with any need to seduce, charm, conquer what you do not really want only for the sake of approval. This is what causes the frozen moment before people, and cuts all naturalness and trust."

I am aware that what I love and seek is illusive, tricky, spritelike. What *ought to be,* and not what is, interests me. Ideas, experiences, and ideals reflected yet distorted by dreams. Also created by dreams.

In between, an all-consuming loneliness. The dreamlike quality of experience both cheats one of reality and yet creates a world of wonder.

I work not by explosion but by infiltration.

The character of luminosity is what is most appealing in adolescence. The Hindus call this a something by which we can become invisible or shine with light.

But when I speak with Gore about the elations, the high moods, he tells me: "I never feel the high moments, only the depressions." Do they really live with less intensity than I do, less color, less feeling? Muted instruments. I was right when I described neurosis as a form of deafness, nearsightedness, a partial atrophy of the senses.

The homosexual fears totality, the absolute in love. So he divides the physical from the love. But now I find that because of my sympathy, and because I see in the homosexual the same hostilities and rebellions toward the willful or possessive or dominant parent, I am in sympathy with their perverse way of circumventing the man-and-woman relationship. I may be destructive or rebellious in such an indirect and subtle way that it is practically undetectable and greatly suppressed, almost imperceptible. I let the young do it. I let the young strike at the assertive elders. I let Miller be aggressive in his writing, and I was able then to continue to be gentle and guiltless, a pacifier rather than a revolutionary element. All my so-called "children" were rebels. They expressed wants and angers of which I was ashamed, and which I repudiated.

We project the unbearable self onto others, so that we can hate it in others and destroy it. These condemned elements are necessary to life. When you kill them, you kill life. But the ideal in me denied them. Everything in me is circuitous, controlled. I see it now. Was that why I protected the destroyers, and those who hurt themselves in their destructiveness, like Henry, June, Gonzalo, Helba?


Because it was Gore who presented me to Dutton, because he watched over the writing of *Ladders to Fire*, encouraged me, I said I would dedicate the book to him.

I do not know if it comes from knowing so many artists, who were defined by Baudelaire as being man, woman, and child in one, or as adults who never destroyed in themselves the fresh vision of the child, but what I see in the homosexual is different from what others see. I never see perversion, but rather a childlike quality, a pause in childhood or adolescence when one hesitates to enter the adult world. The relationship based on identification, on twinship, or "the double," on narcissism, is a choice more facile and less exigent than that between men and women. It is almost incestuous, like a family kinship. True, there may be in one more masculine traits and in another more feminine traits, so that they may balance each other, or mesh; but whenever I came close to a homosexual, what I found was childishness. There was often a parody, too, of parents or grandparents, an attachment to the past (love of antiques), always a fixation on preadolescence, when our sexual inclinations are not yet crystallized, and always some traumatic event which caused fear of woman, hence the hatred of her.

This hatred of woman I had never experienced until I came to America. The Spanish homosexual or the French homosexual loved men but did not hate women. Paradoxically, they romanticized her. My first love was a homosexual. If his desires went to men, his poems, flowers, homages, dreams came to me.

Pablo was completely at ease with women. He romanticized his mother, and his first mistress. The other world seemed like a joyous, facile, promiscuous world, natural, and without permanence. It had (and I always maintained that) an innocence.

In the American homosexual it was the hatred of woman which was a perversity, for it distorted reality, and made expansion impossible. The constant presence of an enemy makes for the opposite of innocence. The homosexuality took on an air of defiance, of surreptitiousness, of treachery in its own eyes. It may have been for this reason that there were no romantic love stories. Homosexual novels were stories of promiscuity, not love. I knew a few loving couples, but one never found them in literature. Did the guilt the culture had bred in them prevent them from acknowledging a love? I always threatened them, that if they did not do it, I would write the first homosexual novel about love, not whoring.

Why is it the young take on this quality of light, and when the friendship ends, this light is withdrawn? Is it that I enhance and light them where there is a vital warmth exchanged? Or when I see into their potentialities? The light has withdrawn from Leonard. Is it that by his writing, his subdued and lifeless statement, he destroyed my illusion of his being alive? When I find not enough life in them, do I turn away? It is the quality of life which illuminates a person for me.

My friendships, instead of being concentrated on a very few, as in Paris, have become fragmented into many. I find only partial relationships. It is totality the homosexual fears. He separates love and sexuality.

Over and over again I discover the diary is an effort against loss, the passing, the deaths, the uprootings, the witherings, the unrealities. I feel that when I enclose something, I save it. It is alive here. When anyone left, I felt I retained his presence in these pages.

Character is timeless. Ageless. We live back and forth in the past, or in the present, or in the future. With the young, one lives in the future. I prefer that. Changes occur constantly according to the vision, image, or myth which possesses one. We do not grow absolutely, chronologically. We grow sometimes in one dimension, and not in another, unevenly. We grow partially. We are relative. We are mature in one realm, childish in another. The past, present, and future mingle and pull us backward, forward, or fix us in the present. We are made up of layers, cells, constellations. We never discard our childhood. We never escape it completely. We relive fragments of it through others. We live buried layers through others. We live through others' projections of the unlived selves.

I refuse to live out my flaws. I bury them and condemn and deny them. Unable to manifest themselves, they inhabit others. In others I accept uncombed hair, a hole in the shoes, a not-too-clean dress, temper, lies, cowardices, treacheries, jealousies. Allowing others to become mad for you, allowing others to complain for you. The guilt involved in this secret participation leads to responsibility for others' lives. If you lack beauty, you live this beauty out in the other. But it is the same with ugliness. The young's attraction for the old is for protection of their future. The need of faith and the elder's vision into the future.

There is a game and play in the children's world which is a

training ground for fantasy and imagination. When this is not killed in childhood it creates the artist and the inventor. You become a Martha Graham, the greatest and most meaningful of our dancers. Every gesture illuminated with meaning. Nothing is lost. Magic powers are in art. To create and transform.

Note from Henry:

The baby seems to have hands like yours and uses them like you do, in Hindu ritualistic gestures. All indications are that it has a high intelligence and superlative good nature.

Was glad to know of your good luck with publishers.

Stanley Haggart on reading my handwriting:

Great powers of love, a love that is compassionate. The inspirer. A believer. You have great faith, a persistent, persevering faith. The most ordinary people could admire your stability of faith. You work until it happens. You persevere. You won't shift from one faith to another. You break through ordinary morality, but to arrive ultimately at a larger kind of morality. You are trustworthy. Your direction is creative, never destructive. There is a great sadness. Intuition strong, but you can get lost and confused emotionally. You have strong emotional power. It should be used daily in relationships. If not it will come out in intensity and unbalance other relationships. I see you as the sun. Your warmth like the sun in Van Gogh's painting. You have achieved poise and confidence, balance. You can do ordinary things like cooking, and you manage to do them more lightly than others, smoothly, magically.

# [February, 1946]

Went to lunch with Teresa [Nin] and Ikle, and met Paul
Mathiesen. Seventeen years old, of Danish descent, very blond,
very charming. His smile is shy, his eyes unblinking and innocent,
and yet from his body come waves of young, playful sensuality.

He came to see me. He sat on the floor and told fairy tales.
One of them was his own. He paints, he writes. He has a gently
caressing voice. He is in a state of reverie. He pursues his reveries
in the middle of a restaurant, crowded rooms. He is a boy in a
fairy tale.

Jacqueline Ford wrote of *Winter of Artifice:* "It hurts too much.
In life there are interruptions, pauses. To take you away and distract
you from your deep feelings. But you live only in them. It's rarified.
It's unbearable."

Theme of America is gigantism, grandiosity. Enlarging self and
surroundings and objects to cover helplessness. Anger is a prelude
to power. It can become creative. I have always considered it
negative. To be controlled. Evil. But it can become necessary to
self-assertion, and to creation. Fear of self-assertion due to guilt:
guilt in relation to weaker ones, fear of injuring them. But even
more, fear of being alone, separated from others, losing relationships, fear of standing alone. Having to find relationships in
*equality,* which is more difficult than in the dependent-protector or
protector-independent relationships. What a relief it will be, the
day I do not feel the compulsion, the obligation, to protect and
to make myself smaller and weaker in order not to overpower
the very young. The gentleness of those crippled by overpowering
parents. My mother was overpowering, had an indomitable will,
and both parents left their anger free, so that they crippled my
anger with fear of consequences (divorce). If you rebel, you lose
your loves.

My world is so large, so full, I get lost in it. My vision is hard to sustain. Last night I felt alone in what I am writing. I have no *twin to my writing*. It is a big burden for a woman.

Gore returns. He wants to meet Christopher Isherwood, because their writings resemble each other. "I would like to have written *Prater Violet*."

Stanley is adept at making homes with very few means. His own cold-water flat is an example of his skill. Like a stage set, everything is made inexpensively, faked. The couch going around the room is of ordinary boards. He brings materials from the television studios where he builds sets for commercials. I loaned him a Japanese doll for a television series. I took it to him and saw him at work. On one set there were four different rooms: one a kitchen, in which the model advertised a vacuum cleaner; another a parlor, in which the model pointed to the rich carpet; and so on. Stanley has a presence, generous, warm, protective. He has the homemaking instinct. And flashes of poetry. When he reads handwriting he is inventive with his intuitions and his own language. At first, Gore had thought of letting him fix up a brownstone on the East Side, where we would all live together. But this plan was not carried out. I saw Stanley create many interiors. His belief was that by creating a certain interior he could change the lives of those living in it, affect them.

Once, on Christmas night, when he invited us, he had cooled the champagne in snow taken from the window sill. Another time, he served *couscous* in a large flat dish on a low, round oriental table. He is gifted, and struggling to keep afloat. He has ways and solutions for doing things with hardly any money.

It is a way of dreaming beauty, as stage designers do, with flimsy or makeshift material, a quality I admire and have often practiced when means were limited.

Today I finished rewriting Part Two of *Ladders to Fire*. I reduced two hundred pages to eighty pages. I like the party section. It is like one of Martha Graham's ballets; it was inspired by them. It is full of rhythm and color. It is like a mobile, a modern painting. It satisfies me. I am exhausted and nervous.

In the sun, yesterday, Gore's eyes were green and gold. I see only his sincerity with me. I know he acts, pretends, and is insincere outside, but I do not see this or wish to know him in the world. He gives me his best self. His open sweetness, his courage.

Party at Maya Deren's. The artifacts on the walls, the dim lights, the photographs and mobiles, African ornaments, furs, drums, always give a sense of primitive tent life. Paul Mathiesen and I danced together. He said: "It's not a dance, it's a spell." Usually it is I who dream. In this case, he is the dreamer, and I stand watching him and seeking to divine what he is dreaming. He is as mute as a statue. He leaves no phrases in your memory. He smiles. Only his face remains in your memory. A half-smile. Another sexual angel?

A wealthy old man is taking him to Yucatán. He brought me his paintings and writings to take care of. He is an elfin boy. He talks as if he were in a trance. And all the time he is sensing everything, far more than he says. He uses very few words. It is a transmission one feels, as if he had another way of communicating. One of the paintings is a self-portrait, in which he sees himself not as a boy but as a faun. Now and then he utters a profound statement, like those made by children, unexpectedly. At other times he seems disoriented in the world, childlike and lost. As if he were the rightful inhabitant and we, clumsy trespassers, not aware of the rituals. He is slim, very fair, with almost white-blond hair, sensitive hands, a slow speech. He might have been born in the North Pole, where men use few words, but he was born in California. He discovered *Under a Glass Bell* when he was in school. His teacher did not approve of the book and he quit school in protest.

The pages on the party conquered Frances. This time the abstraction was successful. She was completely won, as she said, by the humor, the concreteness of the images, the clarity, the impact.

Strange that the highest peak of faith I achieved while I wrote those pages was accompanied by the most acute doubts. Am I mad? Do I see what others do not see? Is it possible to see THROUGH a party at the inner reality, as if people were transparent, and discover that for one reason or another they were not there, but only pretending to be there? I wept. I am breaking through another shell. It is painful.

I write to Leonard every day because he is in hell, his head shaved, his girl's skin spoiled by the hardest training among the coarsest men, living in barracks, never alone. He, the shy one, always folded in upon himself, filled with inarticulate secrets. What will this do to his already atrophied feelings, the atrophy caused by his environment? Where will his feelings hide now, they who are already lying beneath hundreds of layers of defenses, and fears? I write to him because he is lost, trapped, and I do not know if he will survive this. His mother was cold. The army is brutal.

Gore has at times the tense appearance of anxiety. He then appears to move with difficulty into life. His face loses its softness and is set into a mask. (Already!) At those moments I know he is bound by the webs of neurosis. At other times, he is natural. Pleasure and elation are rare in him. He is vulnerable, but has more defenses than Leonard. He can be cynical, sarcastic, and see the weaknesses of others in a cold, harsh light.

Charles Duits tells me I am the only one he feels close to. He tells me about his love for the Chilean girl Luchita. He behaved ambivalently toward her. Her very beauty frightens him. So he is elusive.

I give a Party.

Guests: Luise Rainer and her husband, Robert Knittel; Maya Deren and Sasha Hammid; Stanley Haggart; Woody Parrish-Martin; Kim Hoffman; Sherry Martinelli and Enrique Zanarte; Charles Duits; Louise and Edgar Varèse; John Stroup; Gore Vidal; Claude Fredericks; James Agee.

Took the mattresses off the beds and made a lot of low oriental divans. Invited a flamenco guitarist. Kim played his accordion. Steve, a handsome, suave, elegant Austrian, danced extremely well.

Gore asked me what I put in my nail polish that gives the color a warm gleam.

"Gold," I said.

"As in your writing?"

Enrique Zanarte's somber Spanish beauty, Stanley's intuitive analysis of people, Woody's fantasies, Steve's grace, Kim's music, Maya's films, all bloomed that night. Even Agee, who so often looks a sad Lincoln, and rather dramatic, smiled.

Lectured and read at Amherst. Success. Signed books. Tension and elation. I read the party scene. I made friends with James Merrill, twenty-year-old poet. I answered the mathematicians, who questioned me on the fluctuating point of view, before an audience of sixty people. I was surrounded by young men.

Gore made me go to the PEN Club dinner. I went in an effort to face the world. Was shocked by the mediocrity of the talks. A "literary" world so thoroughly political, intriguing, and commercial, but a world Gore intends to conquer. For the first time I saw a contrast in our aims. His interest is like Miller's: to meet everybody, to win the world.

James Merrill on my work:

I have since been thinking a great deal of your books and what I feel about them. As I attempted to say when you were up here, everything that takes place shifts back and forth between two dreams—the familiar dream of the imagination projecting itself into adventures, situations, moving through and beyond the world; and the other, rarer, dream of the world's moving *in* upon the imagination, objects thrusting themselves through levels of consciousness. Both dreams meet and almost struggle with one another—in a love story like the surrealist one about Artaud, where his vision projects him into the very world that he cannot bear to live in. Somewhere between these dreams of moving out beyond the world, and being violently disturbed by the physical objects in the world (they become, of course, metaphysical), lies what not you but others call "reality," the balance between the magnificent and the tormented dream. It is the way you make these dreams *mingle* that I feel is so astonishing. You move back and forth, from one to another, so that both sides of this "reality" are disclosed, or would be disclosed if we were quick enough to say: "There it is," before it disappears. The passage in the party scene, for instance, where Lillian destroys herself in a long, very realistic monologue—how completely you replace the surface reality with a surface strangeness by speaking of it in terms of color and form, and indeed develop through this all the inarticulate strangeness that such a situation arouses in anyone aware of it. And what is most admirable, I feel, is the assurance you have in describing, in perceiving. I feel so strongly that you are continually saying: These various dreams, these shuttlings of feeling and vision *are* real, are all we have to explain what happens to us. And that is a very compelling and beautiful integrity in everything you write. Even when we are most aware of invention, invention is replaced by the honesty of what you are saying.

This commentary, so much more astute than Edmund Wilson's, is a key to my friendship with the young, who understand what I am doing.

Maya is making a film. She wanted all of us for a party scene. The stars are Maya and a Negro girl, Rita. Gore has a prejudice against Negroes, but he joined us anyway. Maya wanted an undirected party in her studio, in which things would happen, unexpectedly, by the very nature of the relationships. She was looking for the spontaneous, the accidental. Gore and I decided to act pretty well as we do when we are together, a mixture of playfulness, key words, seriousness, and connections with what we are writing.

All my friends had been rounded up: Pablo, Westbrook, Sherry, Enrique, Charles Duits, Caron, Steve, Nancy Banks, a lovely blonde girl who is married to Don, a Negro guitar player, and who invited me to visit them. Tei-ko, a Japanese dancer.

The ensemble of acting did not satisfy Maya. We spent hours under the violent lights. But Maya refused to indicate any theme or direct us into any channel. She wanted things to happen. So, under the strong lights, we moved about as if at a party, forming groups, dancing, talking. It was then I noticed the theme of the party I had written about: that nothing happened because there was no connection of thought or feeling between the people acting, and so no tensions, no exchange of dramatic or comic moments. It was empty. I wanted to tell Maya: Use my words to describe what is happening! But of course film-makers have a contempt for words. So we went on acting out emptiness. Gore and I tried to give a feeling of a bond, an exchange, a vital responsiveness. Nothing came out the way Maya wanted. The cameras turned. We did it over and over again. When we all became extremely tired, all our "poses," our attempts at acting, our self-consciousness disappeared. We let go. And the party Maya wanted materialized. She cheered. Go on, go on, go on. Exhausted, almost on the verge of hysteria, we danced, talked, held hands, or withdrew, or came back, wandered, looked for intimacy. We worked for her for twelve hours.

What Maya sought and could not obtain was something *happening* between the people. It remained empty and disconnected. I know why. It was a dance of shadows, for there was no sensual connection between anyone there. Most of the young men were homosexuals, or else cold toward women, as is Enrique. Rita, the Negro girl, is a Lesbian. Maya is a restless, unsatisfied woman. The men drawn to each other. What is this world without vital relationships between men and women? Where is the passion which overflowed the streets of Paris, every window, every hotel room? Maya was shouting from her director's stool above the lights: "There is a relationship going on! A contact made at the party. Talk as if you were engaged in some relationship."

Oh irony! They couldn't. We couldn't. Out of fatigue, after being under the strong lights, blinding us, from noon until midnight, we became slightly hysterical. We gesticulated wildly to break down the walls. I tried to establish a rapport with Enrique, to stimulate a warmth which might become a fire! It was all warm, but did not spring from a center of passion. It remained, as it is, on the periphery.

Tei-ko, the Japanese dancer, passive, beautiful, and remote. Charles Duits elusive. Nothing strong, assertive, sweeping. And there, under the lights, I saw the drama of our present life: nothing big enough, deep enough, strong enough.

Did the film catch this? How do you catch emptiness, or shallowness, ghostly figures who are erased on the screen as soon as they appear?

———

The greatest suffering does not come from living, from mirages, from the unattainable dreams of Don Quixote, but from AWAKENING. There is no greater pain than awakening from a dream. The deep crying over the dying selves being shed. Giving up the children seems like giving up my own life and youthfulness. The children cannot be companions. Gore cannot be the companion of my writing self, as I had thought. His life is elsewhere. Even if he loves and needs me, he also has other loves and needs. He had a dream of a house in which we would all live together, like the house of George Davis in Brooklyn. There would be guest rooms, and a room for writing, and much life and many friends.

But my efforts at taking him into my life, the life of the artists, and his attempts to take me into his life (wealth, society, famous names, above all the NAMES: So-and-So, and So-and-So) were failures. He did not enjoy the disparate group acting in Maya's film. I did. Meanwhile, Gore introduced me to a renowned international hostess, a wealthy woman with homes in every city. An adventuress who married a wealthy man.

These love-starved children, unsatisfied, are looking, as Otto Rank said, for a return to the womb, for care, faith, love, acceptance, uncritical devotion.

I reread Dr. Esther Harding's book *The Way of All Women*. She states that in woman there must be a relinquishing of the child before she can mature as one-in-herself.

Paul Valéry: A work is never completed, but merely abandoned.

At the Provincetown Playhouse, we gathered to see three films by Maya Deren. The crowd was dense, and some policeman thought he should investigate. He asked: "Is this a demonstration?" Someone answered: "It is not a demonstration, it is a revolution in film-making."
I found Maya's program note deeply interesting:

Man cannot duplicate the infinite intricacy of the living architecture of the wheat stalk. Nature is best capable of its own forms and of the complex inevitabilities which result in such marvelous phenomena. Man himself is such a phenomenon; and the marvelous in man is his creative intelligence, which transcends nature and creates out of it un-natural forms.

In his art—whether architecture or poem—he does not reproduce a given reality; nor does he simply express his immediate reactions of pleasure and pain. He starts with the elements of that reality—the stone, the city, the other man—and relates them into a new reality which, no sooner achieved, becomes itself an element in his next manipulation. In his effort to achieve form he may produce shapes monstrous or divine; but his proud ambition is to create, in the image of his own intelligence, a reality man-made.

In cinema such a concept of creative action has been neglected. The analogy between the lens and the eye, based on the physical similarity between them, has led to a recording of the forms of reality and those of literature, drama and painting. But cinema, to be creative, must do more than record. The mechanism behind the lens, like the brain behind the eye, can evaluate the objects before it, can decide them attractive or repulsive, casual or surprising. Above all, the analogy must be extended to understand that the strip of film is the memory of the camera. Just as man is not content to merely reconstruct an original chronology, but in his art, conceives new relationships between remembered elements, so the film-maker can create new realities by the manipulation of the celluloid memories at his disposal. The labor, the achieved, inspired, intelligent form is a single continuity, a work in progress which is eventually interrupted when the dynamic consciousness which it reflects ceases. From time to time one may pause to give integrated shapes to a stage of one's progress in order to best pursue it further. And so these films have each been brought to an end, in order to be the better abandoned.

Is devotion to others a cover for the hungers and the needs of the self, of which one is ashamed? I was always ashamed to take. So I gave. It was not a virtue. It was a disguise.

# [April, 1946]

Suddenly it is spring. The windows open, the sound of bells chiming on Fifth Avenue, the shops full of flowers, the crowds gay.

Gore buys a house in Guatemala. It was once a monastery. It is beautiful. I must visit it when it is ready.

I help others attain what they want. Gore is physically recovered from the consequences of his frostbite in the Aleutians. It is symbolic that he feels less stiffness. His mother said he could not act, and he acted in Maya's film. His mother said he could not dance, and he danced with me in Maya's film.

I hope this is the end of the TRANSPARENT CHILDREN.

The first person I gave myself to, my father, betrayed me, so I split. Ultimate giving is fatal. I split, split, split, into a million small relationships. And I seek split beings. Divided beings.

Gore's father is enthusiastic about me. "He sees that you are destroying my mother's image, and he always said my mother had been the destructive image for me."

On writing: I am not writing case histories, as Diana Trilling thinks. Psychoanalysis is merely the basic philosophy of my work. I accept its premise, that it is the unconscious which rules and shapes our lives. I am making a new art of storytelling, not stories told as case histories, but stories told with a new vision of the unfolding of character. To say I write case histories is like saying that a poet who studies astronomy, and becomes familiar with the planets' evolutions, ceases to be a poet and is an astronomer.

Letter from Leonard:

You must know you put me in a difficult position. For how am I to answer your offering of a way out of foreign service? On one side lies more than freedom from the army, inspiration, love, comfort and friendship. This is what you hold out to me. This and your own desire for what is best for me. But I see more. I have been nurtured until now by a powerful source, and I cannot help but feel obligated to return to the source something of myself which I do not know how to give, and which cannot be taught but must be learned. It now seems best for me to live awhile by myself, absorbing what has been offered and developing whatever seed of ability I possess in the most honest criticism of solitude. It is not enough to be told that a poem is good, one must feel it is good without influence. I spoke of being nurtured from the outside. This is all very well, but it is not enough. In Japan I will learn whether or not I am fertile or barren. If I am fertile I will be happy and shall return in the manner of Ulysses who has had his search and voyage within himself. If not, I shall return and struggle along with external support. For these reasons I have decided to go to Japan.

People tell me Gore is arrogant and boastful. I have never seen that. Only the tenderness, gentleness, the sincerity, and the thoughtfulness. He does believe in the continuity of relationships; telephone calls, letters, an unbroken dialogue. Companions in life.

Worked well this morning. Wrote pages on the adolescence of Stella; the relationship between Michael and Donald; story of the opening of the tulip, connected with first love scene with adolescents (*Children of the Albatross*).

Monday: Inspired to work. Wrote pages on Sabina and the fire engines. Café life. So much is clear. Writing, too, is a symphony, a ballet, a painting. The arts serve as symbolism for the things which cannot be said in words, only in symbols. The basic orientation and stability is due to psychological reality; analyzed passions, analyzed as they move, not afterward in a static afterthought, as in Proust. All the various women may converge into one because down deep, in the unconscious, there are resemblances.

Also in life women become other women, interchange, identify, and project. Parts of themselves in the other, through the other. There are exchanges, interchanges, and convergences, and parts of ourselves pass into others.

I write about the house in Louveciennes.

A critic on Virginia Woolf:

All of Woolf's characters tend to remain as immensely complex bundles of impressions and sensations. Her values are enclosed in them but for the reader they are not reached through the living experience of which they are the philosophic *reflections*.

This may be said about my work, too. I wanted to give, in *Winter of Artifice*, the pure essence of the personality, stripped of national characteristics, time, and place, the better to penetrate the innermost being, the deepest self. I describe states: insomnia, obsession, frigidity.

Lanny Baldwin said that part two of *Winter of Artifice* was like a volcano. A volcano indeed. Indeed. Volcanoes are safety valves, necessary in asphalt and cement tiles, in cemented lives and asphalted lovers.

A party. Olga and her husband. Bill Ottoway, the Negro writer. William Steig, James Agee. Mrs. Aswell, of *Harper's Bazaar*, Leo Lerman, the Raydons, the Kahlers, Baldwin, Gore Vidal. Gore talked to Ottoway, overcoming his prejudice.

Nancy Banks is married to a Negro guitarist, Don. We made friends during the making of Maya's film. We met at the Calypso restaurant and listened to her husband play jazz. Nancy told me her life story, and I thought about it. It saddened me. Another day I went to their apartment, in a small house near the Hudson. They told me about their child, how they cannot walk through the Village together. They are insulted, and sometimes almost in danger. The child was beautiful. There was hardly any furniture, but many books and records, and much love in the air.

I see Josephine and Pablo. A joyous walk through the city.
Mature people relate to each other without the need to merge.

D. H. Lawrence wrote against merging. But it is this merging I love and seek.

Gore in the world is another Gore. He is insatiable for power. He needs to conquer, to shine, to dominate.

On writing: Writing for me is not an art. There is no separation between my life and my craft, my work. The form of art is the form of art of my life, and my life is the form of the art. I refuse artificial patterns. Stories do not end. A point of view changes every moment. Reality changes. It is relative.

With Wilson it was a matter of bowing to a new regimen, or else seducing, so as to avoid being dominated or overwhelmed or enslaved. Under cover of seduction, one avoids being controlled, influenced, possessed. For this man of power—the father—once overwhelmed me, enslaved me, dominated my life, exerted tyranny, and then betrayed me. He brutalized my childish weakness and dependency. In this father-figure presence, though I am now a woman, I do not feel free or equal, able to continue my growth, my explorations, experiments, adventures. Rather I feel an apprehension that, taking my life in his hands, he may damage me. Impede me, oppress me. In the face of such an attitude, no older man can appear to me in his true light.

Edmund Wilson's opinions, commentaries, and tastes were to be espoused or adhered to as to another dogma. My first experience depersonalized MAN and made him a symbol of someone who misuses his power. A full-powered man was one who misused his power, to dominate woman. The MAN need not be introduced by name. My neurotic vision would pick out the dangerous elements which, incidentally, did not appear in Henry, Gonzalo, or the children. I only saw a man whose will would bend mine, ignore my aspirations, beliefs, deprive me of my liberty, threaten my development.

By his very achievement he was doomed. The very tone in which people spoke of Edmund Wilson, unquestioned respect, doomed him in my eyes. At first I would at times be elated by power: Otto Rank's poetic power gave him the gift of prophecy and drama. But at some point or other, HE asserted his prerogative. *Le droit du seigneur.* Made his claim. And then I used my charm to enslave and abandon first.

While neurosis rules, all life becomes a symbolic play. This is the story I am trying to tell. The childhood creates a set of characters which become myths. Any correlation serves to type them. They are typed and treated according to the pattern. There is no empathy or compassion in neurosis, because the object is seen as a threat, an enemy to be defeated. And from this symbolism (in my case only the power man, never the one who has needs or difficulties in living similar to mine, brothers, sisters, who do not fall into that role) stems the ghostliness, or abstraction, of some of today's relationships. Many couples, many people, are not living with real human beings, but with their ghosts.

Who has not followed for years the spell of a particular tone of voice, from voice to voice, as the fetishist follows a beautiful foot, scarcely seeing the woman herself? A voice, a mouth, an eye, all stemming from the original fountain of our first desire, directing it, enslaving us, until we choose to unravel the fatal web and free ourselves. The story of complete freedom does not appear yet in this volume. I am still in the labyrinth, and I must be willing to get lost before I am saved. It is only when I abandon myself that I am saved. The unreality we are suffering from is what I want to make clear, to dispel. Who knows what shadows from the past dictated to Edmund Wilson his next attraction? The hero of this book is the malady which makes our lives a drama of compulsion instead of freedom.

While I was writing yesterday, the bell rang. Leonard stood at the door. A Leonard who had lost his dewiness, opalescence, transparence, by his life in the army. With rougher hands and skin, and now a lieutenant. A Leonard less shy, with a richer voice. He had chosen to go to Japan.

---

A party at Maya Deren's. Robert Lowry, very fat, like an inflated child, all flesh and small eyes, says: "I expected someone austere, because of the purity of the writing, but you are soft." Griffith says: "There is a quality in your writing which moves me terribly, a kind of courage of the heart."

I sit with Enrique Zanarte, a black-velvet-eyed Velásquez, but he only notes what there is to hate, to feed his detachment. He points to the big woman whose suit does not fit her body, whose hat and veil sit grotesquely on her ugliness. He stares only at the absurd, the black-toothed Willard Maas, the stiff and the incongruous. He observes those who wear façades: mondaine façades, deteriorated or in need of paint. I move away from him because, as I told him, I know all that is there, but what I cannot love and what does not fit into my world, I do not want to see. I talk with Nancy, tied by threads of a many-colored tenderness to her Negro musician, flowing in tenderness of touch with all, because their personal tenderness overflows and spills onto the others. I talk with Sherry. Half of her body is heavy and animal, and the upper half is childlike and fragile, tied by threads of sensuality to many. I seek Pablo's exuberance and physical passion for life and motion. He is always dancing. When he comes up the five flights of my stairs, he leaps like a gazelle, wide leaps, two stairs at a time. I seek Robert Lowry because he gave his energy, years ago, to a printing press, printing and writing, designing attractive small books. I seek James Merrill because his poetry is beautiful.

When I kissed Pablo because of his spontaneous gaiety, others stood in line to be kissed. I abandoned the detached ones, sought only the amorous ones.

Gore was not there, because he was ill. When he came the next day to take me to dinner, he was pale. He brought me poetry he had written at sixteen. He showed me stories he wrote then. One humorous, the other ironic. "In school they made fun of emotion."

And here is the beginning of the shell. The shell is America's most active contribution to the formation of character. A tough hide. Grow it early.

Charles Duits understands the shell. He has a more sophisticated one. It is in his intellectual detachment and analysis. It is in his subtle poetry.

I see Gonzalo every day, but he is dark and heavy, and weighs so heavily on my spirit that I turn to the future. What will Leonard become? What will Gore become? He wants power. Leonard does not even know what he wants. Gore may enter politics. It is in the family.

The game now is between violent and unsubtle men and gentle, tender young ones.

Gonzalo's violence. Out of jealousy, he took down the painting of Paul Mathiesen and destroyed it.

I went to see Nancy, the Negro guitarist, and their child. Their life touched me so much I sat down and wrote a story, "The Child Born Out of the Fog."* I also had in mind Richard Wright and Helen, and their child.

Spent the day at Yonkers, working for Maya's film. Dancing among imitation-Greek columns and statues. Someone bought Cokes and hot dogs. When I ate the hot dogs someone said: "It does not seem right to see you eat hot dogs." Damn the legend! I was having a carefree time and the remark annoyed me. Maya, Sasha, Rita, Nancy, and Sherry would not let me carry anything. Sherry said: "You're a legendary character. I keep thinking that in the future I will look back and say: 'I was here in Yonkers Park with the legendary Anaïs!' " I fell into despondency. Has my writing created this distance? I felt locked out. Locked out of every natural and ordinary life.

But with Gore, whenever I want to act lightly, he does not want it. "You taught me to be happy in the depths."

* Later included in *Under a Glass Bell*—Ed.

The work on Maya's new film was not without its dark moments. Maya, with a true director's domineering power, would telephone and say: "Tomorrow morning at seven be at Central Park, at the Fifty-ninth Street entrance. We have to film before the public gets there. Take a taxi. I will pay for it."

Of course poor Maya never did or could pay. For some of the group this was a heavy burden. At other times we would meet downtown at Grand Street, in front of the shops selling wedding dresses. A surrealist setting, amidst grim, tall, inhuman buildings, dirty streets filled with broken bottles and garbage, with alcoholics sleeping in the doorways, in attitudes which seemed more like those of death.

All gray, brown, black, shabby colors. But in the windows, a world of white satin, lace, white flowers, and airy mannequins floating in clouds of tulle. The most romantic of long trailing dresses, unbelievable survival of periods where beauty and poetry were essential. The ritual of marriage as yet not modernized into ordinary dress. Costumes inspired by the Middle Ages, by days of royal pageants. The high bosom line of Madame Récamier; the Empire dress of Joséphine; the bouffant dress of the eighteen hundreds; the square, low necklines of Queen Elizabeth; the hairdos, ornaments, and veils of Edgar Allan Poe's heroines; the ladies of the castles; the ladies at Spanish court or at bull fights; the Roman matrons at the games. Every graceful, gracious, floating, poetic costume in those windows of Grand Street. A surrealist dream in a poor and shabby neighborhood. A spectacle for dim eyes, hungry faces, shabby bodies. A dream.

We danced among the brides, between reflections of hundreds of brides.

Another time, in Central Park, we suffered a dramatic scene which turned us against Maya. Frank Westbrook is a ballet dancer. His entire life and career depend on his body. Maya planned a scene among the rocks which required Frank to leap from rock to rock. We all felt it was too dangerous. We felt it was too much to ask. A ballet leap on stage, well planned, on an even floor, is one thing; it is quite another to leap from rock to rock and risk breaking a leg. We protested. We said no film was worth that risk. We encouraged him to refuse. I, who had introduced Frank to Maya, felt more responsible than the others; more indignant, too. She imposed her will. She said if he did not do it, he would be out of the film. We laid our coats on the rocks. We watched with fear and anger. He made the leap. But our feeling toward Maya changed. She had a film to make, but we were volunteers. We gave our time, our energy, even our money, and she should be more human. We believed in her as a film-maker, we had faith in her, but we began to feel she was not human. The power of her personality, the unblinking of her blue eyes, the sturdy curled hair growing gypsylike in an aureole around her face; her face square and strong, like a Botticelli, round eyes, full mouth, but far stronger; her determined voice, the assertiveness and sensuality of her peasant body, her dancing, drumming: all haunted us. We spent a great deal of time talking about her. We were manipulated in our life. We had a mixture of admiration for her energy and obstinacy, and rebellion against her dominant presence.

She is the one who gives all the parties. We meet at her house. Sometimes when I arrive with my entourage, my children, my young men, she attempts to hold one of them, and starts what we called her "courtship dance." Once, Charles Duits telephoned me: "I am here alone with Maya. She is doing her courtship dance. Please come and rescue me."

Later he confessed that what frightened him was that she had hair on her chest.

We were influenced, dominated by her, and did not know how to free ourselves. Her film-making fascinated us.


What I like in my adolescents is that they have not yet hardened. We all confuse hardening and strength. Strength we must achieve, but not callousness.

Waking from a dream, the dream of the press, destroyed by Gonzalo. When I do not work there, he spends his time talking with his friends. He is drowned in debts.

I have not been going to the press. I have been writing.

Faced with Edmund Wilson, I felt myself an adolescent. Why? I don't know. But there it was. I felt without authority, vulnerable, stripped of power. I felt that perhaps only by making myself smaller could I avert the storm, or the critical phrase which would fall on me, strike me down. Had I thought of defiance?

Defiance meant war, war meant wounds, and no certainty of conquering. It was the same war I had once waged, with unequal arms, against the overcritical father. Wilson's tyranny and dogmatism, his academic learning, subdued me. It is an error to believe that gentleness is a lightning conductor. On the contrary. He felt my evasions. And the critical phrase came. He read an entire book of mine and could only say: "You've made a mistake in English." With his interest in Henry James he could not read me nor reach me. With his dissertation on Greek art he could not move me. With his new shoes, too polished and formal, he could not touch me. They were too solid and too heavy. His house was not only his house, but the formal house of my father, in Passy. It had the same brown austerity and the same conventional elegance. The same narrowness of windows. He is my father's age. Therefore it ceased to be the house of Edmund Wilson in the present. It became a symbol of the past, to be destroyed and forgotten.

There is a way of living which makes for greater airiness, space, ease, freedom. It is like an airplane's rise above the storms. It is a way of looking at obstacles as something to overcome; of looking at what defeats us as a monster created by ourselves, within ourselves, by our fears, and therefore dissolvable and transformable.

The secret of a full life is to live and relate to others as if they might not be there tomorrow, as if you might not be there tomorrow. It eliminates the vice of procrastination, the sin of postponement, failed communications, failed communions. This thought has made me more and more attentive to all encounters, meetings, introductions, which might contain the seed of depth that might be carelessly overlooked. This feeling has become a rarity, and rarer every day now that we have reached a hastier and more superficial rhythm, now that we believe we are in touch with a greater amount of people, more people, more countries. This is the illusion which might cheat us of being in touch deeply with the one breathing next to us. The dangerous time when mechanical voices, radios, telephones, take the place of human intimacies, and the concept of being in touch with millions brings a greater and greater poverty in intimacy and human vision.

Maya said she did not want to use professionals, because they were empty and without personality. Yet when she gathered together such varied personalities as those I described in the diary, she did not regard them as individuals, and therefore they became meaningless. The meaninglessness part of the film—the party—is empty because the people in it are nonexistent as individuals. Maya did not seek to bring out their personalities. Tei-ko, for example, has an eloquent silence. When she talks it is meaningless and without design because our language is not hers. The themes of pursuit and the chase are never developed. Almost everyone becomes grotesque, rather than significant. It does not add anything to the film that we see magnified the wart on Frank's neck. It alienates us from him as a dancer. He becomes a caricature of himself. In *Meshes of the Afternoon* Maya poetized herself, respected the aura, increased the effect of atmosphere. In this film. [*Ritual in Transfigured Time*] there is no such miracle, except at the end, with the white, vaporous figure. Maya's ruthlessness with people rendered her vision cruel and rather distorted. The first part, the statue sequences, is the best. The party is the weakest. The theme is lost. The sense of quest is gone. There is an emptiness. The theme of interchangeable personalities is not clear, and I might even say that in destroying the characters, Maya destroyed the film. When gestures are broken at the party, heads cut off, it is not human beings who lose arms and heads but the film which loses its meaning. I feel this film is a failure.

Notes for lecture tour:

My basic theme is that of relationship. To explore all the variations, the subtleties of relationships. As it is in moments of emotional crisis that human beings reveal themselves most deeply, I choose to write more often about such moments. I choose the heightened moments, because they bring to bear all the forces of intuition. For this I choose moods, states of being, states of exaltation, to accentuate the reality of feeling and the senses. It is this that I contribute to a feminine concept; the language of emotion, altogether different from that of the intellect. Since I urge spontaneity, improvisation, free association, it would be a contradiction to say I have a plan, a conscious structure. My only structure is based on three forms of art—painting, dancing, music—because they correspond to the senses I find atrophied in literature today; and these forms are those most directly connected with life: the eyes, body, emotions.

It is life I am writing about, at its moments of greatest intensity, because it is then that the meaning shines strongest. I write continually in the mood we are told would be produced if we could know the moment of our death: the intensification of memory. This developed from the use of the diary. Writing in a diary developed several habits: a habit of honesty (because no one imagines the diary will ever be read); a habit of writing about what most closely concerns one; a habit of improvisation on any theme one wishes; habits of spontaneity, enthusiasm, naturalness. The emotional reality of the present. A respect for the present mood. Dreams pass into the reality of action. From the action stems the dream again; and this interdependence produces the highest form of living. I have been able to make these transitions. I have passed from one to the other.

What the poet has to say is as fragile as snow but as powerful as the Deluge. Shall it be the power of feeling which will fecundate the great concrete cities of tomorrow with the necessary water? Feeling will nourish the roots and cause an ultimate flowering, fecundate the million cells revealed by the microscope.

The dismemberment of man, from Joyce to Proust, the breaking down of the cells under the eye of analysis, the fission of uranium atoms, produce chain reactions. Man has to be made whole again by passion and faith. Our faith has been displaced from something outside of ourselves to the inner self. In *Winter of Artifice* I wanted to give the pure essence of the personality, stripped of national characteristics, time, and place, the better to penetrate the innermost being, the deepest self. I describe states of being: insomnia, frigidity, anxiety. By giving impressions of feelings and sensations, such as you might give through music, by enrichment of the sensibilities, I seek to approximate the sensory, emotional way we receive experience.

My way of working resembles that of a composer of music. I start from a word or a phrase which arouses rich associations, and begin variations on this, expansions, improvisations. Always in an effort to extract the largest possible meaning.

When I think of one woman who has oriental characteristics, I see an infinite number of women reflected in her.

I write emotional algebra. All my life I have promised myself to begin at the beginning and tell the whole story very simply, step by step. Then I begin, and the first thing that happens is that my pace becomes rapid, my rhythm breathless, and I am off again, searching for the quintessence of emotional reality. Why does the poet use symbol in his stories? Why does the natural storyteller take his time and deal in a direct way with untransformed events?

Truth and psychological reality are at the basis of what I write, but I have learned that our reality is partly directed by the unconscious and partly formed from former experiences casting their shadows on the present.

I can always produce the realistic incident which caused the writing, which lies at its source. I can produce the true model, the place, the time. But because I insist on extracting the essence, on giving a distilled product, it becomes a dream, where all reality appears in a symbolic form. Everything I write will have to be translated, but by doing this, as when one deciphers a dream, one will learn the language of the unconscious, a valuable language.

I choose the extraordinary moments of life, the heightened ones, because they are moments of heightened revelations, of illuminations, of the greatest riches. They are the moments when the forces of the unconscious rise to the surface and take over. By this choice of the strongest moods, exaltations, states of being, I accentuate the reality of feeling and of the senses. I use the language of emotion and the senses, which is different from that of the intellect.

In *Ladders to Fire* I used modern painting as the best symbol to depict the disintegration of the personality, the fragmentation. Modern painting is used as a key to the character of Jay, revealing his split from reality, his dismemberment. What an overdevelopment of the conscious intellect separated, split asunder, and dismembered can only be put together again by the senses and the emotions. The life of the senses, of feeling, would lead us back to wholeness, to experiencing everything in its totality. Man began to disintegrate under the microscope of analysis, carried to its ultimate perfection by Proust. Man dissolved in the undifferentiated flow of unconscious monologue found in Joyce. But neither of these processes needed to prove fatal to man, any more than the splitting of the atom needed to destroy energy. On the contrary, it released more energy. Analysis of man could release more energy and create a more sincere synthesis. This new dimension, discovered and explored, could well be an instrument to make men more potent and whole.

Some writers expect to know what form to adopt before they begin to write. I feel that form is not a matter of prefabrication, but that it is created by the meaning, the content of the book, by its theme. For me it is an inner eruption, very similar to that created by the earth itself in its perpetual evolutions. They happen according to inner tensions, inner pressures, inner accidents of climate, and it is the accumulation of such inner organic incidents which created mountains and oceans. To discover my own form I have first to dig very deeply into this natural source of creation. And the sources of creation, as in geology, lie very deep at the center of the being, as they do at the center of the earth. Once I have been willing to travel in darkness, to the center of the earth, I find precious coals, metals, stones, and all the elements necessary to life. I also find fire, and without fire no creation is possible, for fire makes coalescence. Fire, earth, and water are all parts of creation, passion, experience, flow. Once I have tapped those sources, writing becomes as natural as singing.

When writing comes with difficulty, it simply means that, like the ancient *sourcier*, I have not yet found the sources of water.

Too great an emphasis on technique arrests naturalness. The material from which I will create comes from living, from the personality, from experience, adventures, voyages. This natural flow of riches comes first. The technique is merely a way to organize the flow, to chisel, shape; but without the original flow from deep inner riches of material, everything withers.

America has suffered from a cult of craft and techniques. Every technique is a craft which is adopted from without, not from inner necessity, or inner vision. It can only photograph and register: nothing else. It cannot impart life. I look at writing as a natural, spontaneous thing, like a torrent. When I see a very meager stream, hesitations, difficulties, premeditations, preparations, and much talk, I know the source is poor.

The theme of the diary is always the personal, but it does not mean only a personal story: it means a personal relation to all things and people. The personal, if it is deep enough, becomes universal, mythical, symbolic; I never generalize, intellectualize. *I see, I hear, I feel.* These are my primitive instruments of discovery.

These discoveries coincided with the discoveries of psychology and science (or rather were influenced and developed by them). Being true to my own experience, I discovered the basic theme of modern literature: man dismembered by analysis, by modern life, by modern technology, achieving a state of nonfeeling dangerous to his sanity and his life.

The primitive and the poet never parted company. When Picasso reached a certain plateau in his creativity, he reached for African inspiration to renew himself. Intellectual knowledge is not enough. Music, the dance, poetry and painting are the channels for emotion. It is through them that experience penetrates our blood stream. Ideas do not.

Much writing in America has confused banality with simplicity, and the cliché with universal sincerity. There is a puritanical suspicion of what may seduce and charm the senses.

There is a prejudice against subjectivity, because it is believed subjectivity is a narrowing of the vision. But this is no more true than to say objectivity leads to a larger form of life. Nothing leads to a vaster form of life but the capacity to move deeply inward as well as outward. What is important is neither subjectivity nor objectivity but mobility, aliveness, the interrelation between them and between all relationships. A man who lives unrelated to other human beings dies. But a man who lives unrelated to himself also dies.

The most important problem for the novelist is that each generation must create its own reality and its own language, its own images. Each one of us must re-create the world.

There is a new dimension in character, and I am seeking a way to seize it. The old single point of view is too rigid.

Man's life is in great part dreamed. This part must be exposed and tracked down. It is part of our reality, our emotional reality.

I work by flashes of intuition, a succession of illuminations. Far more is revealed in a selected moment than in a huge construction of details. The world around the character is described as the character sees it; an emotional landscape. The sewing of a button reveals the carelessness of one man in his relationship to the woman who is sewing.

Moving back and forth in time, because the past interferes in and often takes over the present.

It was Henry James himself who said that if you describe a house too completely, too concretely, objectively, solidly, in every detail, then it becomes impossible for the imagination to conceive of what might happen there. The character of the house overshadows events, creates its own associations with peripheral atmospheres (time, place, history, architecture). The reality of the house swallows the canvas and the storyteller. I go in the opposite direction. I want the least trappings and decor possible.

When Maya asked us to act in her film, we all confessed our individual fears. Frank Westbrook's skin was marked by smallpox and he was sensitive about it. Sasha promised he would bear that in mind. I confessed I was the oldest and feared close-ups. Each one of us had a defect, a flaw, a minor weakness. A heavy leg, or a heavy neck. Sasha and Maya assured everyone that the editing would respect that. Sasha took infinite care with Maya. He made Maya beautiful in her films. The freckles disappeared, the heavy features were softened, the wild curly hair was lighted and airy. So we entrusted ourselves to them.

I remembered this returning from Maya's, where we saw the finished film. We sat shell-shocked and silent when it was over. Frank Westbrook's skin was highlighted and every pore, every tiny pockmark magnified to seem like a crater. A close-up of me, twice natural size, was shiny-skinned and distorted by magnification. Everyone found his flaw there. Maya said: "It is always so. Everyone is shocked when he first sees himself in film or hears his voice for the first time. That is why I made you sign a release. You will get over it."

"Maya, do you mean that though we worked for you as friends, gave you all our time, and often the money we did not have to spend on taxis, you will not consider our feelings and make any change in the editing? You shot so many feet of Frank. Do you think you could find another shot of him from not so close up?"

Kim Hoffman, Steve, Gore, Bill Howell, Pablo. All of them would be disappointed. There was an ugliness in the vision, in the camera eye, in Sasha himself, who witnessed our reaction without a tremor of sympathy. He seemed to feel that the greatness of Maya as a film-maker justified everything, and that our reactions were of no importance.

The curious thing was that the unique qualities of my friends, which Maya had been interested in—Pablo's gaiety and sparkle,

Gore's poise, Steve's beauty, Hoffman's witty face, Frank's dancing and intelligence—none of these were captured. They appeared diluted, watered-down.

You can only see in others what your nature allows you to see. The range of your vision depends on the extent of the personal development.

I found that Maya's prejudice against psychology stemmed from her battle with a psychiatrist-father. She rejected all symbolic interpretation, yet the actions in her films were symbolic, not realistic. She was definitely influenced by Cocteau.

If Maya wanted to portray in the party scene a hypnosis of the senses, the intertwining of relationships, people caught in trances of warmth, the *cabinets particuliers de l'amour,* mutual attractions, she did not suggest it, and it did not take place. What was revealed was emptiness.

Death from disillusion is not instantaneous, and there are no mercy killers for the disillusioned. Because when those who seek to help you merely indicate that you are dreaming, that you are caught in illusion, you can answer truthfully: I am planning and designing the future.

What is the difference between the fragmentation I see around me, and the plurality the German writer Novalis considered a sign of genius?

Is it that rich personalities have many aspects, but do not fall apart?

Gore's family had a house in Easthampton and he suggested I spend a week out there. I rented a room in a picturesque cottage. Claude Fredericks was staying with friends nearby, Moira not very far away, and Madame Pierre Chareau was also staying with friends. I rented a bicycle to get around. A group of us would gather at the beach. Gore would walk down from his chic beach club and join us.

I think he was ashamed that we bicycled through the town.

One night Hugh Chisholm gave a garden party. This was so

157

beautiful that it reminded me of the dreamed party of *Le Grand Meaulnes,* by Alain-Fournier. There were colorful tents and wheelbarrows filled with rose petals, on which rested bottles of champagne. The men and women were out of *Vogue* and *Harper's Bazaar.* It was beautiful to look at, but lacked warmth and naturalness. I did not stay long.

I stood waiting for the light to change at a crossroad. What startled me and made me examine the cyclist waiting beside me was the extraordinary brilliance of his large eyes. They shone with a silver sparkle which was almost frightening, because it highlighted the tumultuous panic close to the surface.

His gestures were free and nimble, the gestures of an adolescent, restless and light. The eyes alone contained all the fever. He had driven his bicycle like a racing car. He had come down upon me as if he did not see trees, cars, people, and almost overlooked the stop signal.

The red light changed to green. He gave a wild spurt to his pedaling, and then stopped suddenly to ask me the way to the beach. The tone in which he asked directions was as if the beach were a shelter to which he was speeding away from grave dangers.

I disliked Easthampton. The cloud of monotony and uniformity which hung over the new, neat mansions, the impeccable lawns, the dustless garden furniture. The men and women at the beach, all in one dimension, without any magnetism to bring them together. Zombies of civilization, in elegant dress with dead eyes. Static. The sign in front of the church: "This is the site of the most costly church on Long Island."

At midnight the place was deserted. Everyone was at home with bottles from which they hoped to extract a gaiety bottled elsewhere. It was the kind of drinking one does at wakes. Only the bars were open, where limp figures clutched at oblivion.

I ran out of sleeping pills. I walked looking for a drugstore. They were all closed. At one o'clock I was still walking, hoping to tire myself and be able to sleep, but I could not overcome my memories of Saint-Tropez: the fiestas, the lively scene at the port, the open cafés, the lights, the dancing, the flags, the banners of yachts.

A car stopped beside me. A tall, white-haired Irish police officer addressed me courteously:

"May I give you a lift?"

"I couldn't sleep. I was looking for a drugstore, where I might find sleeping pills."

I climbed into the car. I said: "I'm homesick for other beaches I have known."

"I was homesick when I first came from Ireland."

"Did you ever see Saint-Tropez?"

"Yes, I did. I was once a bodyguard for a rich man. I'll take you to my home first. The wife and kids are asleep, but I can get you some aspirin."

He left me in the car. He entered his house. He came out carrying a glass of water and two aspirins. I took the water and the aspirins obediently. He focused his flashlight upon a bush in his garden and said: "Look at this!"

I saw flowers of velvet, with black hearts and gold eyes.

"Roses of Sharon," he said reverently, and in the purest of Irish accents. "They only grow in Ireland and in Long Island."

"I'll sleep now," I said.

"Yes, you will. One can only sleep when one has found something to be grateful for. You can never sleep when you're angry."

He gave me roses of Sharon to admire. Driving me home, he spoke of another homesick character.

"He is a young fellow in the Royal Air Force. Aviator all through the war, seventeen when he volunteered. He's grounded now, and he can't take it. He's restless, and keeps speeding, and breaking traffic laws. I stopped giving him tickets. He's used to airplanes. Being grounded is tough. I know how he feels."

The next day we met at the beach. The grounded aviator was there. We were introduced. We took a walk along the beach. John began to talk: "I've had five years of war as a rear-gunner. Been to India a couple of years, to North Africa, slept in the desert, crashed several times, made about a hundred missions, saw all kinds of things. Men dying, men yelling when they're trapped in burning planes. Their arms charred, their hands like the claws of animals. The first time I was sent to the field after a crash . . . the smell of burning flesh. It's sweet and sickening, and it sticks to you for days. You can't wash it off. You can't get rid of it. It haunts you. We had good laughs, though, laughs all the time. We laughed plenty. We would commandeer prostitutes and push them into the beds of the guys who didn't like women. We had drunks that lasted several days. I liked that life. India. I'd like to go back. This life here, what people talk about, what they think, bores me. I liked sleeping in the desert. I saw a black woman giving birth. She worked in the fields carrying dirt for a new airfield. She stopped carrying dirt to give birth under the wing of a plane, just like that, and then bound the kid in some rags and went back to work. Funny to see the big plane, so modern, and this half-naked woman giving birth and then continuing to carry dirt in pails for an airfield. You know, only two of us came back alive of the bunch I started with. My buddies always warned me: 'Don't get grounded; once you're grounded, you're done for.' Well, they grounded me, too. Too many rear-gunners in the service. I didn't want to come home. What's civilian life? Good for old maids. It's a rut. It's drab. Look at this: the young girls giggle, giggle at nothing. The boys are after me. Nothing ever happens. They don't laugh hard and they don't yell. They don't get hurt, and they don't die, and they don't laugh either."

There was a light in his eyes I could not read, something he had seen but would not talk about.

We walked tirelessly along the beach, until there were no more homes, no more cared-for gardens, no more people, until the beach became wild.

"Some die silent," he continued, as if obsessed. "You know by the look in their eyes that they are going to die. Some die yelling, and you have to turn your face away and not look into their eyes. When I was being trained, you know, the first thing they told me: 'Never look into a dying man's eyes.' "

"But you did," I said, suddenly understanding the expression of his eyes. I could see him clearly at seventeen, not yet a man, with the delicate skin of a girl, the finely carved features, the small straight nose, the mouth of a woman, a shy laugh, something very tender about the face and body, looking into the eyes of the dying.

"The man who trained me said: 'Never look into the eyes of the dying or you'll go mad.' Do you think I'm mad? Is that what you mean?"

"You're not mad. You're very hurt and frightened, and very desperate, and you feel you have no right to live, to enjoy, because your friends are dead or dying, or flying still and in danger. Isn't that it?"

"I wish I were there now, drinking with them, flying, seeing new countries, new faces, sleeping in the desert, feeling you may die any moment and so you must drink fast, and fight hard, and laugh hard. I wish I were there."

I saw him two or three times, and then he disappeared. He was in the hospital with a bout of malaria.

I returned to New York. The sea at Easthampton had not renewed me. It was not the same sea.

George Davis persuaded *Harper's Bazaar* to publish the section "Stella" from *Ladders to Fire*. Leo Lerman was asked to write a short introduction. They used a still photo of me from Maya's film.

Irene Selznick telephoned her husband in Hollywood about "Stella." Then she came to see me.

She wanted me to write a play for her. I explained that I felt the way I wrote was the opposite of theater. I had no gift for realistic dialogue or action. The life was inner, and the talk part of that inner awareness.

The appearance in *Harper's Bazaar* gave an illusion of success in the world. It is an ephemeral illusion, as the people who read *Harper's Bazaar* do not care about writing for its own sake. It is a gesture of fashion, like a dress. It only means you are fashionable for the moment

One day the bell rang and, as usual, I stood at the head of the stairs to hear who was coming. I heard puffing and groaning like that of an animal, and some object which was dragged up the stairs, a step at a time, bumping the edges each time, settling, and then moving again. The whole scene accompanied by nonhuman sounds. Finally, a hunchback appeared at the door, with a deformed face that seemed to have been squeezed to become smaller to fit the body. His eyes were weeping from the cold. He carried a carton of books from Dutton, copies of *Ladders to Fire*.

I said: "Come in. You can leave it right there. Would you open it for me? Would you like a cup of coffee?"

"Yes, ma'am."

While I heated coffee, he asked me: "Why did you buy so many books?"

"To give to my friends. I have friends who can't pay such a high price for books."

When he opened the carton, I took out a copy. I was not pleased by the jacket. I had given Dutton a beautiful smoky engraving of a fire with a white ladder running through it. It had been printed in the orange color of cheap imitation-orange candy. But there it was:

"LADDERS TO FIRE by ANAÏS NIN."

"You wrote the book?" asked the hunchback, noticing the name on the paper he was holding out for me to sign.

"Yes, I wrote the book."

"Do you make a lot of money out of a book like that?"

"I get ten per cent of the price of each book."

"That's not very much. Will it be a best seller?"

"The publisher does not think so. He is putting it out quietly, so no one will notice. He does it for prestige. Prestige means someday he may be proud of it. It may be mentioned by a big critic."

"If you don't make a lot of money, and he does not make a lot of money, I don't see the sense of it."

"There is some sense to it. I love to write. Some people love to read. We may have pleasure out of it. Don't you have something you really *love* to do?"

"Yes," he said, "I love fishing. I do it every Sunday."

"It's the same thing," I said.

He labored down the stairs. I was reading my own book as if it were new to me, as if it had been written by someone else, when the bell rang and the same sea-elephant sounds came up the stairwell. It was the messenger from E. P. Dutton.

"You forgot to sign."

"Oh, I'm sorry."

He took another look at me from his very small teary eyes, as if I were a curious specimen, and left with a twist of the mouth intended as a smile.

*Ladders to Fire* was officially published. About three hundred people came to the Gotham Book Mart and feted me as one dreams of being feted, each one carrying several copies of the book for me to sign, for himself, for friends. They said: "Please go on, please do not change. It is so real. It changed my life. . . ." Three days of bookshop parties proved to me that the world for which I write is larger than publishers thought, and also of higher quality and of greater sincerity. The young writers to come will waste less energy in battling, in printing, in talking for themselves. Parties at Young's Bookstore, at Lawrence Maxwell's, at Four Seasons. At Lawrence Maxwell's bookshop a paper crown was offered to me by Eugene Walter.

People do not offer me ordinary compliments, but their feeling, by their eyes and by their silence. All this covered the painful cheap burlesque of the New York *Times* review, entitled "Surrealist Soap Opera"; Diana Trilling's implacable anger; and worst of all, Leo Lerman's betrayal. He telephoned me: "You should lie low and hide after all this exposure of one woman loving another." (The relationship I describe is not even Lesbian!)

I received a letter from a young writer, and later a manuscript. The manuscript won my praise and response. It was subtle and poetic, the words were rhythmic and suggestive. It achieved a quality almost totally lacking in American writing today, that of tragedy.

The mother, scarred by smallpox, lying in a darkened room, unwilling to participate in daylight life, and the boy taken to her for formal visits only. The castle bought in Europe and reassembled in Dallas, Texas.

The loneliness. The formal dining room with candelabra. The garden with statues. And the boy falling in love with a statue. It was born of Proust, but had its own tone, its own atmosphere.

This Kendall is a craftsman. He is a mathematician. His objectivity made his hand steadier, his measures more exact. He described the obstacles, the distances which people maintain to preserve themselves from fervor, contagion, and fusion.

He responded with criticism of *This Hunger*. He was looking for a classical order and form.

Letter from Kendall:

I can only say of your letter that from it I experienced a kind of fluidity of appreciation—a mild, warm wave that broke over a succession of aspects and objects according to some inward rhythm in which your letter was everywhere—that was the beauty, that the advantage, to find myself in the presence of a letter to which everything directly contributed, leaving no touch of experience irrelevant. This wave expresses my feeling about the letter; considering it is for me a matter of prodigious difficulty because, to be quite frank, and I feel that I can be nothing else with you, the fact that you are a woman is for me a matter of the extremest incongruity, for reasons that you must have perceived; reasons that will emerge with, I hope, great sincerity and intensity in the succeeding sections of the novel. Indeed, my complete lack of sense of humor makes me rather dread our future meeting, which I nonetheless anticipate with the greatest expectancy, for I feel that I shall have nothing to communicate except a sadness through my silence.

I was amused, and shocked, too, that the warmth of my praise for his book, my response to his writing, should have been taken for a love letter, and that he is already planning his defenses!

Correspondence growing. I work on my lectures.

I have become aware that homosexuals live in groups, almost communally promiscuous, and sustain each other professionally. Once they feel accepted, they surround you subtly with a barrier made of a chain of friendships. First I met one, and then his friend, and then their friends, and now I find myself surrounded. They bring their gaiety, their brilliance, their gifts, their charm, their beauty, and it is a magic circle. Subtly, they keep Man away, by either parody, mockery, or direct jealousy. They appropriated me.

Was this due to my quest of the artist world? Was it that I found most ordinary men harsh, power-driven, obsessed with their goals, not with life?

Robert Lowry came, and because of his books, his printing press, I was ready to like him. He was brutal in his language, ugly, sinister. Bitter.

James Agee only likes drinking companions. And I cannot drink all night.

With the children, or in spite of them, as a woman I stand in a kind of desert. I have reached an impasse.

The press collapsed under a mountain of debts. Corroded by Gonzalo's irresponsibility. It was closed. Even to move out it was I who had to do the packing, sorting, filing, cleaning. Gonzalo took the small press home. He sold the big one to pay his debts. He began to sell his books, pawn his winter coat, his typewriter.

Neurosis acts like a gray or neutral filter over experience. Gore's letters from Guatemala (which should be full of color, sun, sharpness, vision) sound attenuated, diminished, dulled. Lack of faith, of responsiveness to surroundings and people. A blight. Neurosis is a blight.

Edmund Wilson writes obtusely about *Ladders to Fire*, but he thinks I have made progress in the new part of the book. Although

"the story is a little amorphous, there are charming things in it."
Only the young really understand and respond.

Five o'clock is the hour of my depression. Because the active day
is done, during which I subdue and conquer my disillusions or
disappointments. But five o'clock is the fatal hour, end of work,
beginning of awareness, when the buses are so full you cannot get
on, when the taxis will not stop, when the subway is chokingly
full, when everyone is running somewhere, when the lovers have
chosen each other. Then, at the corner of the street, unable to
reach home, I feel this wave of choking anguish, of homelessness,
rootlessness, loneliness.

Every friend I reach out to here seems incapable of a big friendship. They all shred, dissolve into minor friendships. Instead of
writing in the diary, I have been trying to talk with someone, to
write to someone. They write tight, meager letters, ungenerous,
small, parsimonious.

Letter to Kendall:

There is a misunderstanding. I do not want it to spoil my response
to your work. You must know that I am not only a woman, that I am a
writer, and that I can admire and respond to writing quite apart from
the personality of the writer. I understood your manuscript perfectly and
my response and enthusiasm were not intended for the writer, they went
beyond the personal. It was addressed to the writer and to the tragic
quality of the writing. The description of distance between people
always moves me and my efforts always to decrease such distances may
lead to misunderstandings. Why I allowed myself to express it is because I find the world parsimonious in its responses, puritanical, fearful,
economical. I like warmth and generosity and it was because there is so
little to like wholly that when I find it, I like to say so. I not only know
everything that is implied in the manuscript, but I divined the fear you
felt, the fear that this might make understanding by a woman impossible
and incongruous. Please, dear Kendall, grant me enough subtlety and
above all enough personal experience with your problem. To tell you
the truth, I knew and assumed this beforehand, because I have found
it not a unique case, but a collective one among writers and artists. It is
a problem which has to do with what Eliot called the sickness of modern

love, with people's incapacity to love totally. It is a split and a break within love itself, more serious in America, more fatal, because of Puritanism and matriarchy. What I feared was that you should not be able to accept my understanding of the work. Believe me, you have misunderstood my response, if you interpreted it as a love for the person. It is true that faith uses the language of love, and that they appear to be the same. The truth is that I have always been the very best of friends, and not as a woman, to the kind of person you are, on the basis of sensibility, creativity. I hope this misunderstanding will not distort our friendship and that you will believe me when I say I sensed and respected the obstacle from the first, even in your short story, and that perhaps it was the security this obstacle gave me which allowed me freedom to respond wholly to your writing.

Letter from Kendall:

I must explain to you the reason for what you called the perfection of my writing. I was hoping so much that you would say perfection because I do want to tell you why. For me there is no perfection in my own life. Mine is a life of miserable complexity and unhappiness so that my writing is all that I can rely on. Only in it do I find release from my tensions. I have no life besides my language, at least no happy life. I would unhesitatingly change places with a person whose writing showed less perfection because by showing this the writer would communicate to me that there was some measure of happiness, no matter how little, in his own life. I shall never be able to exist happily except through art, and therefore I must devote to it my entire life. Nothing else must enter my life, for I have often felt at times when I have been wounded terribly by some friend that the wound was actually internal, a physical one which would destroy me, and I feel that I have something to say before my destruction. You too are a person who can be terribly wounded, but there is evidence in your writing of a kind of medicine, or soothing balm, which you possess to apply to your wounds. I cannot tell what this is. In respect to *This Hunger* I must confess that I was perhaps jealous of a joy in living which your language shows, and since there is a kind of communion which your words hold with mine, call it confession, I envied your joy.

Albert Mangones is back.
"Anaïs, I thought you had forgotten me."

"I thought you had forgotten me!"

"You are not easy to forget," he said.

Three years telescoped, and became as if he had been away a few days. He is now thirty years old. He is a Marxist. He wanted to help Haiti. He married his childhood sweetheart, who waited for him eight years. He has a child eleven months old.

What a contrast to all the wordy convolutions of Kendall. Here is a Polynesian island, tropical nature, flowering, flesh dewy and tinted by the sun, eyes glowing, and a mouth shaped for pleasure.

Letter from Kendall:

Thank you for your kind letter of assurance that we can be good friends by virtue of faith in each other's writing, for I have never been able to combine the two worlds of art and actual living: and I feel that with you I will not have to make the effort of impossibility. These two worlds cannot exist for me side by side. I cannot be aware of both at the same time—one must be completely transformed into the other—there is no in-between, no mean—there are only two extremes, and I am not conscious of their inter-relation until that relation creates itself. I cannot create it consciously, simply because I cannot create my everyday living. It remains to me an infinite mystery—I can only say it is complex. The world of art is simple: I can construct it as perfectly as I choose: and my satisfaction comes from knowing that the hours, the days, and the years that I shall spend with my construction represent a living time of perfection, for moving from this perfect world to the imperfect one I have conscious evidence in the written word of my perfect world even though the letter has ceased to exist because of my moving. . . .

So many abstractions to mask the loss of the Garden of Eden! Caresses, tenderness, strength, richness, softness, fire, honey, flesh, the paradise of earth and sensual love.

Albert is sad because he has Negro blood as well as white and he stands caught between the two worlds. He was ejected from the Communist Party in Haiti. So now he works at the United Nations, when he had studied to build houses for the poor of Haiti and wanted to help his people.

# [December, 1946]

Dinner with Kendall at the Hotel Lafayette. He has dark, burning eyes like a Spaniard, and we talk easily. He has a greater love of his poetry than he has of his prose. I have the intuition that it is because the poem is a disguise and the prose revelatory. He is secretive.

He tells me an incredible story. His father does not want him to be a writer. He opposes him in this completely. He is wealthy, but he will not give Kendall time to shape his novel. His face, while he spoke of this, was pained. Then he pulled out of his pocket his father's birthday present to him: a gold fountain pen and a gold pencil. The father did not understand the irony of this. Kendall was bitter about it.

I left for a lecture tour of various colleges. At Harvard, I stayed at Carlton Lake's house. Carlton is cultured, intelligent, sincere, interested in my work for many years, and eager to start a publishing house. A real friendship.

It is almost frightening how I give myself to a situation. The present moment becomes the center. I take an interest in Carlton's life, I enter their lives, his and his wife's secrets, hungers. I felt compassion for the wife, intellectually inadequate, but childlike and genuine, and I helped her to have confidence, to lose her fears. The entire scene becomes glowing and vivid, near. I truly share their life. I experience all they feel. I feel warm and close to them. It all glows with humanity and understanding. We exchanged feelings, parts of ourselves. The reality, the intensity of my two days spent in Carlton's house, confidences, a whole volume of life.

I spoke at the Poetry Room of the Harvard Library, introduced by James Johnson Sweeney. About two hundred people came, when only one hundred were allowed. The room was designed to hold fifty! The lecture and the reading were received with great absorption. No rustle of paper, or coughing.

I wore a black dress and a shocking-pink scarf. I won many people, even some who were openly prejudiced, like Professor Post of Boston University. In the morning, we made a record of my reading of "Ragtime." I was shocked to hear my voice for the first time, to hear the slight French accent, and even more shocked by the young, tremulous voice.

The next day I left for Dartmouth. I had been invited by Professor Herbert West. Before the lecture I was taken into his library. He talked about his loneliness, about academic life, the annihilation of his desire to write, his life only through reading. He took me into the core of his life, a sadness. He was one of the first to write about Henry Miller. Impossible to live a free life in a university. Gossip and watchfulness.

An interesting, roughhewn, warm and human man, but heavy. We talked all evening.

The next morning, after breakfast, I spoke and read to an auditorium filled with some four hundred students. Again I captured their full attention. Professor West said it moved him to see so slight and small a figure facing this hall full of men.

The university plans to publish the lecture.

Kendall sent me two telegrams, one expressing eagerness to see me at Amherst, the other an imaginative answer to my sending him a sea horse. As I opened the telegrams I had a feeling of warmth and intimacy, but one which is no longer singularly attached, which is transferable, not fixed on one person.

But before Amherst came Goddard College. Maya Deren had been there just before me, showing her films. The students were full of resentment because she had insisted on talking about her films *first,* as if to make sure they would look at them in *her* way. They had wanted to see the films before they discussed them with her.

We tried that with the first reading. I read a story first and then we discussed it. But what a grilling, what an obsession with what is left out. They do not understand the writing, but pathetically feel that more factual detail will help them to understand. The hours from eight to twelve were spent in discussion. I am learning to parry attacks, to resist intellectualizations, to avoid irrelevant questions. But I was exhausted.

Then a five-hour drive to Amherst. I was invited to stay at James Merrill's apartment, in a two-story house. Kendall came. We had dinner, with champagne. We were happy, talked exuberantly, fabulously free. Kendall is nineteen, I find, and born February twentieth. No wonder I felt affinities. He is tall, dark-haired. His face is roughhewn, the sensitivity betrayed only in the eyes and in his hands. There is nothing feminine about his appearance, but insecurity in his hesitant speech. When strangers came in to see me, having heard I was there, Jimmy and Kendall did not like it, and did not make them feel welcome. Kendall was talking about the ultimate novel. We were trying to define it. I talked about Fez as the labyrinth; about Nijinsky's diary. Jimmy Merrill has humor and playfulness, which relieved the intensity and anxiety of Kendall.

Jimmy put on records of classical music. He read us a poem. Kendall read a poem. Kendall said he would write an essay on my work. I described my idea of an ultimate novel. Freed of upholstery, of unnecessary detail. We made fun of doors opened and closed, cigarettes lighted, glasses filled, iceboxes opened and closed, as keys to the characters! I told them what Wilson had said about the fact that "Lillian never takes a drink" and yet reminded him of Mary McCarthy. We were so intoxicated with our talks, excitement, so near to a drunkenness with words, with poetry, with projects, that when Jimmy said: "I smell smoke," we did not respond. He went to open the door, and had hardly opened it an inch when smoke poured into the room. He closed the door. He said: "Anaïs, telephone the firemen. I must gather my manuscripts together."

I telephoned the fire department. But the man who answered heard my French accent, and the gaiety in my voice, and believed it was a student hoax. I called out to Kendall: "You talk to him. He does not believe there is a fire because of my accent." We were laughing, uncontrollably, because we could not really believe the fire, because it seemed so absurd, because Jimmy stood there with his manuscripts, and because he said; "Oh, Anaïs, this is a publicity stunt, of course. On the occasion of *Ladders to Fire,* we set fire to the house and we will have to come down a ladder." We opened the windows. The house was only two floors high and we would fall on the grass and on bushes, if the ladders to fire did not arrive soon. We heard the sirens. A huge fireman opened Jimmy's door, ready to rescue us. How do you rescue people taken with uncontrollable laughter? "It was a publicity stunt," we said. He thought it was the champagne. There was a lot of noise around. Neighbors had come to watch. Two engines were standing there. And the climax came when the fireman said: "No danger. It was the lady downstairs, who left a cake in the oven, and that made all the smoke."

I work on a section, "Minuets of Adolescence,"* finding many ways to describe the evasions, vanishings, leaps of adolescent hesitations, using the ballet as a structure.

Letter from Kendall:

Quite impossible to work on my novel here, the flood is damming up within me and will burst through in some sort of violence unless I can escape to my writing as a canal of order. . . .

I seek to convince Gonzalo to return to Peru, where his aging mother calls him, where his family will give him his inheritance. His family is rich and powerful. His brother runs the largest newspaper in Lima.

We argue across a restaurant table and I make a drawing to show him he is stalemated in New York. A job is impossible because of his lack of discipline, his anarchism. He could not even run the press at his own hours, in his own way!

He says he cannot go to Peru because Helba will not go. She does not want to return poor and defeated to the family who rejected her.

* Later published as *Children of the Albatross*—Ed.

Gonzalo offers the same argument: "I cannot go back and face my family as a failure, poor and humiliated as they predicted I would be."

"But you are not a failure. You can take back an armful of beautifully designed and printed books. I will outfit you and give you enough money. In Peru you may find someone to take care of Helba so that you can work on your brother's newspaper."

I did not want to say: "You have destroyed everything, the press, my devotion, my faith." But suddenly I let out a strange, strangled sob at the devastation they had achieved. Gonzalo looked blind and mystified.

He would like to go to France, where his niece Elsa lives, but he does not want to go back there without first seeing his mother, who is so old now. But he cannot face his mother in his poverty-stricken state, and if he does go to Peru the Communist Party will probably want him to stay there. Meanwhile, he has not telephoned for two possible printing jobs, part-time. He has not written to his mother, after borrowing my typewriter to do so. He has not written to France to see what his friends could find for him to do there.

Gore is back from Guatemala. He has built a house and wants me to come and stay there a while. He looks healthier.

At two o'clock I get a telegram from Kendall: PLEASE MAKE APPOINTMENT WITH LIPPINCOTT AFTERNOON OF THE 3RD. I have been struggling to get his novel accepted so that he will be free to write. Just as his writing is orderly, minute, perfect, his handwriting is chaotic and mad. He is unlike Gore, not simple or human but complicated and perverse. But the spark between us generates writing. Writing is our sanity, our gold, our only affinity.

Gore has finished *The City and the Pillar*.

Letter to Gore:

I am going to try and tell you what was destroyed by your novel. It was the myth by which I live. I am a romantic and you are a cynic. It is this difference between us which has been stressed by your book, and not the similarity I had imagined. This is a book without illusion, without feeling, and without poetry. This is no reproach and no criticism. But for me, without feeling, without magic, without poetry, there is no life. Jim, in your story, kills Bob because Bob has not romanticized the sexual relationship they once had, has looked upon it flatly as a mere sexual incident of no importance. That angers Jim: he has idealized the first sexual encounter and for Bob it is nothing. So he kills him. Jim kills the legend in himself, but actually there was no legend, just Jim's need of idealizing reality. Now I read your novel as a revelation of your unconscious. When it comes to painting Maria, she is but a woman who has seen two wars, who has lines around her eyes, and who cannot find satisfying relationships. When all the men have left her, as you say, she will be willing to accept the position of mother which Jim offers her.

Everything in your eyes is diminished and uglified. All quality and beauty comes from one's own vision. In your vision everything is ugly. I like Pablo's exuberance and enthusiasm, and so I overlook his freckles, or his old hands. I like Frank's intelligence, and so I forget about his scarred skin. But you always focus on the faults, on what can be satirized. All the time I thought in your defense that you had been so deeply injured that you lost your faith in people, your feeling about them. But when you come to portray people, all the wonder and beauty of them disappears, and what is left is the ridiculous, the gray, the fault. So you are a realist.

To see only the ugliness, that is what people do when they do not love. Your nausea about people, your ugly vision of them, will only hurt you. You are not aware that when you paint only cruelly, underlining only faults or weaknesses, you are the loser. For you create an ugly world in which there is nothing to love, and what is a lover without an object to love? That is what I call destructiveness. You have been hurt, so from now on you will hurt others! You live without faith, and that will make your world gray and bitter. The only transformer and alchemist that turns everything into gold is love. The only magic against death, aging, ordinary life, is love. Your mother harmed you more deeply than I knew. Or I had counted too much on my power to heal you. I miscalculated. The magic failed. You went off after our friendship, unchanged. As a magician, I feel the failure. A failed magician picks up and leaves. You not only killed Bob, which does not matter much for there are a million Bobs around, but you also killed off Maria.

I did not mail the letter. I made him read it at the Ritz bar.

It shocked him. But if I had to face an aspect of Gore I had not known, he was forced to face an Anaïs he did not know. It was the loss of an invented Gore. Whatever Gore was with me, whatever side he showed me, was not the one he was to show in his life and in his work. He is only twenty years old. He writes a book on a one-dimensional world, sex in a void. A book which will hurt his possibilities in the political world. A prosaic and literal book. The editor at Dutton said: "I hate it." Gore calls on me for help: "Please tell me it is my greatest book." And this is the young man I thought tender and loving and devoted. Did he play a role? Did I cast my own glow on him? Did I imagine this Gore? Was it one aspect of him which came through under auspicious circumstances? Did I deflect his sadism, his cruel vision of others? How could I not see his cynical vision?

Anaïs, you invented a Gore which might have been, but which no longer exists.

To me this was sadder than if Gore had died a physical death.

When *Ladders to Fire* came out, and I could not afford new photographs, I thought of the surrealist's playfulness and gave Dutton the photographs taken by the *Town and Country* photographer who had made me a gift of them. I explained to the publicity department that I wanted them titled by the names of the characters, and only the center one identified as myself. The photos went out, and either through carelessness or malice, they all appeared as photos of me: me with Hejda's oriental, veiled face; me with Lillian's short hair and tailored suit. The very journalists who were always demanding humor as a requisite, demanding jokes, took this with dead seriousness as a part of that decadent surrealism they hated and knew nothing about.

The reaction was totally negative. Not one smile, not one recognition of the roles women play, of disguise and play. The picture in which I posed as the author was not used. The one of me acting out Lillian was misunderstood, and gave rise to the legend that I was a Lesbian. If I had ever enjoyed relationships with women I would not have minded at all. But as that was an unfulfilled part of my life, I felt the irony. I also felt that since it was done with the desire to estrange and excommunicate me from the community, it was malicious. When people do not accept your work, they always find a rationalization for not liking it. The reviewers caught that label to pin onto their total lack of understanding. The other label they used destructively was "surrealist." To them it meant only the pranks of Dali, sensationalism and eccentricity. I was surrounded by homosexuals writing about homosexuality, but the mere fact that I implied woman's love for a woman damned me.

Oscar Baradinski is reprinting *On Writing* from the beautiful Dartmouth pamphlet. I sent him the photograph of me posing as Lillian, circling the face only.

He printed the whole body in the tailored suit, in purple, and from then on whenever anyone did not like my work I was "typed."

I protested to Baradinski. He promised to change the cover at the next printing.

I also protested to Frances Steloff, and she promised not to sell the booklets as they were, but to wait for the new printing.

Leo Lerman asked me for a short autobiography:

Dear Leo:

That was one question I was hoping you would not ask me but answer for me. About myself. Wanted you to make a portrait as you see me; I see myself and my life each day differently. What can I say? The facts lie. I have been Don Quixote, always creating a world of my own. I am all the women in the novels, yet still another *not* in the novels. It took me more than sixty diary volumes until now to tell about my life. Like Oscar Wilde I put only my art into my work and my genius into my life. My life is not possible to tell. I change every day, change my patterns, my concepts, my interpretations. I am a series of moods and sensations. I play a thousand roles. I weep when I find others play them for me. My real self is unknown. My work is merely an essence of this vast and deep adventure. I create a myth and a legend, a lie, a fairy tale, a magical world, and one that collapses every day and makes me feel like going the way of Virginia Woolf. I have tried to be not neurotic, not romantic, not destructive, but may be all of these in disguises.

It is impossible to make my portrait because of my mobility. I am not photogenic because of my mobility. Peace, serenity, and integration are unknown to me. My familiar climate is anxiety. I write as I breathe, naturally, flowingly, spontaneously, out of an overflow, not as a substitute for life. I am more interested in human beings than in writing, more interested in lovemaking than in writing, more interested in living than in writing. More interested in becoming a work of art than in creating one. I am more interesting than what I write. I am gifted in relationship above all things. I have no confidence in myself and great confidence in others. I need love more than food. I stumble and make errors, and often want to die. When I look most transparent is probably when I have just come out of the fire. I walk into the fire always, and come out more alive. All of which is not for *Harper's Bazaar.*

I think life tragic, not comic, because I have no detachment. I have been guilty of idealization, guilty of everything except detachment. I am guilty of fabricating a world in which I can live and invite others to live in, but outside of that I cannot breathe. I am guilty of too serious, too grave living, but never of shallow living. I have lived in the depths. My first tragedy sent me to the bottom of the sea; I live in a submarine, and hardly ever come to the surface. I love costumes, the foam of aesthetics, *noblesse oblige,* and poetic writers. At fifteen I wanted to be Joan of Arc, and later, Don Quixote. I never awakened from my familiarity with mirages, and I will end probably in an opium den. None of that is suitable for *Harper's Bazaar.*

I am apparently gentle, unstable, and full of pretenses. I will die a poet killed by the nonpoets, will renounce no dream, resign myself to no ugliness, accept nothing of the world but the one I made myself. I wrote, lived, loved like Don Quixote, and on the day of my death I will say: "Excuse me, it was all a dream," and by that time I may have found one who will say: "Not at all, it was true, absolutely true."

Everything I write is true, transposed but true. The source of the diary is my life's work. About myself, I have experienced everything and now I am ready to begin all over again. Dear Leo, I have nothing to say. I have not mentioned my flaws. I lack the courage to look at monsters, at cripples, at freaks, at the deformed, the twisted, the sick. I love mushrooms, the tropics, the color black. I suffer from chronic loneliness. I am born under the sign of Venus, the one that appears in the sea shell every morning with a sad expression: "Another long day of love to come." I was intended to live the life of Ninon de Lenclos, my favorite woman. I will never settle down, never have a home. My symbol is a roving ship. I am a writer. I would rather have been a courtesan. The rest is in the diary.

Leo Lerman did not answer.

There was a side of Gore which I saw, which existed in my presence, a Gore which might have flowered if a deeper love had been possible. This elusive, this ready-to-vanish aspect of the young causes me great pain, as when you see the innocence of a child destroyed. What destroys it? What in the world, in others, destroys it?

I went to dinner with him. Same place. But not any longer the same relationship. We had dealt each other deathblows. I would not be, could not be his mother, with no other life of my own. He could not be the son of my writing, the heir, the one whose writing I could love. If he was the Gore of his writing, then he was a stranger to me. Gore said: "Someone said we should write a book together, for you overwrite and I underwrite. You are too warm and I am too cold. I have all that you lack."

# [January, 1947]

Last night I gave a party to end Kendall's loneliness. Invited Bill Howell's sister, a beautiful ballet dancer, and Danny Kenning, her husband. James Merrill, Frank Westbrook, Pablo, Nancy and Carter Harman. As we sat on the floor in the candlelight they all looked young and beautiful. Each one extremely gifted in his own realm. Carter a composer, Nancy a writer and a slim, abstract beauty. I thought all of them worthy of Kendall's love. Carter is open, quiet, with a contagious smile, simplicity, intelligence and feeling fused. He is twenty-seven, slender, blue-eyed, with full lips, blond. He came through the experience of war without neurosis. He was an aviator, went to India. He is writing music for the ballet. He is winning and relaxed.

Nancy is thin and fragile, like a bird, but at the same time cold and hard. It is a marriage of children.

"Your writing," said Carter, "set off music in me, stirred all my desire to orchestrate. I wanted to be a writer just as you wanted to be a musician. I feel the need of words and I have a response to words. I want to compose for singing." He wrote music for some of E. E. Cummings' poems. The rigidity and tension of Kendall was darker by contrast with Carter. Constricted beings. Why do I hope to melt them? They harm me, and I cannot affect their constriction. Was it my father's constriction?

I understand much better now my need for expansion and dilation. Was I afraid of where they would lead me, and did I choose who would act as restraining influences?

Letter from Kendall:

The party was strange, wonderful, full of unknown happenings, made magical by passing glances, by an understanding which I seemed to reach with some rhythmic essence in the dancer Frank. I feel years older. I feel charmed. I feel calm. I feel on the verge of discovery. I shall let the novel speak for me, for I am mailing it for him to read. In my person all my feelings are masked. I cannot speak through myself. I must speak in my writing.

The Poetry Center of Y.M.H.A. presents a reading from the "Prose and Poetry of Anaïs Nin."

At ten o'clock I was reading from *House of Incest*.

At ten, Kendall and Frank were having their first meeting.

At ten, Pablo was listening to a concert of French Renaissance music with Dolly Chareau.

At ten, Bill Howell sat waiting to take me to a party after the lecture.

At eleven, we joined Albert at a Haitian party, and entered into a realm of genuine joy and sensuous responsiveness. Albert is singing and playing the drums.

At three o'clock we walked home on the icy streets. Kendall was attending a graduation party for James Merrill at Sutton Place, a ball for high society and debutantes.

Carter's "Children Songs" heard over the radio. Delicate, innocent, playful.

Bernard Pfriem, a painter, invited his friends for a party at my house: Dorrey, Toshka and three striking figures: Anatole Broyard, New Orleans-French, handsome, sensual, ironic; Vincent, tall and dark like a Spaniard; and Arthur, with mixed Negro and Jewish blood.

Having been as usual dressed too early, in my white clinging dress, heavy gold Arabian necklace, hair piled high, I opened the door and the first to enter was Vincent. He was carrying an album of Afro-Cuban records. He quietly placed one on the phonograph and opened his arms. He is a professional dancer, smooth and supple.

A delirious party, in candlelight, full of incidents. Three friends acted out charades. Dick, rejected by Pablo in favor of someone else, became utterly drunk and went out to the terrace. The banister is not strong. He leaned over it too heavily and it broke. Vincent, at the risk of his life, held on to him until the others pulled them both indoors. Toshka became very drunk and demanded a lover. Someone disappeared with her to the roof. Carter and Nancy did not stay till the very end.

Vincent wanted me to know that he was amazed at himself for having saved Dick's life. He said: "I would not ordinarily do a thing like that. I am a coward. I guess I was trying to surpass myself, my usual behavior, to impress you."

At this party, with people not of my own choosing, I felt a stranger. What made it contrast violently with my dreams was that a bolt of white silk, which Leonard had sent from Japan, had been thrown over the screen like a symbol of the innocence I seek, my withdrawing from cynicism, from drinking. My loved record of Debussy's "Sonata for Violin and Piano," which I consider the saddest piece of music ever written, was broken by my drunken visitors. In contrast with the party I described in *Ladders to Fire,* suspended in the half-dreamed, seeking fulfillment, this one left stains of wine, candle wax on the floor, cigarette stubs, crumbs of sandwiches, empty bottles, ashes, dregs, devastation. I had to clean up, take a bath, erase all traces of it, before I could go to sleep. This taste of the dregs so familiar to Rimbaud, the taste of desecration.

Letter from Kendall:

How very strange that because Frank lost his key I had to enter his apartment Saturday night by way of a fire escape. The symbolism of the act was completely apparent to me, as I am sure it must be to you. There is for me no entrance but the emergency, for I myself am constantly living in a state of accidents, of disasters. And I realize most strongly every day that my only relief is one of writing, that if I ever find a human relationship it will have to come by way of writing, the words must create a path, the relation, the contact between myself and the human. It is fatal to enter by way of emergency. You do understand that ultimately I am incapable of love, because it has assumed such gigantic proportions in my life that I examine it always with every atom in mind. I do not believe there is any love which can endure this kind of analysis.

It is becoming increasingly difficult for me to plunge, yes, plunge into any adventure. I hold myself at a distance, above, beyond, below it, never in its center, but on the other hand, I have not yet forged myself to stone. I shall not plunge into my writing this summer, I shall compose from the greatest heights, with the utmost coldness and cruelty, I shall destroy in my writing everyone I have ever loved, and then finally I shall destroy myself. I shall not feel the slightest of guilt, the least conscience, the smallest responsibility except to my process of destruction. And then I shall be utterly alone, shall exist like a Sphinx in the desert. I'm so glad you are rewriting. You must learn to be terribly critical of yourself in terms of writing, and that will be most difficult because you are perhaps the kindest person I have ever known. The very fact that you are such a wonderful woman hampers your writing, because for you the need of living is strongest. And you are able to live, so by all means do. I cannot, so I must write. But always know that when I am most cruel, I am most weeping.

There is one theme running through all the work of Kendall, Gore, Leonard: this theme of paralysis, inability to love, linked to noncreation. For they are all tied together. Very little is created out of hatred. How did I find myself in a trap, surrounded by homosexuals, by people who cannot live richly and be fulfilled? I know, too, that they are dangerous to other human beings, that they hate those who live or love or write without difficulty. Why do they come to me? Do I allow them to? I understand their difficulties, though they are not like mine at all. I cannot help them. My kindness only embitters them. They cannot possess it all to themselves, because they bring me such a small part of themselves that I cannot fix my whole affection on one.

Anatole Broyard said to Sherry, after dancing with me: "Anaïs is sensual."
Sherry answered: "No, Anaïs is mystic."
Anatole: "No, Anaïs is sensual. Or perhaps a harmony of both."
Vincent said: "You're a strange woman. At the party you did not play the hostess, you did not run things. You were not angry when they broke the records. You seemed to accept that people would

behave like that, but you were so far away, and went further away as the evening went on. . . ."

The manuscript of *Children of the Albatross* lies on the table. I have to write the end.

Kendall writes me a desperate letter: "*Au fond du gouffre.*"

Kendall takes up on a different instrument my complaint at age twelve: "One day I will be able to say I have reached bottom." I answer his desperate plea: "Let me lead you out of the house of incest. I know every turn of the labyrinth. I will not let you destroy yourself."

So today I awakened feeling like a flower, suave, smooth, gentle. I awakened in a pure aloneness which is not loneliness. The typewriter. Work awaiting me. I put on my quilted, ivory-satin housecoat, bought at the thrift shop for five dollars, and went down for the mail. A note from Kendall:

Many go down into the depths and never come up. Only the trained diver can go down those depths and come to the surface again. Again what can I say to your letters when I feel so terribly poisonous before your incredible kindness. Here is a poem I wrote about you:

> Announce your presence like a bell,
> Not loud, but echoing its softness
> Around the infinite sounds of love's
> Issue from the dancer's cell,
> Swirling in vowel of motion
> Nearing the tempo designed for rites
> In the kinetic calmness forming
> Noon's violent religion of shimmering rotation.

With such tribute on my desk I work, smiling, on the pages about the organ grinder and his monkey.

Visits from Albert, from Gonzalo, from Vincent.

Letter from Kendall:

Your letter today about what I was hiding. Yes, I am hiding from myself the dreadful realization that I have for the first time and what I feel to be the last, been unable to resist loving the primitive, the boy. We are both consumed, separately, in loneliness, for we have no way—but there must be a way—of communicating. There is no escape for me at the moment, because I have not the time to write. He is most miserable—I can sense it—and will turn into hate. This is, indeed, the ultimate tragedy of non-communication which Henry James clarified.

Kendall's immensely rich father refuses him an income of two hundred dollars a month while he finishes the novel he is working on.

Gonzalo wore out my faith and devotion. But he repeats that his life was all "bad luck."

I telephoned Kendall on his birthday. I was saddened to hear that he was having a party for young men only. Such a total exclusion of woman must be disastrous to balance!

On my birthday there was a snowstorm. I went out at ten o'clock in the morning because my typewriter had started to skip frenziedly (the right illness for my typewriter), to get it repaired. I went to Gonzalo's to leave money to keep them from starving. I worked on a section of *Children of the Albatross*. Pablo came to fetch me at eight thirty that evening. We went to the Haitian Carnival. In my Spanish dance costume I danced all night. The Haitians did not allow me to sit out one dance. My birthday was a dance with men whose desire is open, strong, proud, whose bodies are alive, flowering, exuding power and passion.

From there we went to the Soho café. My mood changed as we watched a drunkard who had once been a singer, an actor, a master of ceremonies. He appropriated the microphone from the French singer and sang brokenly, lurching all the while, with vestiges of past wit and past linguistics. His eyes were sad, childishly pleading for applause, for one more drink, humble before the authority of the proprietress. A week before, he had come to her, sober, and said: "Will you promise to send me a Christmas card? No one ever sends me a Christmas card. I can't bear that." She kept her promise. He came back a week later, sober, to thank her. He works at the morgue. He kept saying all evening: "I must go to work." He was nicknamed "Cold Cuts" after he had described minutely the nature of his work. He kept saying: "There will be no corpses until six o'clock. It is too cold a night for suicides." He drank down to his last cent, and the owner gave him a quarter for carfare.

I went home and could not sleep. "Cold Cuts" haunted me. I had to write about him.

Anxiety is love's greatest killer. It creates the failures. It makes others feel as you might when a drowning man holds on to you. You want to save him, but you know he will strangle you with his panic.

## [March, 1947]

Sunday I finished *Children of the Albatross*. I am alone. Content. Finished copying and polishing the book, to be delivered tomorrow. I want to write an essay on the similarity between oriental philosophy and psychoanalysis. There is an oriental quality to my work.

Letter from Gore, from Antigua:

I must construct this home as a symbol, whether I live in it or not is not important, it is enough that it is here, but there is no heart to it, of course. These days I am a solo dancer, dancing magnificently with no audience. My attachment to you continues, it grows more poignant, more vast, more hopeless with each day—what can one do with beauty? It is there, it hurts. I have sometimes the feeling that too much of me was left in the womb, it is not a matter of development, rather of what never was—was not born at all. I can never be too long bemused by dreams. I feel a stranger passing through, the books are only shadows I cast before the sun. . . .

Bill Howell and I visited Richard Wright. I had to lead Bill away before he spoiled his relationship with Wright by obstinate argumentativeness. Wright said he disliked Howard Fast for some personal injury he had done him, and Howell set out to argue Wright out of his feeling.

I feel around me a depersonalization of relationships which alarms me, for mine are so personal, and each person is unique and irreplaceable. I consider this a weakening of friendship and love.

I cannot concentrate all my friendship on any single one of my friends because no one is complete enough in himself. I pursue in them echoes, vague resemblances to bigger relationships. I have to make deep relationships out of Howell's gentleness, or Gore's directness, or Leonard's trancelike dreaminess. Mosaics. A construction of small pieces. A bit of a letter, a poem, a tenuous presence, a few words. Pablo leaves his self-portrait on the wall, a mobile, the bird flying from the ceiling. Their tender ways enslave me, but because they are incomplete, not men yet, their presence is erased. But perhaps also because, being a woman, I detected what a psychiatrist could not detect, I became keenly aware that homosexuality was in part, and in most of the young men I know, a stage of immaturity. If two of them made a couple, advanced in living, relied on each other, were devoted and faithful, if I saw around me a big relationship, a great love, I would believe in their maturity. But as a woman, I was allowed to see their fears, their insecurity, their fragmentation, their promiscuity, their vacillations, the shallowness of their sexual encounters. It was their difficulty in living which aroused my sympathy: Gore's body and heart frozen in the Aleutians, Leonard's timidities. Howell's disintegration after the war because he discovered there the source of his difficulties with women. He was coming out of a bar, partly drunk, and was attacked by five soldiers. He did not seek to defend himself. Every time we talked about this he asked me the same question: "Was I a coward? Was it fear?" But one day, when he had drunk more than usual, he added: "The worst of it is that it gave me pleasure. Yes, it gave me pleasure to be passive."

Because I am a woman, the homosexual entrusted me with his childishness. The ephemeral sexual encounters, the disregard of the other's personality, the needs, oh, the endless needs of assurance, reassurance, admiration, encouragement. Something about the psyche as crippled as I was by my father's desertion, something creating difficulty in developing, in assurance, in maturing.

I saw in Pablo expressions of a very young boy. Moments of innocence which lighted his face, gestures of childlike tenderness, not sexual. I saw them fall asleep in the middle of a party, as deeply as children. I saw their spontaneity in art, which I enjoyed: they could draw, write, sing, dance, almost without training, as children do. There were even facial immaturities, immature teeth, hands. All the elements which compose charm and delight, and gifts such as attend the growth of artists, seem to maintain in their personality, in spite of maturity and aging, the sensibilities, the curiosity, the ever-alert responsiveness to life of the child.

This quality, the quality of renewal, perpetual youthfulness, which I liked in the artist, I find in the homosexuals. Except that here it is marred by anxiety, remorse, inhibitions, self-censorship. Why would they not be proud and simple about it? Why do they not have romantic and lasting attachments? Why do they not write romantic novels about homosexual love? There is a furtive quality to it all. Or else it comes out in irony, satire, or mockery of itself. This quality of caricature, which I first met in Henry, I see all around me. It is a subtle, and sometimes not so subtle, distortion, a burlesque which denigrates all it touches, diminishes it, attributes falsity to sincerity, and hypocrisy to sentiment, and denies feeling altogether. In fun, I have often threatened my homosexual friends to write a serious, a deep, a moving book on homosexuality. It seems to me the subject is distorted and its possibilities of beauty avoided. It is always treated with shame, like men's quest for prostitutes.

Kendall showed his distorted and sadistic side in a story he wrote about the party, the party at which he met Frank, and which I thought beautiful. For him the party was an evening of ugliness, I became the seductive and dangerous witch one must destroy, everyone was a grimace, a threat, a party to the ignoble plan to end his loneliness. That which I had done out of compassion for his loneliness became a scene as degraded as a house of prostitution. And the one who whispered all the twisted interpretations into his ear was a young poet who looks like a sensitive and intelligent person, acting like Iago to Othello, only on so low a level that it was quite unbelievable. Was he in love with Kendall, and jealous of my offering him entry into my world? The contrast with the real party, for which I had selected my most gifted, most sincere friends, so shocked me by its grimacing ugliness, presented me with such a repulsive unconscious, that it broke our friendship instantly. The powerlessness which turns beauty into ugliness. This they can do: destroy, belittle, distort.

The child seeking protection and love and then turning against the mother in a fury, because she is a woman, because she belongs to a man, because she is not his to use and misuse.

Letter from Kendall:

I have never known a person whose relationship to myself I have not finally ended by destroying in my ultimate masochism; but I have learned from you that relationships can exist which are too valuable, too dear, too basically spiritual to suffer destruction. I have, I assure you, suddenly developed a sense of values which I never possessed before. There is only one way in which I can heal the wound I gave you by the story, and that healing must be the completion of the novel to the best of my abilities and the dedication of the novel to you.

Strangely enough, I can forgive many things, many acts, many treacheries, many forms of selfishness, exploitation, anything except ugliness in the vision I call cynicism. I think the cynic is the one who projects his inner ugliness onto others. That one trait alienates me completely.

Josephine is singing at the Ruban Bleu. Leonard is still in Korea. Kendall and James Merrill are back at Amherst. Pablo is in Panama visiting his first mistress. Gonzalo comes every day. He looks like a very tired old lion. He works the small press at his home. He has small jobs to do.

I gave a dinner for Richard Wright and Albert, who wanted to meet him.

Albert told Wright about his difficulties in Haiti. He had studied architecture to help his people build low-income housing, like the projects he had seen in America. He went out of his way to assert his African origin, although he was pale, and half-Spanish. But he found himself ostracized by the Negro politicians, the full-blooded local Negroes, because of his light color and his comfortable bourgeois background. His disillusion was with the Left, which could not co-ordinate these inharmonious elements. Nothing that he had dreamed was accomplished; and now, at the United Nations, it seemed to him there was only interminable, legalistic talk. Not enough action for his youthful impatience, his readiness.

Wright was very understanding, and talked of his own disillusions. He was contemplating going to Europe.

Albert thought he should not go, because he was needed here, among his people.

"I can only be useful as a writer, and as a writer here I am strangled by petty humiliations, and daily insults. I am obsessed with only one theme. I need perspective. I need to get away from my personal hurts, my personal irritations. I am so constantly disturbed I cannot even work. I need to live free if I am to expand as a writer."

I supported Wright on this.

Why does everyone here believe that by all of us thinking of nothing else but the mechanics of living, of history, we will solve all problems? Sometimes one has to be away to think properly. I don't think the American obsession with politics and economics has improved anything. It is as narrow an obsession as any other. Richard may be right. He needs a letup from this daily friction.

As soon as one turns away from politics, there is moral indignation. But politics is not the only task there is to do! Each one must do his own well, and it will influence politics indirectly: the doctor, the psychologist, the social worker, the priest, the poet, the writer, the musician. I am tired of this constant "drafting" of everyone to think only of present-day events.

As for escape, ivory towers: The culture on which Japan has based its life for thousands of years was born in a court which was shut off from the outside world, because traveling was too dangerous, because there were no ways of communicating, no ways to expand at the time. So in a closed-in court, turned in upon itself, were born all the rules of aesthetic beauty, literature, architecture, gardening, philosophy, which were to give Japan the admiration and respect of scholars and visitors.

If Richard Wright could be allowed some peace from constant wounding in daily life, his writing might become greater.

Henry was allowed a rest from the restrictions and the sense of limitation into which he was born. Wider forms of culture. Free of abrasive daily injury, Wright might work better, I felt.

Albert did not agree. And Richard was disappointed, because Albert's point of view is the one he hears all the time.

What I did not want to say was that perhaps after a stay in France, Richard might be less neurotic, might trust the friendships which are offered to him. I have tried to be his friend, but I find him reserved and full of mistrust.

Gore telephones me. He fought for me at Dutton. And won. They wanted to wait two years to publish *Children of the Albatross*. They will publish *Children of the Albatross* now!

## [April, 1947]

Carter Harman came to work on the music for *House of Incest.* We worked well, understood each other. He wants to make a dreamlike musical drama of the book. It fills him with music.

Worked with Carter again. I write down what we agree on. He is writing the music.

We went to Lincoln Kirstein's ballet.

Dinner at Nicholas Wreden's apartment. He is my editor at Dutton. Homeliness, bourgeois solidity, comfort, a love of conventional matters. I am bored. Gore is there. He takes me home.

Will Carter Harman become a great composer? Will Gore become a famous writer? Carter is completely emotional, all music. He arrives modestly, with his valise full of scores, and the chronometer.

Leonard's answer to reading his portrait in *Children of the Albatross* was five yards of luxuriant, fire-colored brocade from Korea, wrapped around a secret box, which was the symbol I used to describe his character.

And a note: "I was deeply moved by the book."

Gore does not know what Mr. Macrae, senior editor at Dutton, did behind his back. Every time I had to go to see Nicholas Wreden to discuss something about *Ladders to Fire,* to arrange lecture dates or interviews, I would make a dash back along the corridor to the elevator. But Mr. Macrae, with infallible intuition, would open his office door and intercept me. He would walk me to the elevator, or invite me into his office. In his office, he would show me photographs of his family at a horse-jumping festivity. But the sum of his conversation was always: "*Ladders to Fire* is not selling well. During my lunch hour I sat in the park, and as I looked at the people sitting with me on the bench, I thought: These people will never read *Ladders to Fire.*"

My answer was: "They would if I were sitting on that bench."

Having no suggestions for remedying the slow sales, I decided to try and win his loyalty by showing him the childhood diary, as he is a Catholic, a family man, and a father. He read it and his comment was: "That was a sweet book. Why don't you write like that now, instead of all that bohemian village life?"

Pablo has decided to travel around the world with a friend of his. He took a job aboard a Danish freighter which takes on only about fifty passengers. Pablo was to do all kinds of jobs, whatever was needed: wait on tables, carry valises, clean the deck.

He wanted me to see the boat, but visitors are not allowed on sailing date. He wanted me to be there and say goodbye to him. He would be gone for months.

He suggested I call up the Line, express interest in taking such a trip as a passenger, and ask if I could visit the ship. Yes, they said, I could.

So I arrived on sailing day, well-dressed like a potential passenger, and the Danish captain himself did the honors. First I had to sit with him and taste Danish beer, while Pablo and his friend waited on us. Then he took me to visit the ship. His quarters, the passengers' quarters and, toward the stern of the ship, the crew's quarters. Pablo and his friend hovered nearby. When we reached Pablo's cabin, which he shared with his friend and two other young men, right above his shaving mirror he had already tacked up photographs of his friends. The largest photograph among them was of me, his "Sabina," as he called me, with a dedication. The Danish captain must have seen it. He never let on. I was able to kiss Pablo goodbye, to stand on the pier watching him sail away, a touching figure somehow, on that rather stern-looking ship, without frills or fanfares. A lonely ship, for men only, and how would it be for months and months, for a boy as full of exuberance and life and warmth as Pablo?

*Poetry* magazine, April 1947:

We hear from Paris of a reading of new works by Antonin Artaud at the Vieux Colombier, for which all his friends and backers turned out, including Gide. Half of them could not get inside the theater, and the poet was so agitated that he is said to have been incoherent. Artaud's disturbing poems, according to the normal time-lag, will probably have a vogue in this country sometime in 1960. He has been called by Justin Saget, the *Combat* reviewer, "The last of the true race of *poètes maudits*."

## [May, 1947]

Woody Parrish-Martin is dark like a southerner, always laughing, always lying fully stretched on the floor, drinking and talking. His talk is a series of fairy tales and fantasies with invisible links, full of charm and wit. He is a talking writer. He has difficulty getting to the writing. I love his stories. He also has a mocking spirit. His comments are often critical. I know nothing about his background, but his attitude in life is that of someone with a superior training, who comments rather critically on imperfect human beings. He has style. A subtle thing, in dress, talk, manners. He enters smiling. This smile covers an *enfant terrible*.

In his own apartment he has empty cages of all kinds, which fascinate me. Oriental, Victorian, from various countries. He is gifted on many levels, but they are not analyzable, they do not form a whole. Scattered gifts and scattered personality, scattered stories which, as an artisan, I wanted to preserve, collect, but which dissolved, evaporated.

One story I remember was about a young woman whose lover deserted her. She was forced to marry someone else. In church she wept. She wept real pearls, which the entire village came to collect.

I always hear Woody laugh. This laughter is also his insulating circle. I cannot know him better. He turns everything into a witty game.

Another person for whom I feel a respect and whom I wish for a friend is James Agee. I like his writing, his appearance of one who does not care for appearance, his silence and his seriousness. His clothes are never pressed, he rarely wears a tie, he is often unshaven. He is very tall, and loosely built, very thin and bony. He reminds me of Lincoln without a beard. But when he came to my parties he did not talk very much.

Three formidable barriers stand between me and American writers: one is drinking, which I do only moderately; another is

I do not have the rough, straightforward, tough, plain-spoken manners of masculine women, which inspire them with confidence; the third is, I suppose, my not being a *native*.

It is this which always throws me back into the circle of the young, who are hungry for my presence and for my work. We never drink as the older writers do. We invent and create and write and paint and travel.

The friends I want to have and who do not respond: Martha Graham, Isak Dinesen. (Pablo took a copy of *Under a Glass Bell* to her personally. I never heard the consequences, but I dreamed of her life, her castle, her stories.) Also Anna Kavan in England and her *The House of Sleep,* so much like *House of Incest.*

James Baldwin is writing his first book. He has a winning personality. Here the wall is mostly his obsession with politics. The obsession with politics is perhaps the greatest wall of all for me. The politics they all talk about are not humanistic. They are not psychological. They are abstract and theoretical. They feed on daily news to be reinterpreted. They are an intolerably narrow and rigid form of thought. All the words to say, the ideas, are established by your group leader, or the magazine to which you belong. You are in one group, and do your best to destroy the other group. Books are reviewed solely from the point of view of political affiliation. Friendships are dictated by it, ruled by it, destroyed by it. My search for truths which transcend such compartmental thinking is suspect. It is as if I refuse to go to war, declare myself a pacifist, and am ostracized.

I came to America as a temporary visitor, with a permit to be extended every six months.

Now that the war was over, and I knew I could not return to Paris, I had to leave the United States and re-enter as a permanent resident. This would permit me to start proceedings for naturalization. A great deal of paperwork and red tape was begun.

I considered going to Canada, which was near, or to Mexico, which I had dreamed about. I went to a cocktail party and was talking about all this with a young American from the West. He said: "Do you mean you were about to return to France knowing only New York City? You mean that is all you know of America? New York is not America. You must see it all, especially the South and the West."

Henry's book [*The Air-Conditioned Nightmare*—Ed.] had not given me a desire to see all this, but the young man from the West, and his love of the country, did. I began to think about this country, wondering if I could see it on my way to Mexico.

I found a friend who was driving to Las Vegas to get a divorce, and we agreed to share expenses.

It was when the plans were made that I realized how keenly I wanted to escape from New York, how harsh and abrasive the life was. Like the climate.

A Ford Model A with the top down. The open road leading you on, unwinding. Rhythmic chugging for hours, so that even when you stop you feel as if you were rolling, rolling.

First of all there was the Holland Tunnel, as if New York City had been an enclosed tunnel and I were reaching open freedom. Space. Suddenly the sky opens and takes up most of the space. The sky is the major part of the setting. The earth takes a small part of the stage at first. Clouds changing every moment, at times far off and at times close and threatening. Far ahead, the road looks like a mirage. The trees pass quickly, signs on the road, posters, telephone poles, towns, houses. The clouds travel with you, or lead the way, or point to a storm, or to dawn, or to a hazy twilight, massed capriciously, dissolving, or gathering up density. After the city I became aware of how rarely I lived the moods of the sky, how rarely I had a clear view of it.

After the tunnel, my eyes filled with green: fields, woods, forests, hills, mountains.

The towns, the motels are hallucinatively alike. Where are we? Washington. The motel, the coffee shop, the drugstore. As we rise at dawn, we have breakfast with workmen in coffee shops on the road, open for truck drivers. People eat at the counter, silently. They exchange greetings about the weather. It is cold today, it is damp today, it is hot today.

Rhythm, rhythm, rhythm. Hours of unwinding road. Wonderful names on the map. The Smokies National Park. On the way, we went up a mountain by mistake. When we reached the top it was snowing. It was snowing and the road ended there. It was a dead-end road. We had to turn in the snow, with darkness like an abyss all around us, and return to where we came from.

After the snow, heat and sun as we drove to Roanoke, Virginia. Wide roads, narrow roads, dirt roads, perfect roads. Sometimes we are alone on the road, sometimes surrounded by infernally loud trucks. At times, signs obliterate the landscape. A salesman's landscape.

In Virginia, at a restaurant, we met the majestic old lady who runs the place and who knew Walt Whitman. How strange it is to meet someone who has known a writer I would like to have known. You hope she is a sensitive conductor, who will *put you in touch,* like the clairvoyants, the hypnotists, with one whose death you regret. But not this imposing old lady with a cane. Perhaps she merely fed him when he was hungry. She was uniquely concerned with our appreciation of her cooking and that we should leave nothing on the plate.

The beautiful caverns of Luray, in the Shenandoah Valley.

Two men were convinced from the structure of "Cave Hill" and certain geological evidence that a large cave might exist there. Mr. Andrew Campbell and Mr. Benton Stebbins began a careful exploration of the surface of the hill. After much search in an old sinkhole, among briers and fragments of stone, they found a place where cool air came through the crevices of the rock, escaping into the warmer atmosphere. They were lowered by a rope into the dark and mysterious "Chamber of Silence."

The beauty of the forms and textures in the caves surpasses that of cathedrals, jewels, oriental palaces, crystal chandeliers, damask curtains, spires, the gold roofs of Bangkok, the lakes, the corals at the bottom of the sea. They seem the seed of all design, of tents, pagodas, arches, stained glass windows, panoplies, flowers, and at the origin of fairy tales.

The silence, the fragility, the occasional sound of a drop of water about to be crystallized and sculptured, the mirror-surface of the lakes, the patterns of arrested waterfalls, fixed waves of the sea, suspended rainfall, snowdrop designs. Baffling words: pure image, pure delight.

Always a changing sky, a changing landscape. But no change in the faces yet.

Driving wears down the nerves. The motel is welcome, plain or fancy. Sometimes it is slick and shiny, with lacquered furniture. Another time it is a mountain cabin in the woods, with a brook running beside it. Sometimes there was a real fireplace, and wood to burn; at other times an electric heater. Stretch the cramped legs. Sleep.

North Carolina. Winston-Salem. South Carolina. Atlanta, Georgia. Mobile, Alabama. The landscape grows lush, softer, the people more languid, the motions slow, the streets dusty, and the houses sleepy. It is beautiful and unhurried. Houses are wrapped in verdure, fences in climbing flowers. The fields are of a clear, washed green. No dust. From Mobile, Alabama, to New Orleans. The more southern, the more I respond to it, to perfumes, repose in the gestures, the mantle of nature matching its rhythms, man-to-earth and field-to-man, horses and men, and the little Ford Model A, not as noisy as other cars, less obtrusive, smaller to park, more in keeping with the landscape. Gone the harshness, the brittleness, the violent uproar of the city.

Romantic houses, and most romantic of all the house of Weeks Hall, "The Shadows."

The house half-hidden among wailing trees, so old their branches bend to the ground, moss, ivy, parasitic veils, trailing scarves, dew, smells of old earth and decadent flowers. Pools with moss-green bottoms, peacocks, statues, noble stairs, noble columns, noble doors, noble windows, marble on the floor, scented sandalwood, mirrors, candelabra. And Weeks Hall himself, as old as any man could be, jovial, red-faced, the voice of the house, monologuing its history, tales, memories, guiding so one would not miss the embroidered hunting scene under glass, the embroidered tapestry chairs, the cabinets lined with brocade. The liqueur bottles topped with silver stoppers, but not full enough to satisfy the thirst of the master. Not enough food in the kitchen, not enough servants, not enough of anything to sustain the grandeur of the life that is vainshing. But before vanishing it exudes its perfume of flowers kept too long in their vases, of silk too-long-worn, keeping traces of the many heads which had rested on its pillows, beds creaking, palanquins disintegrating, the poles holding the damask no longer able to hold it, the mattress long gone, the sheets long ago shredded.

Weeks Hall is concerned with the preservation of the house as a museum of southern culture, to be given to the city of New Orleans. But will they maintain it? Otherwise erosion, weather and time will corrode it all, the paintings, the furniture, the engravings and etchings, the photographs, the architect's plans, the fish in the pools. Because of poverty, already so much damage.

At one time, when he was wealthy, he had famous visitors sign their names on a door. By inadvertence, a house-painter painted the door, erasing the famous names. Weeks Hall shipped the door to every person who had once signed it, all around the world, until he recovered the signatures. Here it was.

Concern for the past, even to the extent of protecting the bones of the past. One of his ancestors had asked to be buried in the garden. He did not want to be buried in the New Orleans cemetery with other people. He was buried as he desired. But once, while Weeks Hall was away, a gardener dug too deep for a long-rooted tree, and unburied the ancestor, carelessly. When Weeks Hall returned, he went about the ritual of reburial. To his horror, he found a bone missing. He set the servants and the guilty gardener to searching. If they did not find the bone the dynasty of Weeks Hall would die. He was already an old man, gouty, and with an insatiable thirst for alcohol.

I remembered reading somewhere:

> The learned rabbis of the Jews write:
> There's a bone, which they call Luz.
> No force in nature can do hurt hereto;
> And therefore, at the last great day,
> All the other members shall, they say,
> Spring out of this as from a seed.

The bone was said to be the nucleus of the resurrection body. Weeks Hall must have believed this. His concern was so great.

He was still talking in the twilight. The cicadas were singing.

He had found the missing bone, and all was well. Weeks Hall would not disappear. "The Shadows" would not be cursed by the ancestor.

The road again. Old men sitting on fences whittling pieces of wood, just a gesture, slicing and dropping chips on the ground. In European countries, the same old men carved heads, pipes, dolls, animals, painted them, and decorated their homes. They carved miniature Swiss chalets with their peasant hands.

Gentle landscapes. Rolling fields. Moss-covered trees. Wild landscapes. Blue and purple mountains.

The beauty of the South, luxuriant and intoxicating. Smell of gardenias. New Orleans. Pungent food smells, of herbs and curry, jazz issuing from small cafés, people in the street, relaxed. The coffee with chicory, and the croissant. The courtyards with their overgrown plants, balconies with tracery of iron-lace railings. The flowerpots, the cinnamon, the saffron colors. The leaves are dewy, the faces smile, the winds are caressing, the parks are filled with exotic birds, with flamingos.

To shut out the sun and heat during the day they close the shutters. This brought vividly back to me the days in Barcelona. In the penumbra, with the light of day penetrating in thread-thin slivers of light, there is a sensuous intimacy, of twilight living, as in an arboretum.

In such a place, with marble floor, shuttered windows and wicker furniture, we visited Gore Vidal. He took us to meet a southern painter, Olive Leonhardt. Beautiful face, icy yet intense blue eyes, silver-gray hair. Her paintings are stacked in a room off the entrance hall. She is painting her dreams, she is painting people and New Orleans filtered through her vision. She sees the flaws, the ironies. She published a book of satiric drawings called *New Orleans Drawn and Quartered*.

I saw the painting she had made of me before we ever met, of which she had sent a photograph.* It was me, half-plant, half-tree, half-Ondine, half the girl in *Green Mansions*.

* See Volume III—Ed.

She had made a painting of Weeks Hall's bedroom, the one with the large bed and the broken bedspring, the shredded canopy. It was wonderful. It was the only satiric surrealism I had seen in America. She deserves recognition.

The road again. The small, short routes. The long, monotonous ones. The cities without interest one longs to leave behind. Heavy clouds, light ones. Distance. Everything is always farther. The map deceives. I cannot add miles. Maps and timetables and railroad schedules are mysterious closed books for me. I am not a good co-pilot.

I do not travel backwards, although the sand around the New Orleans seashore, patrolled by sea gulls, reminded me of Saint-Tropez. Because in Saint-Tropez the pine trees grew close to the water, and the bamboo grew thickly. The low, twisted pines. When tired of the sun, we could lie on pine needles. One could undress and dress between bamboo bushes. They rustled. They concealed the lovers. On the road, the girls passed in open cars, bare-breasted. The avidity for pleasure, the gay bathing suits, the swift descent on bicycles down the hill to the port, cooking on the beach the very fish we had fished for. The smell of pine-wood fires. The night club built of bamboo and palm-tree leaves, called "Tahiti." Flowered cottons, sea-shell earrings, sea-shell necklaces, flowers in the hair. The old tourist lady who saw Gonzalo walking with me and said: "These foreigners are overdoing sun-tanning."

In New Orleans I did travel backwards, because the atmosphere was evocative of France. Here, there was a feeling of enjoyment of life as a primary occupation. It was a succulent, lively, odorous, seductive city.

Lake Pontchartrain. Delta country. The Mississippi River. These are places made legendary by writers. The South is rich in writers. It is a fruitful place for a writer. Characters, plants, atmosphere have time to grow and flower to their fullest, like the stalactites in the caves. There is time to record. All this land was heightened and flavored by its writers. The little Ford Model A chugs quickly through some of the towns and places. Some of the figures are seen only in profile, or as they vanish into a house. But one knows them. One knows the Mississippi River, its river boats, its inhabitants.

Little Rock, Arkansas. Oklahoma City. Now we come upon the flat regions, the immense bare landscape, cattle ranches, hedges to keep cattle from crossing the road, and for the first time the human figure seems to have a style, a character, a stance. The walk is assured, booted . . . the pants tight, the hats arrogant. The land is theirs. The cattle cannot cross, but the tumbleweed, this strange round mass of ashen-gray twigs, like a ball of wool, rolls across, driven by the wind. It is very light, it rolls and bounces as the wind sweeps the plains. The wind and the songs start here. There is a song about the tumbleweed.

It is a melancholy sight, first because of the bare and barren land, then because the tumbleweed is weightless and powerless, and is driven here and there by the wind.

Texas, the Panhandle country, flatlands, cattle. The men get taller, and have a grand style of entering a coffee shop, ordering, sitting. They have a style as definite as that of the bullfighter in Spain, the Gaucho in South America, the style of a vocation which has an individual character.

Just before Santa Fe, there was a ranch we visited, in Pecos. It was built by the river. Mountains, river, and trees were stark, all in shades of ash and sand and spring-pea green. I do not know why I suddenly wanted to stay there. The city drains your strength. This place gave strength.

A total break with everything I had known. A bare simplicity. A Lawrencian simplicity. A wooden ranch house, trees, a river. That was all. I felt drawn to it.

But the Ford Model A was leaving in the morning. On to Albuquerque, New Mexico. On to Santa Fe and Taos, to visit Mrs. D. H. Lawrence.

And now we are in Indian country. The bright-colored clothes, predominantly red, the necklaces of coral and turquoise, the long black braided hair. Indians living in hogans made of small timbers, thatchwork, and mud. They weave, they farm. Native corn and grain are still milled on primitive grindstones, as in Mexico.

We climbed toward Taos. I could feel the rarified air, the height, the cold air of the mountains. It seemed sand-colored and half-deserted at twilight, when we arrived. A few Indians in rather tattered costumes sold tourist items. Necklaces, semi-precious stones, woven textiles, blankets. The architecture was of adobe brick, and the white walls and dark wood gave a Spanish air. It was late, and we had to have dinner and sleep first. We could not call on Mrs. D. H. Lawrence until the next day. I had written to her because she had once said that my book on Lawrence was the best. She replied that she would be glad to see us.

The next morning we drove to her house. I expected a tall, imposing woman from Lawrence's descriptions. I found a tiny old lady, all smiles and liveliness. As she led us into the living room, I wondered if it was Lawrence who had seen her as so imposing, like all men who never escape the child's idea of the mother as big and powerful. Age could not have shrunk her so.

The room was immense enough to hold on each wall one of Lawrence's very large paintings, and sometimes more than one. I recognized the fleshy figures, the fleshy tones, trees and figures similar in feeling to Gauguin's nature worship. But these figures were not sun-tanned. They were English. They were in grayer tones, the flesh not rosy as in Renoir or Boucher, but sunless, as if long covered by winter. There was no sun or gold in his paintings, as I remembered from reproductions. They seemed slightly faded. Was it the paint he used? Was it that I expected Mediterranean colors of joy?

Meanwhile, Mrs. Lawrence showed us scores on the piano and we talked about music. She sings German lieder. She would have sung for us if we had stayed longer.

The light was sharp and clear. The light of mountaintops. A modest, quiet man had opened the door for us and then disappeared. He knew people came to talk about Lawrence, and perhaps he felt in the way. In the back of the house, he had his pottery kiln. We went to visit and talk with him.

Mrs. Lawrence was cheerful, talked easily about Lawrence, but admitted she was tired of visitors and monotonous questions. "They ask things they would know if they had read him carefully," she said. She would write her own book.

We did not stay long. As we left, on the way out, the modest man came and with signs led us to the bathroom and the kitchen. He pointed to his paintings on the wall, all very small, as if he did not want to take up too much space, not as much space as D. H. Lawrence. We admired them, and he smiled. Then he led us out. We could have stayed in the cottage up the mountain, where D. H. Lawrence first lived when he came. But I was as reluctant to go into the past of my literary loves as of my human ones. I was curious about tomorrow, about what new places we were going to discover.

North to Denver, Colorado, to Boulder, to the Rocky Mountain National Park, over the top of the Rockies, the Continental Divide, to Fraser, Colorado, Central City, and west through Royal Gorge to Grand Junction, Colorado, the Colorado National Monument. There I began to find things I had never seen, the beginning of those red rocks, like rocks taken out of an intense fire. *Colorado* in Spanish means "red." The Colorado River carries this red sand or red earth two thousand miles to the Pacific Ocean.

West to Utah, south to Moab, driving along the Colorado River. The Arches National Monument, the strange lunar aspect of Utah. The Mormon land. The white salt lakes, the deserts, and the small canyons of gray sandstone, tipped with pale-yellow crowns. Something so subtle, such as one expects of other planets. Here the severity and sparseness was beautiful, like the paintings of Tanguy. The canyons, with their mythical shapes, crenelated towers, castle turrets, like the stalagmites designed under the earth by water. Here it is the wind which is the most skillful and intricate sculptor. The layered geological strata in all shades from gray to gold at dawn, fan-shaped furrows, the feet of birds, fish and shells implanted on the sandstone. The sea has been here. The sandy textures give to all the colors of earth, canyons, hills, rocks, a soft focus, like that of a shredded crayon.

The Indians match the landscape. Other people seem like transplants, and go about their work like visitors, guides, transients. Indifferent, anonymous, not connected to the land. Closed faces, anonymous faces. I cannot remember their faces. I remember the Indians, sharp-faced, proud, haughty bearings. When they are about, then I can link the canyons with the pyramids of Egypt, the Great Wall of China. The land of America, so beautiful, offering snow-capped mountains, African deserts, rivers, caves, mines, treasure, coal, silver, oil, petrified trees, strange flowers, strange birds.

Now traveling through the Navajo Indian reservation. Slept at a ranch in the middle of the fantastic sculptured canyons, in the middle of a soft, sepia-colored sand.

In Utah no sign of the severe and rigid Mormons. But their choice of Utah, with its severe and often bare landscape, its white salt fields, its bare mountains, seemed appropriate to their discipline.

I saw, around the bend of a mountain road, at dusk, a covered wagon. I thought it was a movie prop, could not believe it was real.

I saw the Indian homes carved in the rocks, the highest floors reached by ladders. I wanted more Indians around. They looked sparse, decimated. Weaving rugs, and making jewelry for the tourist.

Blanding and Bluff, Mexican Hat, through Monument Valley to Tuba City, to Lee's Ferry, where the boat starts down the Colorado, to Bright Angel Point and then the north rim of the Grand Canyon.

The earth-red canyons, layered in geological strata, rising to a height of awesome proportions, peak after peak. The work of a myth, a force beyond our grasp, silencing human beings, evoking religions and gods unknown. Temples, pyramids, tombs, palaces.

The colors in a wide range of sepias, reds, maroons, silvered at the top by light.

Standing there stunned by the mass of colors changing in the light, we heard a subtle vibration, a faint symphony of sounds. It was the wind, traveling through changing depths and heights, affected by curves, towers, heights, abysses, issuing prolonged musical whispers.

If one has lost in the city the sense of nature, its greatness and vastness, if one has lost awe, wonder, or faith, the Grand Canyon reinstates this vision of immensity and beauty.

On the way to Las Vegas, the real vast desert, burning and arid. Saguaro forests standing up like fingers of giant hands from the parched sand. The Joshua tree with its strange hairy arms flowering in green, pine-like tips. The cactus in bloom, the violent contrast between the prickly branch and the soft vivid petals of the flower in many colors.

The ocotillo. The fire-red blossoms resemble tassels, or feathery birds at times. There is a desert cactus which is all claws and thorns, and bears no flowers. The desert yucca in bloom appears like a dazzling white Christmas tree, straight and tall, bearing a rich ivory-white flower. All were blooming like spring, and by contrast with the sandy soil, the burnt, lava-like rock, the parched, thirsty earth, they seem miraculous, almost heroic. Compared with the flowers tended by gardeners, watered, protected, set in their appropriate soil and climate, these are defiant and strong, a vivid garden.

I do not describe the places I disliked, such as Las Vegas. Approaching Los Angeles, I smelled in the night the sweet smell of orange groves, exuding a rich perfume.

In Los Angeles I visited Lloyd and Helen Wright. He is the son of the famous architect Frank Lloyd Wright.

I saw first of all a high wall, like the wall of a medieval castle. And a giant tree, which seemed to extend its ancient branches to keep the house from prying eyes. The door on the left led to the architectural offices of Lloyd Wright. On the right, a winding staircase led to the door of his home.

For the first time in many years in America, I entered a home where beauty reigned, in a world created entirely by an artist.

Lloyd Wright stood up. Over six feet tall, gray hair, a full round head with a very high forehead, laughing eyes, and an emotional mouth. He has a powerful voice, gracious manners, a hearty laugh. Next to him a tiny woman with a very sweet voice, sea-blue eyes, large and melting with softness. This is Helen, his wife, who was an actress and now gives dramatic readings of plays.

There was so much to see in the room that one could not become aware of it all at once. It took me all evening to absorb the pre-Columbian sculptures, the exceptionally beautiful Japanese screen, the heavy furniture designed by Lloyd. The room was full of mystery. The uneven shape, the trellised wall made of patterned blocks, the long, horizontally-shaped window, overlooking the patio below, and the old tree that, like a great umbrella, sheltered the whole house; patio and balcony filled with plants and the wondrous cereus, that passionate and exquisite white flower which only blooms once, at night.

The fireplace of soft-green patterned stone was throwing its colors and shadows on the room. The lighting was diffused, indirect, softened by the latticed-stone screened walls.

The colors were soft and blended together. The shelves held books, Japanese dishes of gray and blue with the rare fish pattern, crystal glasses, silver. Helen served a dinner lovingly and carefully prepared to blend with the place and the talk. Everything gave a feeling of luxury created by aesthetics, not by money. By work of the hands and imagination. The atmosphere was rich and deep and civilized.

Lloyd's presence gave a feeling of power. The sensitivity I saw later, when he took me to his office and showed me his drawings and projects, and models for future buildings. His drawings were very beautiful in themselves, the concepts absolutely original and poetic. That was the first word which came to my mind; he is a poet. He is the poet of architecture. For him a building, a home, a stone, a roof, every inch of architecture has meaning, was formed from an inner concept. It was also a triumph over the monotony and homeliness which I had seen from New York throughout the Middle West, in every city.

I saw the model of the Wayfarer's Chapel he was planning for the Swedenborg Society. It was all glass, a perfect symbol for the spirit's transparency, a perfect expression of transcendent acceptance of infinite space. Man's religious spirit on an altar open to the universe through the transparency of glass—candlelight, starlight, moonlight, and golden ornaments shining through, opening out through the sanctuary to the sea, the sky, the trees, and to infinity beyond. He had planted a forest of redwood trees which would form arches over the chapel, like those in Gothic cathedrals, only Lloyd Wright had returned to the natural arches formed by the trees themselves.

I saw his plans for Los Angeles. It could have been the most beautiful city in the world, for everyone to come to see, as people went to see Venice. But architecture had been taken over by businessmen, and Lloyd the artist was not allowed to carry out his incredibly rich, fecund concepts. The room was full of them. When he took a rolled-up drawing from the shelves and spread it over the table, I saw buildings which equaled the wonders of the past. All the images of famous architecture I had read of came to my mind: from India, Japan, Mexico, Peru, the Middle Ages in Europe, Cambodia, Thailand.

Strength was obvious in him, but sensitivity and imagination were in his drawings. Homes, churches, plans for entire cities. A universe of lyrical beauty in total opposition to the sterile, monotonous, unimaginative "box"-buildings now seen all over the world.

He was not only continuing the first poetic and organic concepts his father had developed on the West Coast, where as a young architect he supervised and participated in the construction of many buildings. He was also creating in his own style. He designed and built the first Hollywood Bowl, and many private homes.

I expected Los Angeles to be filled with his buildings. This was not the case. Fame highlighted his father's work, but not Lloyd's—not as he deserved. If his plans had been carried out, the world would have been dazzled by them. His work was on a scale which should have appealed to the spirit of grandeur in the American character, a dramatic and striking expression of a new land. But instead, American architects chose to take the path of imitating Europe, of uniformity, monotony, dullness. In Lloyd's work there was space, invention, poetry, a restrained and effective use of the romantic, surprises always in the forms, new and imaginative use of structural parts, rooms, windows, and materials.

He has a gift for involvement in many-leveled lives, for the variations, caprices, and nuances necessary to the human spirit. Every stone, every roof-tile, every window, every texture or material was designed for the consistent development of his building, its environment, and designed to elevate the quality of people's lives.

Uniformity and monotony kill individuality, dull the senses. Lloyd designed his work to reinforce individuality with poetry, beauty, and integrity. It was planned to create a more beautiful and satisfying human environment. Architecture as poetry.

It was my initiation into architecture as an art. Lloyd is a complete and uncompromising artist. He talks about the organic home, built of materials natural and available to the site; of his respect for trees and the form of a hill; his sense of nature, of the continuity of the natural environment, and of how architecture must contribute to it, not destroy it. To hear him talk about color, materials, textures, forms, was like listening to a painter talk of painting, a musician of composition. In his art he synthesized them all. He drew like a painter, he used words with a biblical simplicity, but his ideas were subtle and complex.

By contrast, the commonplace, shoddy, temporary movie-set houses around him were painful to see. He called them "cracker boxes," shabby, thin, motel-type homes for robots.

---

Some of his houses, which I visited the next day, have the stronghold quality of a castle, a castle for unique individuals, to stem the rising tide of ugliness. Pride. Why did the millionaire father of Kendall not have Lloyd build him an American castle, instead of importing a European one, stone by stone, and rebuilding it in Dallas? What kind of people prefer to live inside of an imitation which has no relation to their personality? The story of Hearst, repeated again and again. And all the other imitations of Italian, Spanish, French, Swiss, and German architecture I had seen on my trip.

The Wright pride. Yes, pride in quality. He supervises his buildings, takes care of every detail: searches for masons who care about stonework, painters who can paint, metalworkers who are skillful. Today, in an age of amateurs, this is a most difficult achievement.

At times his mouth grows bitter; he vituperates, he berates commercialism, he curses greed and land manipulators. He is a crusader for quality. His work suffers indignities. His houses pass into other hands and are mangled, damaged, altered. The acoustically perfect Hollywood Bowl was torn down, rebuilt, and ruined. It is now monstrously ugly.

Lloyd's work belongs to the great moments of architecture, but today's America has no sense of eternity or history. The transient, the meretricious, the imitation, the pseudo rule the day.

We looked over more plans. Projects. Dreams. Dream of a beautiful campus, with individual units to house the students, shaped like a sea shell. A marina with buildings also inspired by sea shells. Certain plans lie gathering dust. They were made for some capricious rich man or woman who was not aware of their beauty. And then, now and then, a fervent, a devoted person, who understands his work and works with him, co-operating to carry out his plans. Out of this came a gay and whimsical nursery school.

His struggle is against uniformity and wholesale design. He speaks out boldly, as Varèse did. If he sounds like a moralist, it is because beauty, quality, and ethics are inseparable. Beauty and integrity. And for them one has to be willing to make sacrifices.

Another visit. The flowers in the room are arranged by Lloyd's big hands with an art equal to that of a Japanese flower arrangement. Friends call him and his two sons the giants of the West. He has gruff ways at times. Helen is there like a diffused light, to create warmth, harmony, refinement, like the cushion and the velvet against the wounds dealt to the artist.

We talk about his bohemian life in New York, with friends such as Djuna Barnes, Theodore Dreiser, Helen Wesley, Eugene O'Neill.

Ibsen would have written about this Master Builder, with one great difference. This architect never falls off the high standards, the heights he established for himself. The mediocre and the deformed sprout around him, like weeds, ugly buildings which do not endure and which look shabby after a few months. He is offended, but he does not surrender. He finds it "futile, offensive, and all-pervasive, but not inevitable."

Among Lloyd Wright's notes and comments on architecture I found the following:

I am concerned with our natural environment, how we can discover and utilize form, and perfect the endlessly varied, stimulating and beautiful services it provides for mankind. It is the architect's opportunity and responsibility to understand and practice the *art* of creating with and out of them a suitable environment for mankind—advancing the art with every conceivable means, including, among others, poetic license and poetic prescience. And now, after billions of years of experience and preconditioning on this earth (from the development of the first one-celled amoeba to our present human complex) we have no valid excuse for not performing superbly.

To see Paul Mathiesen, the Nordic Danish fairy-tale boy, in the melting sun of Los Angeles was strange. The sun made him seem even more ethereal, more remote, his hair whiter, his eyes a vanishing blue horizon. His words had no weight, they were carried away by the wind. Paul took me to see his friend Curtis Harrington. Curtis was a child prodigy of film-making. In college, at seventeen, he had already done a version of *The Fall of the House of Usher,* and a short time later two surrealist films: *Picnic* and *Fragment of Seeking.*

He was devoted to Cocteau and to Maya Deren. He was gentle and unassuming, with his curly hair, a shy smile, and eyes like a contented cat. He was also a historian of film. He had written about the films of the past, even while dreaming of the future.

One evening Paul and Curtis took me to the old section, above Franklin Avenue, where the stars once lived: Ramon Novarro, Valentino, Theda Bara, Douglas Fairbanks, Mary Pickford. What seemed sumptuous then, in the twenties, now seems small and pathetic. We sat on the patio of a deserted house which had been Valentino's. The chairs were broken down, the hammock half-torn off its base, the swimming pool empty. Curtis reconstructed the period for me.

George Leite publishes *Circle* magazine and printed a story of mine. We corresponded. I promised to visit him in Berkeley.

When I arrived, I was amazed by his appearance. He is like a white Gonzalo: six feet tall, round head, black curly hair, big dark eyes. He is of Portuguese descent. He moves impetuously, with a quick jazzed rhythm. Leaped into his old car, drove me to his home, a half-empty cottage, where his wife waited. All I could see were books and records. They had children. They had offered to put me up in the parlor. We sat and drank coffee. George and his wife were like people from a foreign country, after New York. They were inarticulate. Between each phrase, often an unfinished one, they had to move. Books, people, places, were mentioned in a fragmented, incomplete way. Themes were picked up and dropped. I could never recover what was said. There was something disquieting about George. Restless. Evasive. Mobile. He placed records on the phonograph. They were like signals and messages, a secret code. I do not know enough about jazz to classify or name the players. I listened. It was as if we could not speak the same language. Slang, jazz, musicians' lingo, a phrase thrown out, a silence in place of an answer. He drove me to my hotel. He seemed amazed that I left them. It was an unfinished evening.

The Leites took me out. But first of all George insisted I swallow a pill. I did not know what it was. Suddenly the evening became cottony and diffuse. No talk. We went to a night club. In front of the night club, I saw a pool of blood. It was not a pool of blood. It was red wine, from a broken bottle. George seemed to be driving like a maniac. We danced on rubber feet. The jazz music whirled.

Again, they were amazed that we separated. At last I understood. We were supposed to sleep together, the three of us. I kissed them and sent them on their way.

The next morning I left for Monterey, where I had an invitation to stay with friends and to visit Jean Varda. My friends' house was a surprise. They were taking care of a castellated house, copied from a European castle, on a hill overlooking the beach. An incredible setting. Hundreds of empty rooms, empty closets, empty icebox. They were poor. The wife worked at the telephone company, while John wrote his novel. John was there to show the imitation castle to prospective buyers. They gave me a sumptuous room overlooking the sea. No sheets, no towels. There were other visitors. We all met in the kitchen with its empty closets. We put together haphazard meals. We lay naked on the terrace to sunbathe.

John had found a way to delay the sale of the castle. He told visitors that the place was infested with rats. That it was damp, that it needed an enormous amount of repair. That nothing worked: plumbing, telephone wires, electric wires. He discouraged them. The days passed. I would walk down to the beach, but not to swim. It was icy cold. My friends came out shivering, blue.

I went to see Varda at Monterey.

He lives in what was once a stable. A beautifully proportioned, high-ceilinged house, topped by a turret with a flag of Varda's own making fluttering in the wind.

He had said that people cared more for horses than they did for human beings, because stables were more nobly built, with space and height.

As he stood at the door, I loved his laughing eyes, his warm, colorful voice, his bird profile, his sturdy body. He is a builder who built his own home. Goes to the junk piles and picks up wood, old furniture, and magically transforms them. The fireplace is made of bricks and built in the center of the room, as in the peasant houses on Majorca. The smoke goes up the wide pipe through the ceiling. His collages illumine the walls. It is a feast of color and textures. The food is served in big wooden bowls, as for giants, and he uses giant wooden spoons. A ladder leads to the turret. I would have liked to sleep there, with its four small windows opened like an oriental mirador, on a mattress on the floor.

Janko Varda is the only modern artist who creates not the sickly-sweet fairy tales of childhood but the sturdy fairy tale of the artist. The delight and joy of colors, the surprises of shapes and forms, the constant ebullition of invention. Everything that came from his hands was more wonderful than its origin, whether it was a salad, a bedspread, a pillow cover, a curtain, a candelabrum, a candle, a book. Everything was signed Varda. He created his own world. He designed dresses for his loves, jewelry for his mistresses. He was a tireless raconteur of magic tales. His eyes, his voice, and his laughter created joy. He awaited only pleasure. He opened the door only to pleasure.

We ate, we talked. Evening came. He built a huge fire, cooked on it while we sat around it. There was a knock at the door. It was the puppeteers who had come to Monterey. They wanted to see Varda. They came in. They looked like the troubadours of the Middle Ages. They were tattered by travel. They carried the puppets in potato sacks. After eating with us, they offered a show. No light but that of the fire leaping, shadows leaping. And the puppets performing around the round brick fireplace.

Thinking about Varda and his life, his style of life so beautiful, without money, all created out of his hands and imagination. The

Greek artist whose predominant quality is his sense of humor and his creation of magic beauty. The catalogues of his exhibits are a satire of the fashionable double talk used by contemporary critics. I was thinking that someday I must visit Smyrna, where he was born. He was raised in Athens, and just before World War Two he settled in France, in Cassis, a small town by the Mediterranean. His home was a crumbling twenty-room mansion that constantly overflowed with penniless artists, and where he was often visited by Picasso, Braque, and Miró. In 1939 he traveled to New York for an exhibition of his work, and then eventually settled in California. Asked where his home was, he answered: "The world." His address: "The Arts Club."

His collages have an oriental splendor; they are made with brilliantly colored bits of fabric and paper and mirrors. On a base of plywood he pins an arrangement of odd shapes. The first effect is that of an abstraction, but slowly one recognizes a woman, a tree, a house, a castle, a church, a street. A single color dominates the total effect, but with infinite variations emerging from it.

He said to me: "New York is a city of angry people. I am delighted you come to the graciousness of California."

The titles of his collages are a delight:

"Flowers Trapped in a Labyrinth"; "Spiral Woman"; "La Femme Étoilique"; "Machine for Propagating Nihilism"; "When the Woman Rises in the Landscape"; "Women Signalling Under the Moon"; "Aztec Ping Pong Table"; "As Still as Life Can Be"; "Women are Mainly Frugivorous"; "Complete Manual of a Seamstress"; "Still Life Resigned to Stillness"; "Nature Morte, Morte de Mort Violente"; "Still Life in an Advanced State of Crystallization."

He delivers us from the strangle hold of realism, the lack of passion and wit of other painters. He fulfills the main role of the artist, which is to transform ugliness into beauty. I can see him visiting the scrap heaps of any town, picking up wood, discarded boats, furniture, taking them home, reshaping and repainting them into a Byzantine object of beauty. In the barn, he used sheets of tin, thick boards whitened by the sea and wind, bottles, driftwood, sand and stone. With sheets of second-hand glass he opened one wall to the northlight. He laid a cement floor mixed with sand. The grain chutes served as wonderful shelf space, the manger as a deep trough for working materials. He made the chairs, the bedspreads, the dresses for his wife, Virginia. He built a bar by laying an old piece of brown marble across a foundation of empty bottles cemented together. He made masks of driftwood. He made Phoebe, a child-sized mannikin, dressed with winglike sleeves, one leg red and one leg blue. She has spangles of tin foil dotting her dress, and a pink ribbon in her straw hair. She is suspended by a pulley from the ceiling and seems to be a floating angel. For Varda, art is an expression of joy. He wears the same colors he uses in his work: pink pants, or an old rose sweater, green and purple.

His face is ruddy, like a man who lives in nature and who loves red wine. His cooking is as beautiful as everything else.

His gold collages eclipsed the sun, his blues the sea, his greens the plants. The laminated blues dimmed the refractions of the ocean. His treble greens vibrated and made the plants seem dead. With small pieces of cotton and silk, scissors and glue, he dressed his women in irradiations. His colors breathed like flesh, and the fine-spun lines pulsated like nerves.

In his landscape of joy women became staminated flowers, and flowers women. They were as fragrant as if he had painted them with thyme, saffron, and curry. They were translucent and airy, carrying their Arabian Nights cities like nebulous scarves around their lucite necks.

Sometimes they were masked, like Venetian beauties at masquerades. They wore necklaces of solar meteorites and earrings which sang like birds. Velvet petals covered their breasts and stared with enticing eyes. Orange tones played like the notes of a flute. Magenta had a sound of bells. The blue throbbed like the night.

After his scissors had touched them, his women became flowers, plants, and sea shells.

He cut into all the legendary textiles of the world—damask of the Medicis, oyster-white of Greek robes, the mixed gold-and-blue of Venetian brocades, the midnight-blue wool of Peru, the sand colors of African cottons, the transparent muslins of India—to give birth to women who only appear to men asleep. His women became comets, trailing long nebulous trains. Erratic members of the solar system. He gave only the silver scale of their mermaid moods, the sea-shell rose of their ear lobes, corollas, pistils, light as wings. He housed them in façades of tent shelters which could be put up for a moment, then folded and made to vanish when desire expired.

"Nothing endures," said Varda, "unless it has first been transposed into a myth."

He often speaks of paradise. He is in a state of grace with love and joy. He extracts from experience only the elixir of life, the aphrodisiac of desire.

He took no time to weep over fadings and witherings. He concealed his sorrows. Only once did he say to me: "I need the sea. If I could not sail in my boat, I would certainly go mad."

The drive south along the coast from Monterey to Henry Miller's home in Big Sur was steep and dangerous, mountain driving, and Paul's car was not quite equal to it. But as we climbed, the view of the sea below, of the rocks, the pines, the other mountains, was beautiful. It had a strong, Nordic beauty, not the beauty of the tropics, which I love. It was a cold beauty. The sea was lead-color, somber, and carrying no sailboats or ships.

The car drove right into a courtyard, and there was Henry sitting out of doors, typing. He seemed healthier than in New York. He was proud to own the modest cottage we entered. It was simple and uncluttered. I noticed the full bookcases and recognized the old Henry's tidiness. Lepska appeared. She was blond, sturdy, attractive, but spoke very little. There was tension between them. They served us lunch. It seemed to me that Henry was demanding an expansiveness and warmth which was not there. Lepska was silent, but affable in a closed-in way. He criticized her. He was embarrassed. Why? He thought my trip West and to Mexico was a flight from my life in New York, and that he should help me in some way. And he felt acutely the fact that he could not. I made it clear I needed no help.

I was concerned about Lepska. Knowing Henry, I was sure she was young and insecure, and that he would never know how to give a woman confidence in herself. It would be no concern of his, her doubts, fears, her lack of confidence. I was sure he had praised me with exaggerations. The atmosphere was not relaxed, and Paul and I decided not to stay.

When I stepped onto the terrace in front of the cottage, and stood away from Henry and Paul talking, Lepska suddenly and impulsively made a gesture of affection, and said with great intensity: "Anaïs, I love you, and if ever you need me, or need anything, let me know." We embraced, suddenly, spontaneously. There was in her gesture a mixture of distress and desperation, and if I had stayed I am sure we would have reached the confidences which her silence earlier seemed to withhold.

I should not have visited Miller. As soon as one ceases to know a person intimately, the knowledge of them is from the outside, as if you stood at a window looking in. From this day on I would see Henry from the outside, in that sense which I call not knowing. Through others' eyes, through his writing, or through his wife. Other Henrys. Knowing is intimacy. Intimacy takes trust and faith. That was over.

I was just in time to witness a great battle among the people of Monterey, outraged by Varda's creation of a restaurant on Fishermen's Wharf. The newspapers were filled with letters. They said: "Someone who has no sympathy for our traditions has moved in."

Merle Armitage took up his defense: "The matter of aesthetic beauty can hardly enter the argument. No intelligent person could possibly be impressed with the bastard-Spanish confection, topped with an imitation lighthouse astride its roof, known as 'Sonny Boy.' Nor is there anything particularly indigenous to Monterey in the collection of wooden shacks and corrugated iron roofs, plus the inevitable garish neon signs, homemade billboards, and Coca-Cola advertisements which make up Fishermen's Wharf. I was delighted to see Varda's building, and if the town is interested in attracting tourists you will need more, not less imagination, real charm and atmosphere."

Another native wrote of "hallowed traditions, nostalgic memories . . ."

Another answered: "All I see is a conglomeration of cracker-box affairs and corrugated iron shacks. . . ."

And Varda's building for Angelo's restaurant remained.

To celebrate the opening of Angelo's café we were invited to come in disguise. It was difficult to find odds and ends to make costumes out of, in the empty castle, with a wardrobe out of a valise intended for minimum necessities. There were no curtains, no draperies, no paints, no textiles. We did the best we could. I dressed John's wife: from the waist up she was a nun, in brown chiffon, with a cross on her breast. Below was the same chiffon, trailing to the floor, but without a slip underneath, so her legs could be seen in silhouette.

When we arrived, there were some costumes done by Varda which were marvelous. He had dressed some of the young women as his collages. Colored paper cut-outs covered them: blue rhomboids, rose triangles, white squares, orange rectangles, purple parallelograms, green trapezoids, lavender pentagons, gold hexagons, yellow octagons.

The friendship with Varda was situated on such a level of invention, counter-invention, legend and counter-legend, poetry and counter-poetry, our talks were so far out in space, that it was like two magicians ceaselessly performing for each other. We could not rest to wipe off the perspiration, or appear for one moment as human beings, hungry, cold, or restless. Magic must predominate. Varda's attitude in life was that of a Merlin, the enchanter, who must constantly enchant and seduce, fascinate and create. Young women came constantly to him, to be metamorphosed, and it was a marvelous sight to see him create a myth: rename them, reshape them, redecorate them. The Varda touch. They were no longer ordinary women. They were myths. I was a myth, even before we met, because of *Under a Glass Bell*. I possessed one of his loveliest collages. Poetry was like this masquerade of beauty, and I loved it. We all danced and flirted and paired off, and in our disguises denied our everyday selves.

The trip to the West had delivered me of the toxics of New York. It had given me a taste for nature, for people who were natural and gracious, for bigger artists, unconcerned with ambition. I could have stayed on forever, but I had to attend to my immigration problem. I had to make my re-entry into America as a permanent resident by first leaving the United States and making a new entry. If I had not traveled West I might not have wanted to become a permanent resident. It was time to leave for Mexico.

Alice Paalen had told me about an artists' colony at Lake Chappala. It had been described by D. H. Lawrence. I sat on the plane on my way to Mexico City and opened a copy of *Life* magazine. There was a photograph of Lake Chappala, a description of how cold it was, and a reference to black snakes. Already I had decided that although I would find fellow artists there, I would not go. On the next page there was a panorama of Acapulco. The sea, the mountains, the rocks, lush verdure, and a tropical climate. I decided immediately I would go there instead.

When I reached Mexico City, I changed my ticket. There was a plane for Acapulco in half an hour. It was a small plane, seating about ten persons. It flew between high mountains, and bounced continuously. But the first sight of Acapulco, mountains, sea, forests, drenched in sunlight, moved me. We flew over the Pacific, then along the shore, and landed on the beach. As the door of the plane opened, I felt the warm caressing air which immediately turns one into silk. Near the plane, Mexicans were lying in hammocks, under a thatched roof. Some of them came over to help carry the baggage. The tropics took possession of me by softness, warmth, like a drug. It was also an experience to find—after so many years —eyes which really looked at you. They rested on you. They were black, liquid, bright, and intimate. They smiled at you. The smile lingered. The roar of the waves and the salt spray were a few yards away. I felt like taking off my clothes and going into the sea. Three guitars had greeted us, three voices singing, a tender and soft song, a lulling, a caressing song.

I had been told there were only two hotels in Acapulco: the *Las Americas,* which was for tourists and had dancing, a jazz-band, a big pool; and the *Mirador,* which was a Mexican family hotel. I chose the *Mirador* to be with Mexicans, and fortunately so, because it was also the most beautiful. It was situated high on a rocky mountain, overlooking the boiling gorge into which young Mexican divers leaped, dangerously and dramatically. There was a central building, and private cottages spread all over the mountain between passion vines, hibiscus flowers, bougainvillaea bushes, palms. I walked through a labyrinth of steps and tiled passageways to my own cottage. It had a terrace, with a hammock swinging gently, as if awaiting me. It was a simple room. Through the windows I heard a concert of frogs and cicadas. A loud harmonious buzzing. And a whistle, a slightly mocking whistle, which at first I mistook for a man's. It was a bird. Everything stirred and delighted me, the softness in which everything was bathed, the humid glistening leaves, the pungent earth smell as night fell, the sea changing colors like an opal. The sandalwood smell of the furniture. Far off, I could hear the guitars.

I changed clothes and walked to the dining room. The patron came to greet me with old-fashioned courtesy. He was patriarchal, domineering, and protective. I was in the mood to love family life, children, dogs, parrots, nurses, Mexican cooking, Mexican singing, Mexican guitars. Tenderness dissolved me. An emotion which was never allowed to flower in New York. An abandon to tenderness, to warmth of climate and of people, to trust and smiling. It was a mood the singing of the Mexicans created.

In a corner of the dining room, a Mexican woman in native dress made tortillas on a grill. The gestures of her hands as she moulded the paste were rhythmic and ritualistic.

The next morning, the sun seemed not only to cover everything with gold but to penetrate into my very body. The air I inhaled was like a drug of forgetfulness. Every movement I made was pleasurable. The colors of the sea, the sailboats, the flowers, and the papaya on the table, the smooth skin of the Mexicans, everything was a delight to the senses. The communion of eyes and smiles was elating. The festivities of nature anesthetized all thought or sorrow.

Acapulco had once been a fishing village, and before that, Japanese pearl divers had found treasures there. When they were driven away, they destroyed the oyster beds. It remained a simple fishing village until the artists arrived. The train did not come all the way and donkeys provided the only transportation. The artists were followed by the real-estate men and the hotelkeepers, but Acapulco remained a village where the wind was like velvet, and the sea as warm as a mother's womb.

The first person I met was Doctor Hernandez. He had the broad face of Mayan sculptures, the aquiline nose, the full mouth slanting downward while the eyes slanted upward. His skin was light olive, from a mixture of Indian and Spanish blood. His smile was like that of the natives, open and total, but it came less often and faded quickly, leaving a shadow over his face.

I was seeking a new territory, the territory of pleasure, and I felt Doctor Hernandez was not the proper guide to it.

I felt like saying to him: "Give me a little carefree time before making me aware of the dark side of Acapulco's life."

Everything was novel to me. The green of the foliage was not like any other greens; it was deeper, lacquered and moist. The leaves were heavier, fuller, the flowers bigger. They seemed surcharged with sap, and more alive. Just as the people seemed more alive.

The bungalows, some of them with roofs of palm leaves, recalled African native huts.

Doctor Hernandez and I sat drinking coffee on the terrace, where everyone gathered to watch the sea and the stars, and the boys diving from the high rocks.

He said: "In the tropics, white men fall apart."

"I've heard that," I said, "but I never believed it. I have seen too many people fall apart in New York. People always blame external circumstances for their disintegration. The white man who falls apart in the tropics I am sure is the same one who will fall apart anywhere."

The sun was setting with all the pomp and splendor of an oriental ceremony. The palms had a naked elegance.

The eyes of the Mexicans were full of burning life.

Even twilight came without a change of temperature or alteration in the softness of the air.

There are so many kinds of drugs. Some for remembering and some for forgetting. Acapulco is for forgetting. Will Doctor Hernandez let me forget? There is no permanent forgetting. We may seem to forget a person, a place, a state of being, a past life, but meanwhile what we are doing is selecting a new cast for the reproduction of the same drama.

And one day will I open my eyes in this beautiful, overwhelming place and see that I am caught in the same pattern, repeating the same story?

Already I had met the Doctor, lucid and aware, saying: "Awareness, awareness. Come with me and see the illness and the poverty."

How could it be otherwise? The design comes from within. It is internal.

And yet, the next morning, swimming in the tropical sea, listening to the guitar playing and the singers on the beach, eating the freshly caught fish, drinking coconut milk from a shell, looking at the conch shells brought in by the beach boys, lying in the sun. I remembered that the definition of *tropic* was "turning," changing," and I felt a new woman would be born here.

# Index

Acapulco: visit to, 222–24
adolescence: understanding of, 94–95
Agee, James, 132, 133, 141, 165, 195
*Air-Conditioned Nightmare, The,* 12, 197
Alain-Fournier, 158
Allendy, Dr. René, VII
Amagansett, N.Y.: visit to, 22; 75
America: in the 1940s, VIII; love of polemics in, X, 91; suffering from realism, 66; gigantism in, 129; creates a shell, 144; writing in, IX, 153–54, 195–96; re-entering as permanent resident, 196, 222; architects imitating Europe, 211
*Americas, Las,* Hotel (Mexico), 223
Amherst College, Mass., 170, 171, 189
Amiel, Henri Frédéric, 73
Anderson, Sherwood, 85
Angelo's Café (Monterey, Calif.): opening party, 221–22
Armitage, Merle, 220
Artaud, Antonin, VII, 134, 193, 194
Arthur, 180
Aswell, Mary Louise, 111, 141
*At Land* (film), 68
Austen, Jane, 88

Baldwin, James, 196

Baldwin, Lanny C., 32, 49, 54, 62, 70, 141
Banks, Don, 135, 141, 145
Banks, Nancy, 135, 141, 144, 145
Bara, Theda, 214
Baradinski, Oscar, 176
Barer, Marshall, 45–46, 72, 76, 78; portrait of, 80; letter from, 80; 81, 92, 95, 98, 99, 105, 107, 108, 111, 112, 114, 123
Barer, Rabbi, 81
Barnes, Djuna, 10, 213
Baudelaire, Charles, 38, 125
Beardon, Romare, 61
Berkeley, Calif., 214
Bernanos, Georges, 71
Big Sur, Calif., 6, 12, 16; visit to, 219–20
"Birth" (story), 37
Bonaparte, Josephine, 146
*Book of the Dead,* 101
Boston University, Mass., 170
Botticelli, Sandro, 76, 147
Boucher, François, 205
Bowen, Elizabeth, 112
Braque, Georges, 217
Braud, Paul, 50
Breit, Harvey, 18
Breton, André, 31, 103, 112
Brooklyn, N.Y., 19
Brouwer, Desclee de, 34

Brown, Frances, 13, 15, 16, 18, 28,
30, 32, 36, 40, 43, 45, 46, 47, 48, 49,
60, 62, 63, 64, 65, 66, 69, 70, 81,
89, 91, 96, 98, 105, 131
Brown, Tom, 16, 45, 46, 48, 49, 80
Broyard, Anatole, 180, 182
Bryn Mawr College, Pa., 30
Burton, Richard, 109

Café Society (N.Y.), 67
Campbell, Andrew, 199
Capote, Truman, 110, 111
Caron, 135
Central Park (N.Y.): filming in, 146–
47
Chants du Maldoror, Les, 37, 48
"Chaotica, Hotel," VI
Chappala, Lake (Mexico), 222
Chareau, Madame Pierre, 60, 157,
180
Charles à la Pomme Soufflé (N.Y.
restaurant), 106
Charles Restaurant (N.Y.), 121
Charles Street (N.Y.), 46
"Child Born Out of the Fog, The"
(story), 145
Children of the Albatross, 140, 172,
183, 184, 186; manuscript finished,
191; 192
"Children Songs" (composition), 180
Chisholm, Hugh, 157
Choix des Élues, 10
Churchill, Winston, 114
Circle (publication), 11, 15, 44, 214
City and the Pillar, The, 173
Cocteau, Jean, 68, 76, 78, 157, 214
"Cold Cuts" (nickname), 184–85
Combat (publication), 194
Company She Keeps, The, 61

Conservatory (Paris), 50
Cortot, Alfred, 50
Covici, Pascal, 103, 104, 105, 112
Criterion, The (publication), 5
Crosby, Caresse, 15, 17, 61
Cummings, E. E., 179

Dali, Salvador, 67, 176
Dartmouth College, N.H., 170
Davis, George, 137, 161
De Brun, Elsa, 40
Debussy, Claude ("Sonata for Violin
and Piano"), 181
de Falla, Manuel, 50
de Guerin, Maurice, 73
de Lenclos, Ninon, 177
de Rougemont, Denis, 103
Deren, Maya, 67, 75; visit to, 76;
90–91, 92, 96, 98, 101, 102, 104,
111; party at, 131; 132, 133, 135,
136, 137; on her films, 138; 139,
141; party at, 144; 145; work on
film, 146–47; 149, 156–57, 161,
170, 214
Dinesen, Isak, 196
Doctor Kerkhoven, 93
Don Quixote, 98, 137, 176, 177
Dorrey, 180
dreams: and the unconscious, 40; 73;
and reality, 98
Dreiser, Theodore, 66, 213
Dudley, John, 12
Duits, Charles, 16, 18, 22, 23, 42, 60,
62, 71, 72, 95, 98, 99, 105, 107, 108,
111, 114, 132, 135, 136, 144, 147
Dukas, Paul, 50
Duncan, Isadora, 8
Durrell, Lawrence, 6, 44
Durrell, Nancy, 6

Dutton, E. P. (publisher), 104, 111, 114, 125, 175, 191, 192; episode with messenger, 162–63
*Dyn* (publication), 15, 57

Earhart, Amelia, 115
Easthampton (N.Y.), 157, 158, 161
Eisenstein, Sergei, 61
Eliot, T. S., 66, 67, 117
Elizabeth I, Queen, 146
Elsa (Gonzalo's niece), 173
Emerson, Ralph Waldo, 66
Ernst, Max, 15
*Esquire* (publication), 80
Estelle, 81
*"Être Étoilique, Une"* (essay), 5
"Eye's Journey, The" (story), 15, 57

Fairbanks, Douglas, 214
*Fall of the House of Usher, The* (film), 214
Fast, Howard, 186
Fez (Morocco), 171
Field, Marshall, 74
*Finnegans Wake*, 22
Ford, Jacqueline, 129
*Forgotten Village, The* (film), 76
Four Seasons (N.Y. bookstore), 163
Fowlie, Wallace, 6, 36, 38; visit from, 44–45; 48, 66, 67, 74, 99
Fraenkel, Michael, 44, 61
*Fragment of Seeking* (film), 214
France: liberation of, 24; dream of returning to, 25; memory of, 32–33
Frances, Esteban, 103
Fredericks, Claude, 132, 157
Fredericks, Millicent, 112
Freud, Sigmund, 35, 86, 122

Friar, Kimon, 104

Gallon, Jean, 50
Gallon, Noel, 50
Garrigue, Jean, 105
Gauguin, Paul, 205
"Gemor Press," 3, 12, 31; collapse of, 165
Gide, André, 38, 194
Giraudoux, Jean, 10
"Givor" (pseudonym of Wolfgang Paalen), 57
Goddard College, Vt., 170–71
Goldberg, Samuel, 16
Gonzalo, IX, 3, 4, 11, 12, 16, 17, 18, 19, 23, 26, 27, 28, 30, 31, 32, 59, 72, 82, 89, 107, 108, 123, 124, 125, 142, 145, 148, 165, 172–73, 183, 184, 189, 203, 214
Gore, Senator, 106
Gotham Book Mart (N.Y.), 32, 34, 90; party at, 163
Graham, Martha, 120, 121, 122, 128, 130, 196
*Grand Meaulness, Le*, 157
Grand Street (N.Y.), 146
*Green Mansions*, 202
Griffith, Richard, 144
Guggenheim, Peggy, 103
Guriananoff, Gregory Psnikow, 69

Haggart, Stanley, 119, 130, 132, 133; on A.N.'s handwriting, 128
Haitian Carnival (in N.Y.), 184
Haitian Flag Dance (in N.Y.), 16
Hall, Weeks, 200; visit to "The Shadows," 200–02, 203
Hammid, Alexander, 75, 76, 132, 145, 156

Harding, Dr. Esther, 59, 137
Harman, Carter, 179, 181, 192
Harman, Nancy, 179, 181
*Harper's Bazaar* (publication), 123, 141, 158, 161, 177
Harper Brothers (publisher), 103, 104
Harrington, Curtis, 214
Harvard University: lecture at, 169–70
Hauser, Caspar, 47, 64, 73, 74, 82, 89, 91, 101
Hayter, William, 3
Helba, 26, 32, 48, 125, 172, 173
Helion, 103
Hemingway, Ernest, 66, 106
Herkovitz, Harry, 18, 19, 20, 21, 24, 29, 30
Hernandez, Dr., 224–25
Hitler, Adolf, VIII, 22
Hoffman, Kim, 112, 132, 133, 156
Hogarth, William, 83
homosexuals: fears of, 125–26, 127; in groups, 165; childishness of, 187–89
*House of Incest*, 18, 34, 58, 180, 196; music for, 192
*House of Sleep, The*, 196
Howell, Bill, 156, 180, 186, 187
Hugo, Ian, 17, 30, 64

Ibsen, Henrik, 213
Ikle, 129
*In a Yellow Wood*, 123
Isherwood, Christopher, 84, 130

Jaeger, Martha, 13–14, 15, 16, 17; visit to, 19; 22, 60, 62, 63, 69

James, Henry, 148, 154, 184
*"Je Suis le Plus Malade des Surréalistes"* (story), 37
Joan of Arc, 177
John (pseudonym), 158, 159–61
John, 215
*Joie, La*, 71
Joyce, James, 92, 102, 151, 152

Kahane (Girodias), Maurice, 44, 58
Kahler, Mr. & Mrs., 141
Kavan, Anna, 196
Kendall (pseudonym), 164; letters from, 164, 167, 168, 172, 179, 181–82, 183–84, 189; letter to, 166–67; 168, 169, 170, 171–72, 173, 179, 180, 182, 183; poem from, 183; 184, 188, 189
Kenning, Danny, 179
*Kenyon Review* (publication), 38
Kiesler, Frederick, 103
Kirstein, Lincoln, 192
Kleeman Gallery (N.Y.), 102
Kline, Herbert, 75
Knittel, Robert, 74, 132
Kollwitz, Käthe, 17
Kreiselman, Miriam, 36

"Labyrinth, The" (story), 101
*Ladders to Fire*, 77, 114, 116, 117, 120, 125, 130, 152, 161, 162, 163, 165, 172, 175, 181, 192
Lafayette, Hotel (N.Y.), 169
Laffont, Robert, 58
Lake, Carlton, 169
La Pensée, Henry, 39
Laughlin, James, 5
Lautréamont, 48

Lawrence, D. H., VII, 35, 58, 61, 85, 86, 115, 142, 205, 206, 222; T. S. Eliot on, 66

Lawrence, Frieda, 204, 205; visit with, 205–06

Leite, George T., 12, 38, 44, 214; visit with, 215

Leonard W. (pseudonym), 36; letters from, 36–37, 37–38, 80; visit from, 42–43; 44, 45, 46, 47, 48, 54, 57, 60; letters to, 60, 64–65, 73–74; 62, 64, 70, 71, 73, 75, 88, 89, 91, 94, 98, 99, 104, 112, 115, 116, 117, 126, 132; letter from, 140; 143, 145, 181, 182, 186, 187, 189, 192

Leonhardt, Olive, 202; visit with, 202–03

Lepska, Janina M., 36, 219–20

Lerman, Leo, 16, 97, 101, 109–11, 123, 141, 161, 163; autobiographical sketch for, 176–78

Letters to a Young Poet, 64, 73

Life (publication), 222

Lincoln, Abraham, 133, 195

Longchamps (N.Y. restaurant), 79

Los Angeles, Calif., 208; Lloyd Wright's plans for, 210–13

Louveciennes (France), VII, 50, 141

Lowry, Robert, 144, 165

Luchita, 132

Luray, Caverns of, Va., 199

Maas, Willard, 144

Mabille, Pierre, 61

Macdougal Alley (N.Y.), 99

Macdougal Street (N.Y.), 3

Macrae, Elliot, 192

Magazin du Spectacle (publication), 58

Mangones, Albert, 17, 167, 168, 180, 183, 189–91

Maritain, Jacques, 6

Marquand, John P., 84

Martinelli, Sherry, 107–08, 132, 135, 144, 145, 182

Marx, Karl, 122

Mathiesen, Paul, 129, 131, 145, 213, 219, 220

Matta, 105

Maugham, Somerset, 38

Max and the White Phagocytes, 58

Maxwell, Lawrence, 163

McCarthy, Mary, 41, 61, 79, 83, 87, 90, 93, 171

Memoirs of Hecate County, 80, 95

Merrill, James, 134; on A.N.'s work, 134–35; 144, 171–72, 179, 180, 189

Meshes of the Afternoon (film), 68, 149

Mexico: Miller plans to travel to, 11; 196, 197, 219; A.N. in, 222–25

Mexico City, 15, 222

Miller, Henry, VII, IX, 4, 16, 18, 19, 20, 21, 24, 28, 31, 36, 37, 38, 59, 66, 71, 74, 82, 91, 108, 125, 134, 142, 170, 188, 190, 197; letters from, 5–8, 11–12, 30, 44, 58, 128; letters to, 21, 36, 61–62; visit with in Big Sur, 219–20

Miller, June (Henry Miller's second wife), 18, 19, 20, 21, 40, 125

Mills College of Education, N.Y., 107

Minotaure, Le (publication), 67

Mirador, Hotel (Mexico), 223

Miró, Joan, 217
*Miroir du Merveilleux,* 61
"Mohican, The" (story), 37
Moira (pseudonym), 16, 22–23, 33, 157
Monterey, Calif., 215, 219; vs. Varda, 220–21
Moore, David, 61, 71, 72, 76, 78, 79
Moricand, Conrad, 16, 60, 110
Museum of Modern Art (N.Y.), 49, 100, 103, 117

Nabukova, Tatiana, 69
*Nation, The* (publication): review of *This Hunger,* 86–87
neurosis, 143
New Orleans, La., 200, 202, 203
*New Orleans Drawn and Quartered,* 202
New School of Social Research (N.Y.), 16
*New Yorker, The* (publication), VIII, 5, 84, 98
*Nightwood,* 10
Nijinsky, Vaslav, 8, 171
Nin, Joaquin (Anaïs Nin's father), 4, 33, 51, 83, 106, 139, 148
Nin-Culmell, Joaquin (A.N.'s brother), 49–52
Nin-Culmell, Rosa (A.N.'s mother), 50, 129
Nin, Teresa, 129
Noguchi, Isamu, 99–100, 103, 117
Normandy (France): Allied landing in, 19; breakthrough at St.-Lô, 23
Novalis (Friedrich von Hardenberg), 157
Novarro, Ramon, 214

Olga (pseudonym), 8–10, 12, 69, 74, 119–20, 141
O'Neill, Eugene, 213
*On the Town* (musical), 78
*On Writing* (pamphlet), 176
*Origines* (publication), 78
Orlikova, Capt. Valentina, 10–11, 39
Orwell, George, 5
Ottoway, Bill, 141

Paalen, Alice, 57–58, 60, 222
Paalen, Wolfgang, 57
Pablo (pseudonym), 28–29, 42, 43, 44, 45, 46, 48, 49, 58, 60, 64, 65, 70, 71, 72, 76, 92, 95, 96, 99, 105, 107, 108, 111, 112, 114, 126, 135, 141, 144, 156, 174, 179, 180, 184, 187, 189, 193, 196
Parrish-Martin, Woody, 119, 132, 133; portrait of, 195
*Partisan Review* (publication), 42
Pecos, N. M., 204
PEN Club, 134
"Petrouchka" (composition), 38
Pfriem, Bernard, 180
Picasso, Pablo, 60, 154, 217
Pickford, Mary, 214
*Picnic* (film), 214
Poe, Edgar Allan, 18, 146
*Poetry* (publication), 28; cited, 193–94
Port Jefferson (N.Y.), 69
Porter, Bern, 11
*Portfolio* (publication), 61
Post, Prof., 170
*Prater Violet,* 130
Premice, Josephine, 17, 45, 67, 72, 108, 109, 112, 141, 189

*Print* (publication), 28
Proust, Marcel, 17, 38, 52, 53, 74, 140, 151, 152, 164; Leon Pierre Quint on, 53–54
Provincetown Playhouse (N.Y.), 137

*Que Viva Mexico* (film), 61
*Quinquivara*, 32
Quint, Leon Pierre, 52, 53, 74; on Proust, 53–54
Quintero, Emilia, 50
"Quintet for Piano and Strings" (composition), 49

"Ragtime" (story), 96, 170
Rainer, Luise, 15, 18, 28, 36, 43, 44, 45, 74, 132
Random House (publisher), 103
Rank, Dr. Otto, VII, 59, 69, 75, 99, 124, 137, 143
Raydon, Mr. & Mrs., 141
Récamier, Madame, 146
Reichel, Hans, 57; story of, 15
relationships: notes on, 150–51
Renoir, Pierre Auguste, 205
rhythm: in writing, 55
Rilke, Rainer Maria, 64, 73
Rimbaud, Arthur, 6, 38, 181
Rita, 135, 136, 145
*Ritual in Transfigured Time* (film), 149
Roanoke, Va., 198
Rodin, Auguste, 53
Roosevelt, Franklin D., 43, 114
Rosenfeld, Paul, 90
Rothschild Residence (Paris), 33
Rouault, Georges, 61
Rousseau, Henri, 49

Ruban Bleu (N.Y. restaurant), 121, 189

Sablon, 43
Saget, Justin, 194
*Saison en Enfer, Une*, 37
Sainte Catherine Press (Belgium), 34
Saint-Exupéry, Madame, 103
Saint-Tropez, 158, 159, 203
Sarasate, Pablo de, 50
*Scenario*, 58
Schrafft's (N.Y. restaurant), 3
Schola Cantorum (Paris), 50
Sekula, Sonya, 103, 112
Selznick, Irene, 161
Shankar, Uday, 8
Shelley, Mary, 103
Shelley, Percy Bysshe, 97, 103
Smith, Lawrence, 45
Smith, Tony, 45
Sokol, Thurema, 16, 17, 36
*Soviet Russia* (publication), 120
Stebbins, Benton, 199
Steig, William, 141
Steinbeck, John, 75, 122
"Stella" (story), 161
Steloff, Frances, 32, 90, 176
Steve (pseudonym), 133, 135, 156
Stravinsky, Igor, 38
Stroup, John, 18, 132
Stuart, Mary, 104
*Sunday After the War*, 5
Sweeney, James Johnson, 169

Talbot-Martin, Elizabeth, 119
Tambimuttu, J. M., 28
Tanguy, Yves, 61, 206
Taos, N.M., 204

Tarkington, Booth, 38
Tei-ko, Miss, 135, 136, 149
Texas: style of, 204
*This Hunger,* 18, 28, 38, 64, 67, 70, 78, 81, 82, 83, 89, 96, 106, 112, 116, 120, 164, 167
Tibet, 6
*Times, The* (N.Y.), 163
Toshka, Miss, 180, 181
*Town and Country* (publication), 39, 123, 175
Trilling, Diana, 82, 121, 122, 123, 139, 163; review quoted, 86–87
*Tropic of Cancer,* 61
Tyler, Parker, 96

*Ulysses,* 92, 102
*Under a Glass Bell,* VII, 3, 8, 16, 25, 28, 35, 36, 37, 44, 60, 62, 65, 78, 84, 85, 90, 104, 107, 110, 131, 145, 196, 222

Vaharoff, Nikolai, 69
Vail, Pegine, 103
Valentino, Rudolph, 214
Valéry, Paul: quoted, 137
Van Gogh, Vincent, 128
Varda, Jean (Janko), 6, 7, 36; letter from, 7–8; visit with, 215–19; vs. Monterey, 220–21
Varda, Virginia, 218
Varèse, Edgar, 132, 212
Varèse, Louise, 132
Vassilinoff, Vassily, 69
Vence (France), VII
Verlaine, Paul, 38
Vidal, Gore, 104; visit from, 105–06; 107, 111, 112–17; horoscope

of, 118; 119, 121, 123, 124, 125, 130, 131, 132, 133, 134, 135, 136, 137, 139, 140, 141, 142, 144, 145, 156, 157, 165, 137; letter to, 173–74; 175, 178, 182; letter from, 186; 186, 187, 191, 192, 202
Vidal, Nina (G.V.'s mother), 124, 134, 174
Vieux Colombier (Paris Theater), 193
Viking Press, The (publisher), 103, 104, 112
*Villager, The* (publication), 3
Vincent, 180, 181, 182, 183
Vinez, Ricardo, 50
*Vogue* (publication), 158
"Voice, The" (story), 37

Wahl, Jean, 17, 22
Walter, Eugene, 163
Washington, D.C., 198
Washington Square (N.Y.), 45
Wassermann, Jakob, 47, 93
*Way of All Women, The,* 137
Wesley, Helen, 213
West, Herbert, 170
West, Rebecca, 37
Westbrook, Frank, 92, 135, 146, 147, 149, 156, 174, 179, 180, 181, 188
Whitman, Walt, 66, 199
Wilde, Oscar, 176
Williams, Tennessee, 102
*Williwaw,* 114, 123
Wilson, Edmund, VIII, 5, 18, 37, 41, 42, 61, 65, 79, 80, 87–89, 90, 92–93, 95, 97, 98, 99, 100, 101, 105, 106, 108, 115, 116, 119, 135, 142, 143, 148, 165, 171; visit with, 82–

84; reviews *This Hunger,* 84–86;
on Joyce, 102

*Winter of Artifice,* 7, 25, 28, 35, 37,
83, 88, 129, 141, 151

Wolfe, Thomas, 66

women: conflicts of, 25; as nature,
33

Woodward, James, 23

Woolf, Virginia, 141, 176

Wreden, Nicholas, 192

Wright, Frank Lloyd, 208, 211

Wright, Helen (Mrs. Lloyd Wright),
208–09, 213

Wright, Helen (Mrs. Richard
Wright), 145

Wright, Lloyd, 208–09; work and
architectural concepts, 209–10,
211–13

Wright, Richard, 102, 145, 186;
dinner for, 189–91

writing: on, 152–53

Yonkers Park (N.Y.), 145

Young's Bookstore (N.Y.), 163

Young Men's Hebrew Association
(Poetry Center, N.Y.): reading at,
95–96; 104, 180

Zanarte, Enrique, 108, 132, 133, 135,
136, 144

Zilka, Berthie, 23, 24, 26

Zilka, Mr., 22

Books by Anaïs Nin available in
paperbound editions from
Harcourt Brace Jovanovich, Inc.

*The Diary of Anaïs Nin, 1931–1934*
**(HB 157)**

*The Diary of Anaïs Nin, 1934–1939*
**(HB 174)**

*The Diary of Anaïs Nin, 1939–1944*
**(HB 199)**

*The Diary of Anaïs Nin, 1944–1947*
**(HB 239)**

*A Photographic Supplement to the Diary of Anaïs Nin*
**(HB 293)**

2284